We believe that everyone needs to challenge themselv
Leigh has made it easy by stimulating your senses for
adventures. Go for it!

The Amazing Race Canada contestants

Several years of traveling around the world have taught us how good we have it in our own beautiful backyard of Canada. Leigh's book is an amazing showcase of that, and her dedication in compiling these top adventures is extremely admirable. She is an absolute authority in all things outdoors, and we have already added several of these amazing adventures to our own to-do list!

Dalene and Pete Heck
2014 National Geographic Travelers of the Year
HeckticTravels.com

Discover Canada: 100 Inspiring Outdoor Adventures isn't just for hard-core, outdoorsy types. This book is for anyone who's ever felt the pull of the great outdoors. Leigh has created a fantastic guide that will inspire you to get off the couch and get back to nature with these approachable adventures. Leigh is a true travel expert. She's been pretty much everywhere, experienced more than I could ever hope to in my lifetime, yet remains remarkably ego-free. By thoughtfully matching the appropriate season and best activity to soak up the true essence of the destination, explorers will be well rewarded, thanks to her guidance. Now go on and turn this bucket list into your reality.

Jody Robbins
Award-winning travel writer and blogger
TravelsWithBaggage.com

Every time I receive an email from Hike Bike Travel regarding outdoor adventures I begin to salivate like one of Pavlov's dogs. When I open one of her posts, I am transformed from my room to a wild and rugged Canadian adventure. Suddenly, I am in a pristine forest, a wilderness lake, or a mountain range with breathtaking views. I am no longer surfing the web. I am now canoeing, kayaking and hiking, thanks to Leigh's gorgeous photography and engaging prose. This book is a must for those who love Canada; the perfect coffee-table addition to take people from their living room into the wilds of Canada, and a great resource for those who want to follow in Leigh's footsteps. Just be sure to also buy a bib.

Ted Nelson
travelingted.com

Discover Canada: 100 Inspiring Outdoor Adventures should be a must-read for every Canadian! It demonstrates how much our country truly has to offer, and gets me excited to visit more of it with inspiring photography. Leigh has included activities suitable for the casual day-hiker to more challenging multi-day adventures, so there's something for everyone. This book will make you proud to be a Canadian and will be the push you need to get out and experience more of our beautiful country.

Laurel Robbins
Adventure travel blogger
MonkeysandMountains.com

Leigh is an adventurer we should all admire. Whether it is bike riding in Spain, kayaking the wonders of Canada or hiking through some magnificent wilderness, she always takes you along with her — celebrating the highs, but often celebrating the tough times more! She challenges herself and always comes out the other end with positive, informative and accurate information for her readers, who can then vicariously enjoy her adventures. Her latest work, *Discover Canada: 100 Inspiring Outdoor Adventures*, is inspiring! It brings together many of her experiences into one easy-to-read guide. With an easy-to-follow layout, it is brimful of accurate information drawn from her personal experience. Throw in some wonderful images and this guide will motivate you get out and enjoy many adventures across Canada. What's stopping you?

Frank Wall
Our Hiking Blog
Author of Food to Go: How to Eat Well in the Wild

Discover Canada: 100 Inspiring Outdoor Adventures is the perfect addition to any "bucket list", making glad the adventurous Canadian and visitors to Canada who are even more happy they came. The book highlights great outdoor venues for hiking, backpacking etc. throughout the entire country. Leigh McAdam has brought together in this book all her skills as a travel/adventure writer to celebrate the incredible offerings of outdoor excitement Canadians can well be proud of. A must read!

Phillip Ferranti
Author of 140 Great Hikes in & Near Palm Springs

Discover Canada: 100 Inspiring Outdoor Adventures is written with an easy-to-read enthusiasm, illustrated with superb photographs and peppered with down-to-earth information on hiking, biking and kayaking across Canada. Leigh's adventures will inspire those who enjoy the outdoors to never stop exploring!

Anne & Laurence Yeadon-Jones
Authors of the Dreamspeaker Cruising Guide *Series*
dreamspeakerguides.com

Leigh McAdam has explored more of Canada than anyone I know. I have been an avid reader of her popular blog, HikeBikeTravel, for many years and she would be the first person I would turn to with any question about the Canadian outdoors. Her new book, *Discover Canada: 100 Inspiring Outdoor Adventures*, is a great resource for anyone who would like to explore more of this beautiful country from coast to coast at any time of the year. The carefully selected adventures in each of the provinces and territories are rated from easy to difficult, so there's something for the experienced outdoors-person as well as beginners or families with children, and everyone in between. Readers can't help but be inspired to experience many of these uniquely Canadian adventures for themselves.

Lisa Goodmurphy
Family Travel Blogger
GonewiththeFamily.com

A comprehensive and well-respected guide to Canadian adventures for the outdoors lover. A book worth investing in.

Barbara Arnold
Owner
Hidden Trails International Horseback Riding and Outdoor Vacations

Discover Canada

100 Inspiring Outdoor Adventures

DISCOVER CANADA

100 Inspiring Outdoor Adventures

Leigh McAdam

GRANVILLE ISLAND
PUBLISHING

Library and Archives Canada Cataloguing in Publication

McAdam, Leigh, 1957–, author
      Discover Canada : 100 inspiring outdoor adventures / Leigh AcAdam.

Includes index.
Issued in print and electronic formats.
ISBN 978-1-926991-46-7 (pbk.).—ISBN 978-1-926991-57-3 (ebook)

      1. Outdoor recreation—Canada—Guidebooks. 2. Hiking—Canada—
Guidebooks. 3. Cycling—Canada—Guidebooks. 4. Skis and skiing—Canada—
Guidebooks. 5. Canoes and canoeing—Canada—Guidebooks. 6. Backpacking—
Canada—Guidebooks. 7. Canada—Guidebooks. I. Title.

GV191.44.M312 2014   796.50971   C2014-907378-X
                                                C2014-907379-8

The activities described in this book involve risk. Though the author tried to make
this guide as accurate as possible, we make no warranty of its content and disclaim
all liability arising from its use. Users of this book are solely responsible for their
own safety.

Editors: Cynthia Nugent and Adriana Van Leeuwen
Proofreader: Renate Preuss
Book designer: Omar Gallegos
Indexer: Bookmark: Editing and Indexing

Granville Island Publishing Ltd.
212 – 1656 Duranleau St.
Vancouver, BC, Canada V6H 3S4

604-688-0320 / 1-877-688-0320
info@granvilleislandpublishing.com
www.granvilleislandpublishing.com

First published in 2015
Printed in Canada

To my husband and best friend John,
for his tireless support, sense of adventure and
good humour, even under adverse conditions.

To Kristen, for inspiring me with her efficiency
and her efforts to make this book a success.

And to Matt and Grace,
for your love and encouragement.

Contents

Introduction

The outdoors has called to me for as long as I can remember. I was lucky to grow up in Ottawa where so many great outdoor locations were at my fingertips: the Gatineau Hills for skiing, the Rideau Canal for skating, the Ottawa River for canoeing and countless bike paths available for cycling.

Then when I turned fifteen I was bitten by the travel bug. It was a summer when Ottawa suddenly felt too small and boring, especially when I heard that a 600-mile bike ride around England and Wales was being offered to Ottawa high school students. I pestered and browbeat my parents, promising to do anything they asked until they finally agreed to let me go.

That cycling trip was my first serious outdoor adventure. It was unforgettable on many levels and forty years on I still remember the camaraderie, the satisfaction of making it through a tough day, and the excitement of feeling totally alive. It was intoxicating and I never wanted to lose those feelings.

But life brought me to Toronto, where hours of highway traffic separated me from anything that felt like the real outdoors. That's not to say that I didn't take advantage of canoeing in Killarney Provincial Park or hut-to-hut skiing in Algonquin Park, but the frequency of those outings was rare, especially while raising a young family.

Then in the early '90s our family moved to Boulder, Colorado — and life changed for the better. Now with easy access to the great outdoors, we could escape to the mountains most weekends. We climbed 14,000-foot peaks; we camped and backpacked; backcountry-skied to mountain huts and downhill-skied the big-name resorts. We developed confidence in ourselves and in being in wild places. The one thing we didn't do was go anywhere near the water. Something had to change.

Georgian Bay, ON

Sea kayaking was becoming more popular around that time, so we booked our first kayaking trip out of Tofino on the west coast of Vancouver Island. There we had our first west coast experience of deserted white sand beaches, challenging seas, seabirds, animal life and that state of bliss which comes from relaxing by a campfire after a day on the water. We were hooked. Kayaking, not only on oceans but on lakes and rivers, opened up a world of possibilities.

In 2002, we moved to Vancouver where, for the better part of the next ten years, summer holidays and weekends were spent exploring the waters around Vancouver Island, Desolation Sound, the Sunshine Coast and the city itself.

Now I live in Calgary. I didn't want to come at first, but I've learned that there is much to love about the city, especially its proximity to the Rocky Mountains. Hiking and backpacking to some of the world's most beautiful mountain lakes and peaks has replaced sea kayaking, and fortunately, we can still kayak on the many nearby lakes and rivers. Calgary also borders Saskatchewan, which led me to discover, as you'll read in this book, that the province is rich in beautiful wild places and holds so much more than wheat fields.

I've written a number of adventure guides to places outside Canada, as well as maintained my popular travel blog, **HikeBikeTravel.com**, for the last four years. Now I want the world to know that some of the best places on the planet for an outdoor adventure are right here. My hope is that this compilation will inspire you to get out there and be active while getting to know this fantastic place called CANADA.

How I Chose the Adventures

Choosing just 100 adventures from the potentially thousands that a country the size of Canada can offer was a difficult task. The second-largest country in the world, Canada is bordered by three oceans, creating 202,280 km (125,691 mi) of coastline. It is crisscrossed by mountain ranges and boasts hundreds of rivers, thousands of lakes and a land mass greater than all of Europe. Keep in mind, too, that there are nine natural UNESCO World Heritage Sites, thirty-six national parks, eight national park preserves and several hundred provincial parks, all offering a slice of some of the most interesting and dramatic pieces of Canada.

To whittle down the list I took into account the following factors:

- I had to personally experience each of the adventures. Research is useful but it's on-the-ground, first-hand familiarity with each and every adventure in this book that allowed me to decide whether it deserved to make the top 100. If it didn't live up to its billing, it got the boot. All 100 adventures are unique Canadian experiences.

- The list should show Canadians and visitors the country's geographic diversity.

- I wanted to cover all four seasons. Canada offers outdoor adventures year-round. Even so, most of these suggestions are for summer and fall, the time when people take vacations and get outside. I also feel it's better to embrace than simply endure our long winter, so I looked for ideas to get even the worst winter couch potatoes outside. Spring, with its reputation for balm and blossom, actually has the most unpredictable weather; lakes are cold, and campgrounds, if they're open, are soggy. Knowing that eastern Canada enjoys better springs than the west, I've located my April and May trips there.

- Cost was a consideration. As much as I would like to hike or kayak in every national park in Canada, those in the far north are simply out of the financial reach of most people. Nunavut, Canada's newest territory, is the size of Western Europe, but it's particularly hard to access, so is represented by only one adventure, even though it merits many more. If you can afford it, there are phenomenal hiking and kayaking opportunities all across the hauntingly beautiful Arctic. Fortunately, the Yukon and Northwest Territories are at least partially accessible by car in the summer, as well as by air. You could spend a lifetime up there; I have just provided a taste of the possibilities.

- Outstanding natural beauty influenced my choices, particularly for hiking, backpacking and kayaking trips. What better way to get the sense of the wild Canadian landscape than by visiting places with spectacular mountain or coastal scenery?

- Locomotion was another factor. I've limited the adventures to certain ways of getting about: walking, hiking, backpacking, road cycling, canoeing, kayaking, rafting, skating and cross-country skiing. Apologies to the downhill skiers, surfers, stand-up paddle boarders, horseback riders, fishermen, golfers and whomever else I've left out.

I realize the result is not a comprehensive list, and that I've probably missed some of the gems that only locals know. But I hope the winning recommendations in this book will widen the scope of possible adventures for my fellow Canadians and visitors alike. Please visit my website, **HikeBikeTravel.com**, to post comments and suggestions for the next edition. I'm looking forward to hearing from you.

Ratings are subjective. What's hard for one person might be a walk in the park for another. It depends on your physical conditioning, prior experience and, to a lesser degree, age. For those reasons, it's difficult to rate a hike, a bike ride or a kayaking trip. I have tried to explain my rationale, but it seems there are always one or two adventures that don't quite fit the criteria.

Rating difficulty for hike and backpack trips

EASY: Mostly flat, well-maintained trails, less than 10 km (6 mi) long; family-friendly.

MODERATE: Trails are generally in good shape but there may be elevation changes of up to 760 m (2,500 ft). Trails are longer, up to 18 km (11 mi) in a day.

DIFFICULT: Trails may include rough terrain with uneven footing and river or stream crossings. Most adventures labeled difficult have more than 760 m (2,500 ft) of elevation gain and require long days of hiking — even if the distances are shorter than a moderate day. Any backpacking trip greater than three days is considered difficult because of the amount of food you must carry.

Rating difficulty for single and multi-day bike rides

EASY: Flat; typically less than 30 km (19 mi) in a day; family-friendly.

MODERATE: Expect more hills and greater mileage — up to 50 km (31 mi) in a day.

DIFFICULT: Hills are steeper and there are lots of them. Generally mileage is anything greater than 50 km (31 mi) but there are exceptions. Some rides are short but with many steep hills, like the Fundy Trail.

Rating difficulty for kayak and canoe trips

EASY: Water is calm and waves and currents are minimal to non-existent, distances are short; family-friendly.

MODERATE: A full day trip where wind and waves may be a factor but distance traveled is less than 15 km (9.3 mi). If canoeing, frequent short portages are a possibility.

DIFFICULT: A long day on the water, covering more than 15 km (9.3 mi), with wind and waves your constant companion. Currents may be an issue. Portages, if there are any, are longer or encounter rougher terrain. All wilderness trips far from civilization are rated difficult.

Throughout the book, look for a symbol below each title indicating the grade (level of difficulty). Easy adventures are represented by ■□□□, moderate ones by □■□□, difficult adventures by □□■□, and very difficult adventures by □□□■. Some adventures can have more than one level of difficulty depending on certain circumstances. For example, if an adventure could be moderate and/or difficult, this is represented by □■■□. If it could be easy all the way to very difficult, it would be ■■■■. You'll find different combinations in the book.

Rating difficulty for cross-country ski trips

Ratings for all of the cross-country ski adventures are in line with how each hill is rated by the park or organization that owns it. It's been my experience that ease or difficulty is related to the steepness of the hills on the trail.

All **skating** adventures are easy. **Rafting** is easy unless you're in Class III whitewater, in which case it becomes moderate.

Auyuittuq, NU

Managing risk and staying safe while participating in any outdoor adventure should be the goal of every outing. But you can't eliminate all risk and, in reality, that is part of the thrill of an outdoor adventure. Not everything is within your control, but most accidents can be prevented if you educate yourself and go prepared. If you're new to the outdoors, start off with shorter trips, perhaps with a tour so you can learn from the guides. Take the time to understand the risks, carry the 10 essentials and learn from your mistakes. Here are some of my thoughts on how you can make your next adventure a safe one.

THE 10 ESSENTIALS

Always carry the 10 essentials; these items are your survival insurance in case of an emergency.

1. A map. Nowadays people rely on a GPS but you should always carry a map and know how to read it, just in case your batteries die or your GPS gets broken or stolen.
2. A compass. And you should know how to use it.
3. A flashlight or headlamp with extra batteries and a spare bulb. Keep it in a waterproof bag.
4. Extra clothing. You'll have to decide how much you need to carry. Remember that cotton kills when it's wet.
5. A one-day supply of extra food that doesn't require cooking, such as energy bars and dried fruit. Always have extra water and a means of purifying it.
6. Sunglasses. On longer trips consider taking an extra pair and some duct tape to make a repair.
7. A Swiss Army–style pocketknife with scissors, a screwdriver, a can opener and at least two folding blades.
8. Matches stored in a waterproof container with a piece of sandpaper.
9. A firestarter. This is a lifesaver when wood is wet or you really need to start a fire quickly to warm up.
10. A first-aid kit in a waterproof bag. The contents will vary depending on what the adventure is, but at the very least carry an assortment of bandages, moleskin, adhesive tape, gauze bandages, cleanser, Neosporin and a triangular bandage. Add pain killers like Ibuprofen, Benadryl for allergic reactions and any other drugs you might think helpful.

OTHER NECESSARY ITEMS

- Sunscreen and a lip balm with a high SPF.

- Insect repellent is an absolute essential in many parts of Canada, depending on the time of year. Also, be wary of ticks. They are carriers of Lyme disease and Rocky Mountain spotted fever. During peak tick season wear long pants and sleeves and check your body thoroughly after each adventure.

HYPOTHERMIA

Hypothermia is the excessive loss of body heat that can eventually lead to death. It's preventable and reversible if you know how to treat it. It commonly occurs when it's wet and the temperature is between 0 and 10°C (32–50°F). Most of us in Canada have suffered the mild hypothermia of shivering and chills. But as it progresses, watch for impaired coordination, slurred speech and fuzzy thinking, followed by slowing pulse, shallow breathing, blue skin and finally, loss of consciousness. Irregular heartbeat is the last stage before death.

Hypothermia can happen quickly. In the outdoors, the possibility of it happening is high, especially on wet, windy days when the temperature is cool but not cold. Wear synthetic clothing, as it wicks the moisture away from your skin. Cotton kills because it doesn't dry quickly. Eat high-calorie foods regularly to stay energized. Stay tuned to other group members, who may not be aware of what's happening to them.

The key to dealing with hypothermia is to act fast. Change into dry, warm gear as soon as you feel the onset of shivering. Toss on rain gear and get out of the wind. Seek shelter. Eat sweets and have a hot drink. If someone is already incoherent, then the best thing to do is to set up a shelter. Remove the person's wet clothes and climb naked into a sleeping bag with them. Keep the person conscious and try to get them eating sweet foods, which provide energy quickly. Start a fire if you can and when possible seek medical help.

WILDLIFE

BEARS

Say the word Canada and the first thing that pops into people's minds is bears. They are around, but fortunately they're rarely a problem. Even so, if you're travelling through bear country, it's very important that you get to know your bears and take all the steps necessary to mitigate any kind of bear–human interaction. Remember, just your voice is usually enough to scare off a bear and it works far better than bear bells. Nonetheless, always carry a can of bear spray that is no more than two years old.

Black bears are much smaller than grizzly bears and lack the shoulder hump. If you see a bear print and it's got claws, then a grizzly has been through the area. Also look for signs of bear scat. If you find fresh scat, make a lot of noise and leave the area. Keep your campsite clean. Hang your food off a pole or a tree or bring bear-proof containers to store your food. Keep your tent scent free.

If you meet a bear and it doesn't take off, do the following:

- Keep an eye on the bear but don't make direct eye contact.

- Provide the bear with an escape route.
- Speak in a calm voice — which is easier said than done.
- Remain in a tight group; four people being the magic number to avoid an attack.
- Make yourself look taller.

Should the bear head in your direction:

- Use bear bangers, flares or whatever noisemaker you have.
- Yell and speak loudly.
- Use bear spray if it gets within 4 m (13 ft) but make sure the wind isn't blowing in your direction or you'll become incapacitated.
- If a bear charges, stand your ground; it's usually a bluff.
- Never run away from a bear, swim for it or let your dog off the leash as their barking will further agitate the bear.
- **If it's a black bear**, back away slowly. Do not climb a tree and do not play dead. If it attacks, fight back with everything you've got!!
- **If it's a grizzly bear**, back away slowly and try to climb higher than 3.6 m (12 ft) in a tree or it can pull you down. If it attacks, protect your head and stomach and play dead.

For all the days and weeks I have spent in the wilderness over a period of decades, I have seen bears perhaps a dozen times. In all instances, it has taken off or I've been able to back away without it following me. Go into the wilderness prepared and educated; don't avoid it altogether just because of bears.

Cougars

Cougars are present in many parts of Canada, especially on Vancouver Island and in the Rockies. Chances of seeing one are very rare. You should feel privileged if you do see one. They are solitary animals found in dense forest or rocky areas. They can grow to a length of 2.4 m (8 ft) and the average male weighs 56.7 kg (125 lb). Although cougar attacks are rare, it's important to know what to do.

- Don't hike by yourself if you are travelling through known cougar country.
- Always provide the cougar with an avenue of escape.
- Pick up small children and form a group. Try to make yourself look large by waving sticks.
- Speak in a calm voice. Don't look a cougar in the eye. Back away slowly but never turn your back on a cougar.
- Do not run or make sudden movements as this can trigger an attack.
- If a cougar attacks, fight back with whatever is on hand including sticks, stones and your fists.

Moose

Moose can be found in most parts of Canada but especially around lakes, streams and muskeg in the boreal forest. Although they give the appearance of looking docile, they are not. It's highly unlikely you'd be killed by a moose but they can inflict significant damage with a kick.

Fortunately a moose provides you with warning signs indicating that you should leave the area. If they smack their lips, flatten their ears, show the whites of their eye, toss their head up in the manner of a horse or if their hair bristles on the back of their neck or hips, it's time to leave. Once you do, they'll leave you alone. Should they charge, get behind a tree, as their eyesight is poor.

OTHER CONCERNS

LIGHTNING

Getting caught in a lightning storm is never a pleasant experience, especially when you're high on a mountain or out on a lake. These tips may save your life.

- Seek shelter in a substantial building if at all possible.
- Monitor approaching storms, especially if you're on the water or high on a mountain, and take cover as soon as you can.
- Stay away from tent poles and cooking gear.
- Crouch on a sleeping bag, plastic sheet or anything that helps shield you from wet ground.
- Never be the tallest object in a meadow.
- If you're caught on a mountain or hilltop, lose elevation as fast as you can. Get into a crouch position with feet together. When lightning hits the ground it spreads out along the surface and causes the formation of a ground current. This current can travel up one leg and down another. That's why it's so important to crouch with your legs together. Do not lie down.
- Avoid all metal conductors including wire fences, metal sheds and even ice axes.
- If you're with a group, spread out!!! You should be at least 15 m (50 ft) apart to minimize injuries. Again, assume the crouch position.
- Remove any metal jewelry; it can cause severe burns.
- Close your eyes to protect your vision and cover your ears to prevent hearing damage.
- Tuck your head into your knees to minimize the chance of a strike to the head.

STREAM CROSSINGS

Spring can be an especially deadly time to cross a fast-moving stream. To prevent injury and drowning, refer to the blog 12 Safety Tips for Safely Fording Rivers and Streams found in the following address:
hikebiketravel.com/30262/12-safety-trips-for-safely-fording-rivers-streams/

BUGS

Depending on the time of year, you may have to deal with bugs. June and early July are usually the worst time, but peak bug activity varies across the country. You may encounter a combination of blackflies, mosquitoes, no-see-ums, deer flies and horseflies. I do my best to avoid prime bug times as it really can ruin a trip. If you have no choice, then at least go prepared. Take a bug jacket and a lightweight head net. Carry insect repellent. Products with 30% DEET usually work on every-thing but the flies. Wear light-coloured clothing, don't use fragrances and avoid eating bananas. Choose your campsites wisely, avoiding any near standing water. Windy points work well.

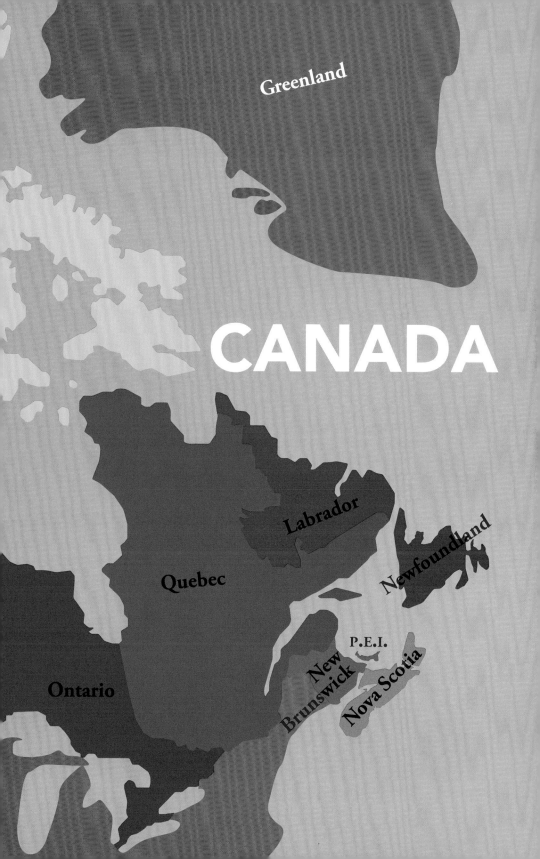

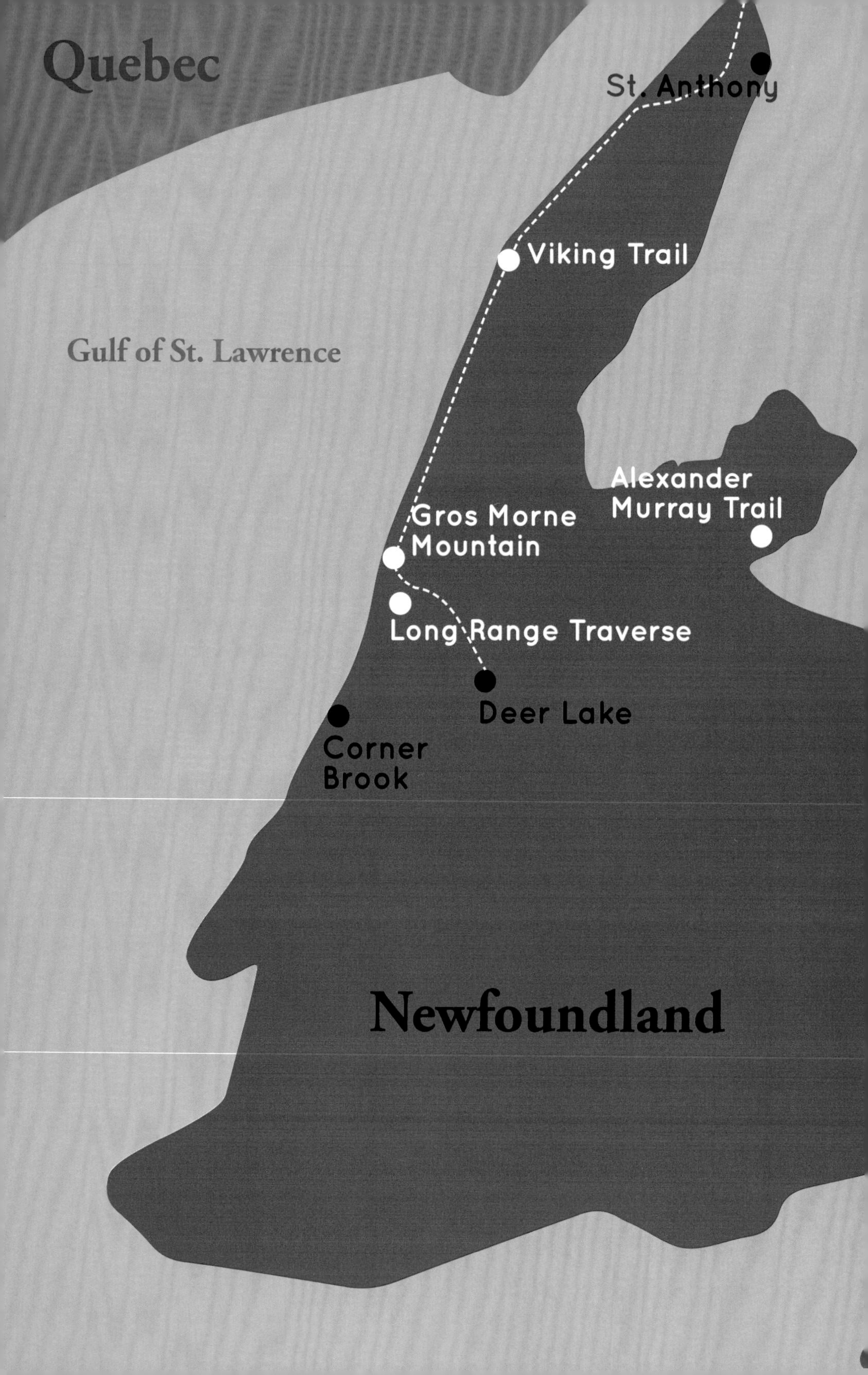

Quebec

Gulf of St. Lawrence

St. Anthony

Viking Trail

Alexander
Murray Trail

Gros Morne
Mountain

Long Range Traverse

Deer Lake

Corner
Brook

Newfoundland

Newfoundland Adventures

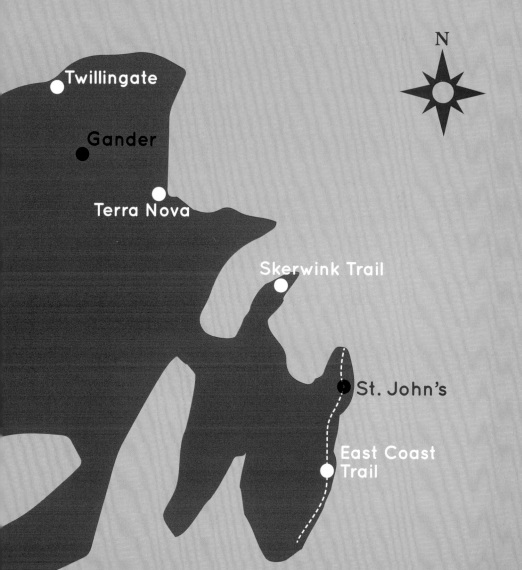

Atlantic Ocean

N

Twillingate

Gander

Terra Nova

Skerwink Trail

St. John's

East Coast Trail

Hiking
The East Coast Trail
on the Avalon Peninsula

■ ■ ■ ■

You're in for a treat if you decide to hike Newfoundland's East Coast Trail, rated by National Geographic in 2012 as one of the ten best adventure destinations in the world. Running from Cape St. Francis in the north to Cappahayden in the south, it offers 265 km (165 mi) of rugged and very beautiful coastal scenery via a series of twenty-four connected paths, each with its own northern and southern trailhead. Along the length of the trail you will be treated to a display of fjords, rugged cliffs, headlands and vertical columns of rock called sea stacks. You'll hike past Cape Spear, the most easterly point in Canada — where, with luck, you'll see icebergs and whales. Lighthouses, ecological reserves, abandoned settlements and wildlife encounters are also in the cards.

You can choose to do the trail in its entirety over a couple of weeks, or you can hike a section or two at a time. The trail winds through wilderness linking a total of thirty-three communities, including St. John's. There are highway signs pointing to trailheads, and once on the trail there should be no difficulty following it. Unless hiking the whole trail, the hard part lies in deciding what section to do and working out the logistics of getting to and from trailheads without retracing your steps.

For day trips, you can simply base yourself in St. John's. If you're there on a weekend, it's easy to carpool and join a hike led by a volunteer from the East Coast Trail Association. Some of the most scenic day hikes include Sugarloaf Path, Stiles Cove Path, Spout Path and the Cape Spear Path. All are very different and each appealing for different reasons. The level of difficulty of the twenty-four trails varies: sixteen are rated easy or moderate, and the rest are either difficult or strenuous. The East Coast Trail website, **eastcoasttrail.ca**, is a great resource with detailed information about each section of the hike.

Another option is to do the full trail, either on your own with a backpack or with the help of the tour company Trail Connections. If you camp, there are five wilderness campsites along the trail and one campsite in a provincial park. Alternatively, get a taste of Newfoundland hospitality and stay in a B&B. Many B&B hosts are very accommodating and will pick you up at trailheads at pre-arranged times. Failing that, try booking a local taxi. But be warned that you will need to be prepared for a full wilderness experience because the distances between villages can be large and there isn't much infrastructure in place.

If you are attracted to the idea of immersing yourself in a landscape of rugged east coast scenery while breathing in generous doses of the Newfoundland whiff (the Newfoundland term for good salt air), then you're going to love this trail.

HIGHLIGHTS: Dramatic coastal scenery, coves, rock faces, cliffs, pocket beaches, occasional icebergs, interesting flora, lighthouses, historic communities

DISTANCE: 265 km (165 mi) of developed trail

TIME NEEDED: 1–14 days

GRADE: Easy to very difficult depending on what section you hike and whether it's wet or dry

WHERE: The trail runs from Cape St. Francis at the tip of the Avalon Peninsula to Cappahayden in the south.

HOW: Do it on your own or sign a waiver to do a weekend hike with volunteers from the East Coast Trail Association.

WHEN: April to November, but you could snowshoe many sections of the trail in the winter.

COST: Free

DON'T FORGET: Warm clothes, rain gear, bug repellent, walking poles, gaiters. You can buy a map in St. John's or download one from the website.

OPTIONS: Pick one section of the trail to hike at a time.

TOUR COMPANIES: Trail Connections. Or join a guided weekend hike with the East Coast Trail Association.

INTERESTING FACT: In 2010, Hurricane Igor toppled 5,000 trees onto the trail. The trail has since been cleaned up.

Hiking
The Skerwink Trail
on the Bonavista Peninsula

■■□□

The Skerwink Trail has received its share of accolades, including a ranking as one of the top 35 trails in North America and Europe by *Travel & Leisure* magazine in 2003. It offers more scenery per linear foot than any other trail in Newfoundland, at least according to John Vivian, the founder of the trail. Located in Trinity East on the Bonavista Peninsula, the Skerwink Trail follows the north and south coasts of Skerwink Head, a rocky peninsula separating Port Rexton from Trinity Harbour. It's best hiked in a clockwise direction so you can take advantage of the views of Trinity Harbour as you hike south from Skerwink Head.

The trail starts off flat and proceeds arrow-straight along an old rail bed. Just after the one-kilometre post, the coast comes into view and remains in sight for the next 3 km (1.9 mi). The hiking through this section is exceptional with a different first-class coastal view every few minutes. Should you be afraid of heights or if you prefer trees to coast, there is also the option to hike an inland portion of trail between kilometres one and two. But really, it's the coastal trail that packs the visual punch.

Chances are your progress along the coast will be slow, not because the trail is overly strenuous but because there's so much to look at. Views of improbably shaped sea stacks rising out of the water and narrow cliff-faced beaches keep stopping you in your tracks. Photographic opportunities abound. And if you're lucky, whales and icebergs can be seen in season. But even with all that grand coastal scenery, the highlight for me was watching a couple of baby foxes playing.

The Skerwink Trail is one of the best-maintained trails I have ever hiked. There are signs every kilometre so you can track your progress; steep sections are accessed with stairs; boardwalks abound and lookouts come with benches. Along the coast, trees have been trimmed so you can continually enjoy the views. But do exercise caution, especially if you are hiking with children; the drop-offs are severe and any fall will probably be your last.

Don't miss the Skerwink Trail if you're anywhere near the Bonavista Peninsula. It's a superb hike, and one you'll be talking about for years.

HIGHLIGHTS: Coastal landscape, sea stacks, sea caves and arches, capelin beaches, bird life, humpback and minke whales, moose, occasional icebergs

DISTANCE: 5.3 km (3.3 mi) loop

TIME NEEDED: 1.5–2.5 hours at a minimum, more if you're an avid photographer or you want beach time

GRADE: Easy to moderate and family-friendly

WHERE: Located 11 km (6.8 mi) northeast of Trinity via Highway 239 and 230 N, and 270 km (168 mi) north of St. John's

HOW: There is a parking lot across from the trailhead, but no public transportation.

WHEN: May to early October

COST: Free, though you can donate to Friends of Skerwink to help with trail maintenance.

DON'T FORGET: Dogs must be on a leash. Bring wind- and rain-proof gear. There is one outhouse within five minutes of the trailhead.

OPTIONS: Hike the 7.7 km (4.8 mi) Murphy's Cove–Lodge Pond Trail in Trinity Bay North, or the short Upper or Lower Gun Hill Trails out of Trinity.

TOUR COMPANIES: None

INTERESTING FACT: 'Skerwink' is the local name for a seabird called a shearwater.

Hiking
The Coastal Trail
in Terra Nova National Park

■ □ □ □

If you've ever driven the highway between St. John's and Gander or Deer Lake, you've driven through Terra Nova National Park. Although the drive is pretty, you do need to get off the road to appreciate the park. Terra Nova lacks the grandeur of Gros Morne, but what it does offer is a taste of the boreal forest where it meets the North Atlantic Ocean.

Terra Nova became Newfoundland's first national park in 1957. With 400 sq km (154 sq mi) of space, there's plenty to explore. There are twelve hiking trails, covering over 100 km (62 mi) and ranging from short half-hour jaunts to multi-day trips. Choose the family-friendly 9 km (5.6 mi) Coastal Trail if you'd like to include some beach time and a swim.

The Coastal Trail starts by the Visitor Centre, although some people start at the southern end of Newman Sound. Its mostly flat terrain, with only a few minor hills, means it can be comfortably hiked in half a day. The trail sticks to the coast as it heads south through a forest of black spruce along Newman Sound. Though it's primarily dirt, some boardwalks — fringed with ferns and wildflowers like lady's slipper and blue flag — protect sections of the fragile bog. At the halfway mark, you need to cross a road; Pissamare Falls is here, but it can easily be missed as there isn't much water flowing.

There are plenty of beach access points, with the best beach being at Sandy Point, where you can enjoy a breeze from all directions. The water isn't deep, so it's perfect for kids. You can still find engine parts from a sawmill — a remnant of the logging industry which thrived in the area from the mid-1920s to the mid-1950s. In fact, five schooners were built there.

Playground equipment, picnic tables and cooking shelters mark the end of the trail. Simply retrace your steps to return to the parking lot. As you head back, especially in the area of the mudflats, keep a close eye out for ospreys, eagles, terns, greater yellowlegs and spotted sandpipers. Newman Sound, one of ninety-two Canadian Wildlife Service Bird Sanctuaries in Canada, offers migrating birds a plentiful food source and safe refuge.

HIGHLIGHTS: Beaches, swimming, wildflowers, mudflats, eagles, osprey, shorebirds

DISTANCE: 9 km (5.6 mi) return

TIME NEEDED: 3 hours

GRADE: Easy and family-friendly

WHERE: Start at either the Visitor Centre parking lot at Salton's Brook or at Newman Sound.

HOW: Purchase a park pass and go.

WHEN: May until late October

COST: $5.80/adult, $2.90/youth

DON'T FORGET: Layered clothing, bathing suit, bug spray on a calm day

OPTIONS: There are more than 100 km (62 mi) of hiking trails in the park. For an overnight trip, hike the 48 km (30 mi) Outport Trail. For a great view, hike the 8 km (5 mi) Ochre Hill trail.

TOUR COMPANIES: None

INTERESTING FACT: The appetites of the park's large moose population make it hard for the forest to regenerate, as a single moose is capable of eating 18–27 kg (40–60 lb) of vegetation per day.

Hiking
The Alexander Murray Trail
in King's Point

□ ■ □ □

As you drive into King's Point, look north and search for the network of stairs visible on the ridgeline heading towards the high point of the Green Bay area. That's your destination if you're planning to hike the Alexander Murray Trail, a beautifully built trail known as one of Newfoundland's best-kept secrets.

The start of this hike is located at the entrance to the tiny community of King's Point behind the Visitor Centre. Sign the logbook, read any notices explaining the current condition of the trail, then cross the first of several brooks into mixed forest. In five minutes, not only will you begin the 2,200 stairs of the trail, but you'll reach Grouse Brook and see the first of many signs showing your exact location as well as the distance and time to the next point of interest.

Moose Barrens, located at the 1.4 km (0.9 mi) point, is the start of the loop section of trail. Head in a clockwise direction for Corner Brook Gorge. In theory, you could hike the loop in either direction, but you'll have more energy if you take the two hundred stairs (and change) required to get out of the gorge earlier in the hike. The stairs start in earnest after the Moose Barrens. They will be a great test of your aerobic capacity, but the reality is that they make the hike a whole lot easier than it would be without them.

On a hot day, the gorge and waterfalls are a refreshing place to rest or go for a dip. Afterwards, climb back to the main trail and up what feels like the never-ending stairs until you reach a rocky section that takes you to the summit, known as the Haypook. Viewing platforms and picnic tables offer superb views of the southwest arm of Green Bay as well as the Gaff Topsails, three drumlins rising above the surrounding land on the southwestern horizon.

The descent from the summit on a combination of stairs and dirt trail passes Roswell's and Gull Brook Falls and a campsite. Generally, the descent on the well-spaced stairs is very pleasant, but there is one washed-out bridge where you'll have to wade across. From there, continue through some boggy areas to reach Moose Barrens and the main trail. You'll be back at your starting point within thirty minutes.

Alexander Murray, the trail's namesake, believed this part of Newfoundland was as picturesque as any he'd seen in the world. Hike this trail and see if you agree.

HIGHLIGHTS: Waterfalls, Corner Brook Gorge, views of the southwest arm of Green Bay and the Gaff Topsails, icebergs in season

DISTANCE: 8 km (5 mi) round trip plus 335 m (1,100 ft) of elevation gain over a total of 2,200 stairs

TIME NEEDED: Allow 3–5 hours.

GRADE: Moderate

WHERE: The trail starts by the entrance of the town of King's Point in central Newfoundland, 12 km (8 mi) off the Trans-Canada Highway via Highway 391 approximately 132 km (82 mi) northeast of Deer Lake.

HOW: Park at the welcome centre where you can load up on water and food during business hours.

WHEN: May to October

COST: Free, but you can make a donation for trail maintenance.

DON'T FORGET: Bug spray, sunscreen, water

OPTIONS: Try the nearby 6 km (3.7 mi) King's Cove Hiking Trail in Harry's Harbour, where you'll find picturesque coves and beaches.

TOUR COMPANIES: None

INTERESTING FACT: The trail is named for Sir Alexander Murray, head of the Newfoundland Geologic Survey from 1864 to 1883 and the person responsible for producing the first geological map of the province.

Kayaking in
Iceberg Alley
out of Twillingate

■ ■ ■ □

As mythical as mingling with giants, kayaking with icebergs in Iceberg Alley is an experience that should be on every wilderness bucket list. The coastline that stretches south from Labrador to the southern tip of Newfoundland is one of the top places in the world for seeing these frozen behemoths, and Twillingate, Newfoundland is where iceberg viewing and kayaking come together.

The peak viewing time in Twillingate is May, but icebergs can linger into July. Every year is different, depending on how many icebergs calve off the west coast of Greenland and how quickly they move. You can check the location of icebergs in advance of your trip by consulting **IcebergFinder.com**. The prime time for kayaking with icebergs is June and early July; any earlier and you may be dealing with pack ice in Twillingate Harbour.

There is something almost supernatural about paddling at eye level with icebergs. Powerful and unpredictable, they're also incredibly beautiful, and each one is unique. But they can roll over with little notice, taking you with them if you happen to be too close. They can also calve without warning, and the resultant wave can easily flip you. To be safe, keep a distance of at least twice the height or the length of the iceberg.

Most visitors to Twillingate will want to hire a kayaking guide; iceberg season is no place to paddle on your own without someone who understands icebergs. Even if you do have considerable kayaking experience, you might find it intimidating to be on your own around icebergs. Local knowledge will also come in handy in judging wind and waves, and how far out of Twillingate Harbour you should paddle.

When I was there, I was lucky to have a relatively calm day which allowed me to kayak towards Twillingate's Long Point Lighthouse, then circumnavigate Burnt Island in just three hours. But a big part of the pleasure of kayaking in this part of the world is simply watching the icebergs, especially when they start to move. And, if your timing is right, you could see humpback whales as well.

Experienced kayakers might want to consider an overnight paddle to the southeast coast of Burnt Island, a beautiful spot where you can enjoy the sight of floating ice from a beach-front campsite. If you're not a kayaker, hike the trails around the Long Point Lighthouse. Exceptional coastal views, rocky clifftop hiking and icebergs will ensure a memorable hike.

HIGHLIGHTS: Icebergs, rugged coastline, whale sightings, bird life, Twillingate

DISTANCE: Up to 15 km (9.3 mi) if you circumnavigate Burnt Island

TIME NEEDED: From 2.5 hours to a half day

GRADE: Easy to difficult depending on wind and wave conditions

WHERE: Twillingate is located 112 km (70 mi) north of Gander via Highway 330 and 331 off the Trans-Canada Highway.

HOW: Book a tour with OQ Close Encounters.

WHEN: June through till mid-September

COST: Tours start at $69 pp.

DON'T FORGET: A wetsuit (provided when you paddle with a tour company), fleece jacket, raincoat, sunscreen, sun hat

OPTIONS: Hike the Lighthouse/Lower Head Trail for superb views of icebergs in season.

TOUR COMPANIES: If you don't kayak, consider the option of a zodiac tour with OQ Close Encounters, or arrange a boat tour with one of five companies in the Twillingate area.

INTERESTING FACT: Ninety percent of Newfoundland's icebergs come from glaciers in western Greenland. Their journey to the coast of Newfoundland can take several years.

Cycling
The Viking Trail
through Gros Morne National Park

□ ■ ■ □

If you have an adventurous spirit and are prepared for some challenging cycling, then take the 600 km (373 mi) trip up the rocky coast of Great Northern Peninsula through picturesque fishing villages with names like Sally's Cove, Cow Head and Brig Bay. You'll have the opportunity to meet the people of Newfoundland, who in my experience rank as some of the friendliest and most generous on the planet. Where else in the world would complete strangers offer you their car so you can drive to dinner instead of cycling in the rain?

A ten-day itinerary is ideal for this multifaceted trip. Start in Deer Lake and cycle 89 km (55 mi) across the rocky barrens to beautiful Trout River. On the second day, take a boat to Norris River and continue 42 km (26 mi) to Rocky Harbour. Get off the bike on day three and explore Gros Morne National Park. Although you could cycle straight through, this UNESCO World Heritage Site contains one of the best examples of plate tectonics in the world. At the very least, take a boat ride up the fjord or hike to the top of Gros Morne Mountain (see Hiking Gros Morne Mountain).

On the fourth day, head 50 km (31 mi) north to Cow Head, allowing time to do a boat tour of the fjord. On day five, cycle 101 km (62 mi) along the coast to Hawke's Bay, and on day six, travel 86 km (54 mi) to St. Barbe, visiting the Port au Choix National Historic Site along the way. Once there, allow a day to ferry over to Labrador. Whale sightings are common and the cycling, though hilly, travels through a beautiful elemental landscape. Besides, when are you likely to return to Labrador?

On day eight, pray that the wind is at your back, as it's 125 km (78 mi) across a desolate stretch of the northern interior barrens to Pistolet Bay. It's even farther if you don't plan to camp. On day nine, bike 72 km (45 mi) to L'Anse aux Meadows, this trip's second UNESCO World Heritage Site, where you'll see the wood-framed sod houses of an eleventh-century Viking settlement — evidence of the first European presence in North America. If your timing is good, you may see an iceberg float by, too.

After that, it's back to Pistolet Bay. On the final day, enjoy an easy 30 km (19 mi) to St. Anthony, where you'll take your shuttle back to Deer Lake. Of course there are variations to this itinerary depending on what company you choose and whether you plan to camp, but the one day you spend cycling across the barren lands is a tough one, no matter what.

HIGHLIGHTS: Rugged coastal scenery, unexpected moose encounters, Gros Morne National Park, whale-watching, L'Anse aux Meadows, music, outdoor theatre, exceptionally friendly people

DISTANCE: 523 km (325 mi) plus an additional 72 km (45 mi) to visit L'Anse aux Meadows. If you cycle in Labrador, add at least another 30 km (19 mi); more if you're up for it.

TIME NEEDED: A minimum of seven days, ideally 10 days to allow for side trips

GRADE: Moderate to difficult

WHERE: Start in Deer Lake and finish cycling in St. Anthony's near the tip of the Great Northern Peninsula.

WHEN: June to September

HOW: It's best to join a tour unless you take your own bike and figure out a shuttle back from St. Anthony.

COST: Highly variable depending whether you're self-guided or with a tour company

DON'T FORGET: Rain gear

OPTIONS: Whale-watching and kayaking around Bonne Bay are two additional side trips.

TOUR COMPANIES: Freewheeling, Pedal and Sea Adventures, Atlantic Canada Cycling

INTERESTING FACT: The area has been inhabited for at least 7,500 years, starting with the now-extinct Maritime Archaic Indians, the extinct Dorset people and the Vikings.

Hiking
Gros Morne Mountain
in Gros Morne National Park

□□■□

If you only have time for one hike while you're in Gros Morne National Park and you're looking for a killer view, plan on the challenging hike to the top of Gros Morne Mountain. The return is no picnic either. But for incomparable views of Ten Mile Brook Pond, the Long Range Mountains and Bonne Bay, plus the chance to stand on the second-highest peak in Newfoundland at 806 m (2,644 ft), it's well worth the effort.

Also called the James Callaghan Trail, after a peace- and nature-loving British prime minister, it starts with an easy 4 km (2.5 mi) climb through the woods on a combination of dirt and rock paths, boardwalk and stairs. When you emerge at a viewing platform near a knot of small ponds, you'll find a marvellous vista of the gully up to the top of Gros Morne Mountain, as well as Bonne Bay unfolding to the south.

For some, this will be enough hiking for one day. But if you want to keep going and know you can return to the trailhead before dark, continue to the summit and back on an 8 km (5 mi) loop, which takes four to six hours to complete. It begins with a strenuous 500 m (1,640 ft) climb up a steep and rocky scree slope (returning this way is not recommended). Once at the massive summit, rock cairns and rock-lined paths lead the way across the flat top. You're now in a fragile Arctic-alpine environment with plants and animals that are normally only seen hundreds of kilometres farther north. Tread lightly.

To return, descend across the mountain to the spectacular lookout over the U-shaped Ten Mile Brook Pond. Plan to eat lunch just below this spot so you can get out of the constant wind. Then, continue your descent via the northeast flank of the mountain, guided by fluorescent fog markers. The trail is in great shape through here, with lots of boardwalk and one section of 177 well-built stairs — I counted.

Once you reach a small lake and the Ferry Gulch Campsite, it's 2.5 km (1.6 mi) of rough terrain back to the viewing platform. It's also blisteringly hot through here on a sunny day, so make sure you refill your water bottles in the lake — remembering to treat or filter it.

The Gros Morne Trail can throw anything your way, including high winds, temperature variations and thick, disorienting fog. Water, especially at the summit, can also be an issue, so take at least two litres per person. Despite the hazards, it's a great trail; just don't overestimate your abilities.

HIGHLIGHTS: Views of Ten Mile Pond and the Long Range Mountains, wildlife sightings including black bear, moose, woodland caribou, Arctic hare and rock ptarmigan, Arctic tundra habitat

DISTANCE: 16 km (10 mi) partial loop with 800 m of elevation gain

TIME NEEDED: 6–8 hours

GRADE: Difficult and not recommended for small children

WHERE: The trailhead is located 7 km (4.3 mi) southeast of Rocky Harbour off of Highway 430.

WHEN: Late June through till September; the trail opens once the rock ptarmigan have hatched.

HOW: Obtain a park permit and map at the Visitor Centre.

COST: $9.80/adult, $8.30/senior, $4.90/youth

DON'T FORGET: Water, warm clothes, rain gear, hiking poles

OPTIONS: Reserve a backcountry campsite at Ferry Gulch. It can accommodate three tents. Another excellent hike in the park is the Green Gardens Trail, a coastal trail close to the Tablelands.

TOUR COMPANIES: Gros Morne Adventures, Clem Trekking Adventures

INTERESTING FACT: Gros Morne is one of the few places in the world where the ocean crust and rocks making up the earth's mantle are exposed on the surface.

Backpacking
The Long Range Traverse
in Gros Morne National Park

□□□■

A real test of your mettle and your navigation skills is the challenging Long Range Traverse. This unmarked wilderness hike is located in Gros Morne National Park on the west coast of Newfoundland. The route — there really isn't a trail — takes you through world-class scenery that includes awe-inspiring views of fjords and rock-covered plateaus, rolling hills and numerous lakes, ponds, streams and rivers. Fortunately, the reward for hiking the trail more than makes up for any discomfort, be it physical or mental.

The trip starts off with a beautiful boat ride to the end of Western Brook Pond. But once the boat drops you on the dock, you are well and truly on your own. The Traverse only sees about 500 backpackers per year, so you may not see another human soul. What you will see are moose, and perhaps the odd caribou or black bear. The park gives every group a Spot transmitter for emergencies. Should you be late to re-emerge after your trip, the park personnel will prepare for a rescue, but will delay for 24 hours if you have been caught in dense fog or bad weather.

The hike is typically done over three to five days. The odd group does it in two, but that's just a marathon and doesn't allow you the chance to soak in the beauty of your surroundings. Three long days are just doable, provided you don't make any navigation errors — a common occurrence, judging from the reports I've heard.

To my mind, four days is ideal. But if dense fog appears, be prepared to stay put until it clears, unless you want to risk a navigation nightmare on your hands. The route on the first day is the easiest to follow. Stay right of the waterfall and you'll pop out where you need to on top of the gorge. But the next few days present some navigation challenges.

You should never be hiking in tuckamore (a disorienting landscape of impenetrable krummholz vegetation), and game trails don't always take you in the direction you want. Be prepared to pull out your map and compass repeatedly; use a GPS only as a back-up. Also be prepared for a couple of river crossings. You know you're near the end of the trip when you catch sight of Ten Mile Pond with Gros Morne Mountain rising in the distance. It's mostly downhill from there, though the trail to Ferry Gulch is one of the steepest I've ever encountered. Once there, it's another 6.5 km (4 mi) on a well-marked trail back to the parking lot.

This is an exceptional trail and one every keen backpacker will love.

HIGHLIGHTS: World-famous views, scenic boat ride, lakes, wildlife, grand mountain scenery, wildflowers

DISTANCE: About 35 km (22 mi) if you don't make any navigation errors, and a 700 m (2,297 ft) elevation gain

TIME NEEDED: 3–5 days

GRADE: Very difficult

WHERE: The trailhead is accessed via a boat shuttle on Western Brook Pond. Trail starts at dock at end of the fjord. It's a 3 km (1.9 mi) walk to boat shuttle from the parking lot, located 27 km (17 mi) north of Rocky Harbour via Route 430.

HOW: Reserve months in advance and book a boat shuttle via **Bontours.ca** to take you to the end of Western Brook Pond. Arrange Pittman's or VIP Tours taxi to boat shuttle or for pickup at end of hike.

WHEN: Late June to late September

COST: $24.50 Long Range reservation fee; Long Range fee $83.40 pp. Boat shuttle is $32.50 pp with minimum of six people. Taxi fare is about $40 from parking lot to boat shuttle.

DON'T FORGET: Permit issued only if you pass a navigation test proving good map-reading and compass skills. Obtain Map 12H12 for the Long Range Traverse at the Visitor Centre or outdoors store. Bring warm clothes, rain gear, first aid kit, insect repellent, bug net, 2 days of extra food.

OPTIONS: The North Rim hike from the boat landing can be combined with the Long Range Traverse, but as of this writing the trail is in rough shape. Contact the park at 1-709-458-2417 for the latest information.

TOUR COMPANIES: Gros Morne Adventures, Clem Trekking Adventures

INTERESTING FACT: The Long Range Mountains are the eroded remains of mountains formed 1.2 billion years ago.

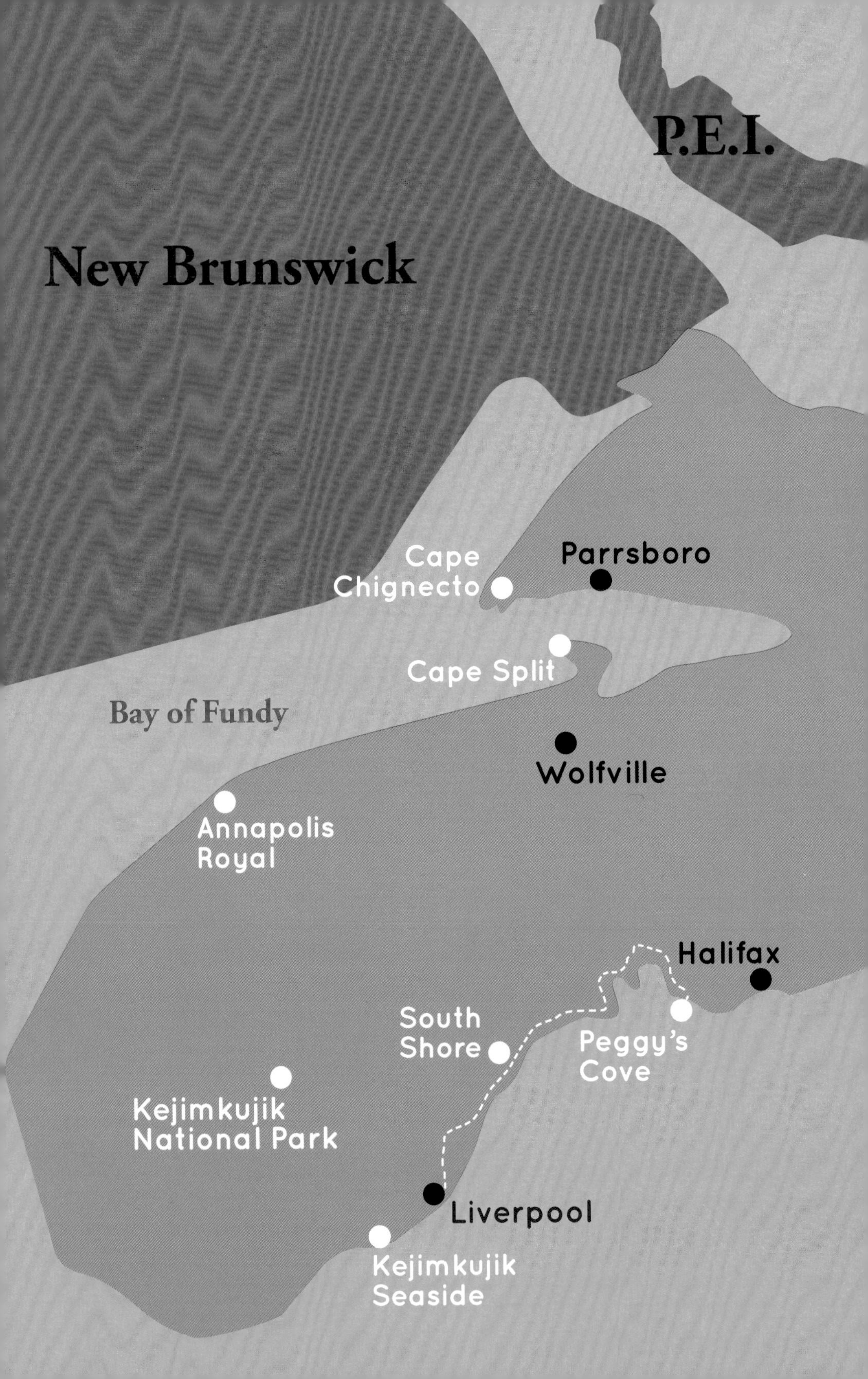

P.E.I.

New Brunswick

Bay of Fundy

Cape
Chignecto

Parrsboro

Cape Split

Wolfville

Annapolis
Royal

Halifax

South
Shore

Peggy's
Cove

Kejimkujik
National Park

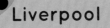
Liverpool

Kejimkujik
Seaside

Gulf of St. Lawrence

Cabot
Trail

Sydney

Nova Scotia

Atlantic Ocean

N

Nova Scotia
Adventures

Kayaking
The Peggy's Cove Area
out of East Dover

□ ■ □ □

If you've ever clambered over the rocks at Peggy's Cove and stared out to sea, hypnotized by the waves rolling in and smashing onto the rocks below, you probably wouldn't have thought that kayaking there would be a good idea or even possible. But it is.

One look at a marine chart will tell you why: the countless islands and islets east of Peggy's Cove allow for safe kayaking by absorbing much of the power of the waves. An adventurous beginner should consider paddling in a double kayak, but if you've got solid intermediate paddling skills, challenge yourself from the seat of a single. However, in these waters it would be sensible to engage a guide; between the currents, swells and wind, it's helpful to have someone with local knowledge. And with a guide you are able to get into places that look far more dangerous than they actually are, including a few spots where you can paddle up towards a big breaking swell, which will then surprise you by dissipating before you're engulfed. And there are sections — depending on what the tide is doing — where you'll have fun slithering your kayak over kelp-covered rocks to get to open water.

Launching in East Dover, I set out with my guide for a day of exploration. Initially the water was calm, but once out of the bay near the pretty community of West Dover, we were into confused water with lots of bounce. The paddling then became challenging enough to require my full attention. For lunch we pulled up onto an unnamed island — basically just a huge chunk of granite — in Polly Cove which had a great view of Peggy's Cove. It was hard not to be awed by the dramatic and desolate beauty of the area.

After lunch, you can head back the way you came, or take the exceptional side trip to Dover Island, which might end up being the highlight of your day. Essentially a mile-long slab of granite, Dover Island is a mecca for rock climbers. Land your kayak in a safe place and walk to the west end of the island past weekend campsites and through fields filled with pretty wildflowers. Park yourself on a flat rock out of the wind and sit back to watch the timeless beauty of the breaking waves. You can make it back to East Dover from here in under an hour. This is a one-day trip that will stay with you for years to come.

HIGHLIGHTS: Spectacular rocky coastline, erratics, quaint fishing villages, views of Peggy's Cove from the water, Dover Island

DISTANCE: 8–10 km (5–6 mi) for a full day, approximately 6 km (4 mi) for a half day

TIME NEEDED: A half to a full day

GRADE: Moderate. You should be an intermediate paddler for a single kayak or an adventurous beginner for a double kayak.

WHERE: Start in East Dover, a 10-minute drive east of Peggy's Cove and 38 km (24 mi) from Halifax.

WHEN: Mid-May until mid-October

HOW: If you've got strong paddling skills, charts and your own kayak, launch in any quiet bay in East or West Dover. Otherwise, engage a guide.

COST: Prices start at $45 for a sunset tour.

DON'T FORGET: Sunglasses, sunscreen, windbreaker, footwear that can get wet

OPTIONS: Paddle South offers rentals and tours out of Mahone Bay, 87 km (54 mi) west of Peggy's Cove.

TOUR COMPANIES: Nova Shores Adventures

INTERESTING FACT: North America's only official lighthouse post office is located in Peggy's Cove.

Cycling
The South Shore
of Nova Scotia

□ ■ □ □

Cycling the south shore of Nova Scotia is a fantastic way to discover its charms. You can slow down and breathe the fresh salt air, poke about historic small towns and fishing villages, meet local artisans, and eat all the lobster rolls and pie you can manage. Hills make the cycling moderately difficult, but the distances are short. It's roughly 130 km (81 mi) from Peggy's Cove to Lunenburg via the Aspotogan Peninsula. There are side roads aplenty to explore, but resist them. Shorter cycling days make time for all the other fun things to do.

Start at Peggy's Cove, a fishing village built on time-smoothed granite and erratics (rocks left by retreating glaciers). Allow time to wander the village and visit the lighthouse. After that, continue towards Hubbards via St. Margaret's Bay on winding, shoulderless roads through a hilly landscape that transitions from rocky coast to tree-lined beaches. Take care not to miss the memorial for Swissair Flight 111. Once you reach Hubbards, you can continue directly to Chester, a seaside resort town of manicured lawns, gardens and old money. Alternatively, you can cycle 58 km (36 mi) around the rock-strewn coastline of Aspotogan Peninsula past deserted beaches and sleepy, picturesque fishing villages.

The road from Chester to Mahone Bay is more trees than views, but once you reach Mahone Bay you're in for a treat. This very pretty town has three waterfront churches and numerous galleries and studios. Join a kayaking tour and explore a few of the three hundred islands of Mahone Bay.

After that, make your way to Lunenburg via Indian Point, exploring the back roads as you go. But leave time for Blue Rocks, a small fishing community calling itself Lunenburg's answer to Peggy's Cove. A twenty-minute bike ride later, you'll be in Lunenburg, a UNESCO World Heritage Site and the best example in North America of a planned British colonial settlement. The folks here aren't afraid of a little colour; pink, orange, bright blue and lime-green houses beg to be photographed.

If you've still got the energy and the time, cycle out to the Ovens, just 15 km (9 mi) from Lunenburg, to explore the park's hiking trails and seaside caves. From there you can continue on quiet coastal roads as far as Liverpool, about 70 km (44 mi) away via a ferry from La Have.

The back roads and towns on the south shore of Nova Scotia are sure to enchant. One trip here is never enough.

HIGHLIGHTS: Colourful fishing villages, lighthouses, coastal scenery, beaches, Lunenburg, Peggy's Cove, Mahone Bay, Chester, local cafés, galleries

DISTANCE: Up to 175 km (109 mi), depending on your time and energy

TIME NEEDED: 1–4 days

GRADE: Moderate

WHERE: Between Peggy's Cove and Liverpool along the south shore of Nova Scotia

HOW: Bring your own bike, rent a bike from Freewheeling Adventures in Hubbards or join a tour group.

WHEN: May to early October

COST: Allow for bike rentals, meals and accommodation. There are lots of B&Bs as well as camping choices.

DON'T FORGET: A bike repair kit

OPTIONS: Explore Tancook Island by bike via an 8 km (5 mi) ferry ride from Chester.

TOUR COMPANIES: Freewheeling Adventures, Pedal and Sea Adventures, Great Explorations

BEFORE YOU GO: Read *The Last Best Place: Lost in the Heart of Nova Scotia* by John Demont.

INTERESTING FACT: Some of the houses in Lunenburg date back to the 18th century, which is very old by Canadian standards.

Hiking in
Kejimkujik
National Park Seaside

■☐☐☐

Kejimkujik National Park Seaside boasts 22 sq km (8.5 sq mi) of wild, rugged and isolated coastal scenery. It is also home to bogs dotted with orchids and thick coastal forest made up of stunted balsam fir and white spruce. Located on the southwest shore of Nova Scotia, it's a special part of the province that feels untouched by humans, even though it has a long history of habitation.

Within the park there are two superb hiking trails: the 5.2 km (3.2 mi) out-and-back Harbour Rocks Trail and the 8.7 km (5.4 mi) Port Joli Head loop. They can be done individually in just a few hours, but it's also possible to combine them.

The access for both is via a flat trail that winds from the parking lot through dense forest. There are no views through here, but the trail boasts plenty of wildflowers. Once you get to the first well-signed intersection, you have to decide which of the two hikes to do. Head right to continue on the Port Joli Head trail or stay left for Harbour Rocks.

The Port Joli Head trail is divine. A combination of boardwalk and gravel paths takes you through bogs laced with a mix of wildflowers, including pitcher plants and wild iris, to a large viewing platform overlooking Boyd's Bay, and from there to the coast. The coastal section of trail is surprisingly tough going, as it's on cobbles, but it's very pretty. Look for lobster traps washed ashore and admire the views over to the beaches at Thomas Raddall Provincial Park.

As you hike around the tip of the peninsula at Port Joli Head, stop and admire the stone buildings left from the days when a thousand sheep roamed the area. Keep a close eye out for black bears through here; I saw a mother bear and two cubs.

Harbour Rocks is the next landmark. The rocks and the islets are basking spots for hundreds of seals. You might see Eider ducks and cormorants, too. The highlight for many, though, will be the glistening white sand and turquoise waters of St. Catherine's River Beach, just a short distance away. The sand here is of the talking variety: it squeaks when you walk on it because the quartz grains are all of a uniform shape. This beach is also the nesting ground for endangered piping plovers, so much of it is off-limits to the public from late April until mid-August.

Hiking the trails at Kejimkujik National Park Seaside is bliss. It's a rare treat to experience such coastal wilderness.

HIGHLIGHTS: Secluded rocky coves, wild-flowers, beaches, rugged coastal scenery, wildlife including seals, black bears and seabirds

DISTANCE: The Harbour Rocks Trail is 5.2 km (3.2 mi) out and back; the trail around Port Joli Head is an 8.7 km (5.4 mi) loop.

TIME NEEDED: A half day

GRADE: Easy and family-friendly

WHERE: Approximately 174 km (108 mi) west of Halifax and 25 km (15.5 mi) southwest of Liverpool via Highway 103 and St. Catherine's River Road

HOW: The park is only open during the day.

WHEN: The hike is best done between May and October.

COST: Free

DON'T FORGET: Bear spray, food, water

OPTIONS: Spend the night camping in Thomas Raddall Provincial Park — just 10 minutes away by car — as there is no camping in Kejimkujik Seaside.

TOUR COMPANIES: None

INTERESTING FACT: The earliest inhabitants of the park, the Maritime Archaic Indians, lived here 4,500 years ago.

Paddling
The Lakes and Rivers
of Kejimkujik National Park

■■□□

Kejimkujik National Park in Nova Scotia's interior offers paddlers a choice of lakes and rivers to explore, with no whitewater except on some stretches of the river in spring. Novice paddlers can spend a few hours practising their strokes on the peaceful Mersey River — more akin to paddling a swamp in southern Georgia, minus the Spanish moss and alligators — while experienced paddlers have wilder choices.

Kejimkujik Lake, the largest in the park, offers a portage-free experience, which will be appealing to many. It's shallow, so whitecaps form quickly, especially in the afternoon when the wind often blows up. It can become treacherous in short order. Fortunately, mornings and evenings are generally very calm and peaceful. The lake is dotted with islands, and there are plenty of bays and beaches to explore from the nine wilderness campsites scattered around the lake. It's also possible to explore a section of the lake in a day.

Two other areas of the park are accessible if you're prepared to portage. The easier of the two and the best for inexperienced canoeists is the Big Dam Lake–Frozen Ocean Lake combination, accessible via a short 400 m (1,312 ft) portage. Over two to three days, paddle 26 km (16 mi) in two very different lakes — despite the fact that they're joined by a narrow passage. One lake is spring-fed with clear water, and the other is bog-fed with dark water. Choose from ten backcountry campsites dispersed around the two lakes.

The 48 km (30 mi) Peskowesk Lake System is another option. Longer portages are required, but the reward is a true wilderness canoeing experience on lakes boasting the classic Canadian Shield landscape without the people. There are at least eleven backcountry campsites to choose from, spread over five different lakes.

Although the Kejimkujik experience might not meet the wilderness canoeing requirements of hardcore wilderness paddlers, it does offer an outstanding and accessible adventure to visitors and residents of Nova Scotia.

HIGHLIGHTS: Beautiful islands, wildlife, sandy beaches, windswept stands of white and red pine, great swimming, fishing

DISTANCE: Variable depending on campsite location and how much exploring you do

TIME NEEDED: 1–7 days

GRADE: Easy to moderate depending on the length of the trip, wind and wave conditions

WHERE: Kejimkujik National Park is 167 km (104 mi) northwest of Halifax, off Highway 8.

HOW: Make backcountry reservations 60 days ahead. Call 1-902-682-2772, when lines open first Monday in May. In summer, campsite stays limited to two nights.

WHEN: Late May to mid-October

COST: $5.80/day park fee, $24.50/night backcountry camping fee, $4.90 reservation fee. Reserve and rent canoes and kayaks at Jake's Landing from Whynot Adventure.

DON'T FORGET: Water filter, bug repellent, rain gear

OPTIONS: All lakes and rivers in Kejimkujik are linked with portages, so it's possible to create circuits lasting many weeks. Such a trip would include the lakes and rivers of the 1,000 sq km (386 sq mi) Tobeatic Wilderness Area.

TOUR COMPANIES: Whynot Adventure

BEFORE YOU GO: Read *The Tent Dwellers: Sports Fishing in Nova Scotia in 1908* by Albert Bigelow Paine — interesting book to non-fishers, too.

INTERESTING FACT: For centuries the Mersey River was the major transportation route for the Mi'kmaq people to travel to the coast every summer to fish and collect seafood.

Cycling
The Back Roads
of the Annapolis Royal Area

■■■□

Annapolis Royal, called the "most livable small town" by one UN agency, sits at the western end of the Annapolis Valley on the south bank of the scenic Annapolis River. It's a quiet, picturesque part of Nova Scotia that's perfect for exploring from the seat of a bike.

Unfortunately, there is nowhere to rent a bike in town, so you'll have to bring one with you. On the other hand, the town has published an excellent bicycle map with sixteen routes ranging in length from 8.2 km (5.1 mi) to 102 km (63 mi). There's a huge variety of countryside to explore; study the map and choose a route suiting your interests and ability. Suggested routes include a challenging coastal tour along the Bay of Fundy, a ride down to Kejimkujik National Park and a dirt-road ride to Belleisle Marsh.

For a pretty out-and-back ride with little traffic, head across the Annapolis River Causeway. This is a remarkable spot, especially when the tides are changing: you can see and feel the power of the churning water. It's the only place in North America currently generating energy from tidal flux. At the end of the causeway, head west towards Victoria Beach on a road that offers views of the Annapolis River, the Annapolis Basin and the Digby Gulf. Plan a stop at Port-Royal, which was a French colonial settlement in the early seventeenth century and is now a National Historic Site. You can take a tour or just admire the view. You'll pass a lighthouse as you continue cycling the gently rolling hills of this very pastoral ride. Retrace your route to Annapolis Royal from Victoria Beach.

Another interesting but hillier ride takes you along the south shore of the Annapolis Basin past colourful character homes — some long abandoned — to the village of Bear River. Stop for wine-tasting at the Bear River Winery, and if you time your arrival in the village to coincide with lunch, you can pull up a chair at one of the waterfront cafés built on stilts and enjoy a view of the tidal Bear River. Explore the town on foot before continuing on a loop that will take you back to Annapolis Royal on quiet back roads bounded by fields of wildflowers. One more winery — the Annapolis Highlands Vineyard — might beckon you to stop. If not, you'll be back in Annapolis Royal in under an hour.

Annapolis Royal is a delightful destination with a surprising amount to offer. No matter what your cycling ability, there will be a route for you.

HIGHLIGHTS: Pastoral scenery, wineries, lighthouses, Bear River, Bay of Fundy, Garrison Cemetery lamplight tour, waterfront boardwalk in Annapolis Royal

DISTANCE: Highly variable depending on your interests

TIME NEEDED: 2–3 days to properly explore the area

GRADE: Easy to difficult, depending on what route you take

WHERE: Start in Annapolis Royal and explore one of the 16 published cycling routes. Annapolis Royal is 200 km (124 mi) northwest of Halifax and just 108 km (67 mi) west of Wolfville.

HOW: Either bring your own bike, rent one at Valley Stove and Cycle in Wolfville, or rent from Freewheeling Adventures in Hubbards.

WHEN: May to early October

COST: Free

DON'T FORGET: Bicycle lock, water bottles, sunscreen

OPTIONS: Ride the back roads along the coast of the Bay of Fundy all the way to Wolfville.

TOUR COMPANIES: Pedal and Sea, Bike New England, Easy Rider Tours, Backroads

INTERESTING FACT: For an outstanding history lesson and unforgettable evening, take a candlelight tour of the Garrison Cemetery, located on the grounds of Fort Anne in Annapolis Royal. It is the home of the oldest English gravestone in Canada, dating back to 1720.

Hiking to
Cape Split
in Blomidon Provincial Park

□■□□

There is only one reason to hike to Cape Split: expansive views of the Bay of Fundy. They are your reward for slogging up a trail which at times is unremarkable. Grassy meadows atop 60 m (200 ft) cliffs are the setting for these views. In summer you'll share them with a flock of noisy, nesting gulls.

The scene at the end — rock spires in the Bay of Fundy, lichen-covered cliffs, a rock pillar overgrown with grass — will quite literally take your breath away, especially if you're foolish enough to venture up close to the edge of the cliffs. The cliffs are constantly eroding, so use common sense if you're someone who likes to court danger.

The most tedious section is at the beginning of the 8 km (5 mi) each-way hike. Fortunately, you can dispatch with that part of the trail in thirty minutes. From there, the woods thin and offer a forest walk with a more open feel. At times, it's even quite pretty. And for two weeks in May, the wildflowers through here are prolific. The Cape Split Purple Trillium is the star flower in the spring. If you're hiking when the trees have leafed out, you'll only get a few peekaboo views of the water below. As you get close to the trail's end, you can't miss the network of side trails taking you out to the cliff edge for a view. Exercise extreme caution here as the cliff edge can be obscured by vegetation and it's a long way down.

Although the hike to Cape Split is reported to be a 16 km (10 mi) round-trip, it doesn't feel that long. In fact, the signs suggest allowing four to five hours, but I did it quite comfortably in seventy-five minutes each way. It's perfect for families. Leashed dogs are also allowed on the trail.

As a side note, it's possible to find agates around the shores of Cape Split, but because of the huge fluctuation in tides it's worth going with someone who knows the area and the hazards. On the beach where Little Split Rock is the dominant feature, it's possible to find agates when the tide drops because they glisten when wet.

I think it's well worth enduring the tedium of the early section of the trail to enjoy the scene at the end of it. Choose a sunny day, if at all possible, to maximize your viewing pleasure.

HIGHLIGHTS: Stunning Bay of Fundy views off of Cape Split, a chance to see standing waves caused by the tide, bird life, spring wildflowers

DISTANCE: Approximately 16 km (10 mi) return according to the government sign, though I think that's high by several kilometres.

TIME NEEDED: 2.5–5 hours return, depending on your hiking pace

GRADE: Moderate

WHERE: The trailhead is 35 km (22 mi) north of Wolfville — about a 40-minute drive away. The trail takes you to the tip of the Blomidon Peninsula.

HOW: Take exit 11 off of Highway 101 to 358 North. Drive to Scots Bay and look for the Cape Split signs.

WHEN: April to November

COST: Free

DON'T FORGET: Binoculars, water and a picnic. The last 5 km (3 mi) or so of the road to the trailhead is heavily potholed, so exercise caution.

TOUR COMPANIES: None

INTERESTING FACT: Turbulent tidal currents can be heard roaring for miles at the mid-point of the incoming tide. The sound has been called the 'Voice of the Moon.' They are captivating to watch.

Kayaking in
Cape Chignecto
Provincial Park

The Cape Chignecto area is a wild, unspoiled landscape best appreciated from the water. A kayaking trip provides the chance to get close to rock spires, arches, cliffs, even a rock amphitheatre and the legendary Three Sisters rock formation often referred to as the crown jewel of Cape Chignecto Park. There are pristine beaches, albeit rocky ones, once you're past the Three Sisters — perfect for camping, if you're lucky enough to have the time to do a longer paddle.

It's possible to do this trip on your own, but remember that twice a day a billion tons of water move in and out of the Bay of Fundy, so conditions can change rapidly. The difference between low and high tide is over 12 m (39 ft). Local knowledge about tides and currents goes a long way here.

Fortunately, Nova Shores Adventures operates out of nearby Advocate Harbour and specializes in tours. Although it's possible to launch in Advocate Harbour, Spicer's Cove — just a thirty-minute drive away — provides access to some of the best scenery on the coast. You have to meet in Advocate Harbour, then you're sent on your way with a map to reconvene a half-hour later in Spicer's Cove.

Departure times are strictly dictated by the tides. Plan to leave at high tide so you can take advantage of kayaking in and around the Three Sisters. You must kayak around one headland, an area that can be tough to paddle on windy days or if the current is especially strong. Be prepared to dig in and paddle hard for about fifteen minutes through here. Then, it's basically smooth paddling through to the Three Sisters, an area that's fun to paddle because of the wave bounce and the photography opportunities. If the winds have been cooperative you should have time to continue to a beach just a twenty-minute paddle away for some rest and relaxation.

On the return to Spicer's Cove, the wind is typically at your back and seas are generally calmer with a falling tide. The change in the Three Sisters is remarkable; once the tide has fallen they are only accessible on foot.

Spicer's Cove is also unrecognizable at low tide. What had been water is now beach, and it's a long way up to the launch site. This is where the kayak carts come in handy. The ground is firm enough to hold the weight of even a double kayak, and in a matter of minutes, with little effort, you're back to your starting point.

Kayaking is an excellent way to experience parts of Cape Chignecto Provincial Park that are otherwise only accessible via a long, arduous hike.

HIGHLIGHTS: Wild rock formations including the Three Sisters, towering sea cliffs, inspiring coastal scenery, desolate landscapes, world's highest tides, seals and seabirds

DISTANCE: About 5–6 km (3–4 mi) return

TIME NEEDED: From 5 hours up to 3 days

GRADE: Generally moderate; the wind determines the difficulty.

WHERE: Start at Spicer's Cove, about 28 km (17 mi) and a 30-minute drive from Advocate Harbour. Advocate Harbour is 227 km (141 mi) by road northwest of Halifax.

HOW: Either do a self-guided trip with your own kayak or book a tour with Nova Shores Adventures. There are no nearby places to rent kayaks.

WHEN: Late May to early September

COST: Approximately $95/adult plus tax for a day tour

DON'T FORGET: Camera, binoculars, rain gear, kayak cart

OPTIONS: Start at Spicer's Cove and finish at Advocate Harbour three days later. Campsites are located at Seal Cove and Refugee Cove.

TOUR COMPANIES: Nova Shores Adventures

INTERESTING FACT: The red rhyolite cliff face at Spicer's Cove is a result of volcanic eruptions that happened over 400 million years ago. It gets its red colour from the oxidation of iron-rich minerals in the lava.

Backpacking
The Coastal Trail
in Cape Chignecto Provincial Park

☐ ■ ☐ ☐

Cape Chignecto Provincial Park is located on the Bay of Fundy near the small community of Advocate Harbour. It's the largest park in the province (4,200 hectares) and offers a mix of outstanding coastal scenery complete with dramatic 200 m (600 ft) red cliffs, sheltered coves and remnants of old-growth forest.

The physically demanding 51 km (32 mi) Coastal Trail requires three to four days. It can be done in either direction, but you do have to plan what campsites you're going to stay in before you make your reservation. You have the option of tenting or booking a hut. The huts lack the wilderness feeling as there are dirt roads leading to them, but they do offer a dry, bug- and bear-proof roof over your head. They are outfitted with bunks, a wood-fired stove, picnic tables, treated water and outhouses.

Cabins are for single group use, even if your group is one person. However, the cabins aren't as close to the water, so if it's views and beaches you want, plan to tent. Be warned, though: the beaches that make the best campsites are reserved for the use of kayakers. Hikers need to camp in the woods. There are seven campsites and four cabins, so you need to plan your itinerary. Most campers hike 12 km (7.4 mi) to Refuge Cove on the first day, 17.1 km (10.6 mi) to Seal Cove on the second day and head back to the starting point at Red Rocks on the third day.

The hike to Refuge Cove is definitely the most challenging portion of the trail with its steep ups and downs, but strong hikers can be finished in four hours. The trail starts with a beach walk, providing it's not high tide. Then a set of steep stairs delivers you up to the main trail. From there until Refuge Cove it's primarily a forest walk, and some of it — the fog forest — is as green as anything I've ever seen.

From Refuge Cove, the trail gets far more interesting. Numerous lookouts along the way to Seal Cove offer spectacular coastal vistas. Some of the beach views are breath-taking. You spend more time hiking on clifftops than you do walking on beaches. Abundant wildflowers and seabirds are an added attraction. The most enjoyable section of the whole hike lies between Little Bald Rock and Seal Cove, though after Seal Cove the spectacular Three Sisters, a set of basalt sea stacks, loom off in the distance.

Up next is the abandoned town of Eatonville. The final stage of the hike continues from Eatonville to the intersection just west of McGahey Brook. This section of trail is poorly marked and in need of some attention. Lots of downed trees make the hiking tough. But in a few hours you'll be back on the beach and thirty minutes from your starting point at Red Rocks. The Coastal Trail is a marvellous experience offering world-class coastal scenery without the crowds.

HIGHLIGHTS: Rugged coastal scenery, pristine coastline, fantastic 200 m sandstone cliffs, highest tides in the world, fog forest

DISTANCE: 51 km (33 mi) for the whole loop; it's possible to do a car shuttle and knock off the least interesting 14 km (9 mi) from Eatonville back to the Visitor Centre.

TIME NEEDED: 3–4 days to do the full loop

GRADE: Moderate

WHERE: Located on the Bay of Fundy outside of Advocate Harbour, about 250 km (155 mi) northwest of Halifax

HOW: Book with Nova Scotia Provincial Parks at the beginning of April (call 1-888-544-3434) or take your chances and book reservations once you're at the Visitor Centre. Decide ahead of time where you are going to spend the night.

WHEN: April through November; permission is required to camp or stay in huts outside of that time.

COST: $25.90/night for backcountry campsites, $57.65/night for wilderness cabins that sleep 4–6 people, $9 reservation fee, $5.40 entrance fee to the park

DON'T FORGET: Hiking poles, sturdy hiking shoes, bear spray, rain gear

OPTIONS: Choose one of the easy front country trails for a day hike. Alternatively, hike to Seal Cove and back from Eatonville to get a taste of the dramatic coastal scenery.

TOUR COMPANIES: None

INTERESTING FACT: Eatonville was at its peak in the 1890s, when 350 people involved in lumbering and shipbuilding called the place home. It is now a ghost town.

Cycling
The Cabot Trail
on Cape Breton Island

□ □ ■ □

Bicycling Magazine calls the Cabot Trail one of the best multi-day bike rides in North America, and I would heartily concur! Throw in the fact that Cape Breton Island is one of the least spoilt islands in the world and I think you might see the allure of a visit.

The Cabot Trail is a 300 km (186 mi) loop that will take most mortals five to seven days to complete. Because it's a loop, you can in theory start anywhere, but I found Baddeck to be a good place to start because of its proximity to Sydney and plane connections. It's also the first decent-sized town you hit if you're driving from Halifax.

Baddeck is famous for its association with inventor Alexander Graham Bell, so take time to visit the museum named after him before you head out. And if it's a beautiful sunny day, you can't go wrong with a few hours in a kayak or sailboat on the beautiful Bras d'Or Lakes as well.

From Baddeck, the bike ride takes you through the pastoral Margaree Valley, also home to world-class salmon fishing. Then it's out to the coast and north through a mix of Acadian and Gaelic towns. The dramatic coastal route to French-speaking Cheticamp is peppered with small craft shops and galleries, which can be great to hang out in on rainy days. Cheticamp itself is the hooked-rug capital of the world, and touring the galleries there may give you a new appreciation for the artistic heights this craft can reach.

From Cheticamp, continue north through the spectacular Cape Breton Highlands National Park, where you can expect to be physically challenged. Two major climbs — one with grades of 13 percent over 3 km (2 mi) — will test your conditioning program.

The east side of the Cabot Trail offers lovely surprises, including beautiful pink rocky shores, secluded beaches, inspiring vistas and quaint fishing villages. From food to golf, Scottish influences are everywhere. Golfers will want to stop in Ingonish and play the famous Highland Links Course. From there, it's one last big climb up Cape Smokey before the final leg into Baddeck.

HIGHLIGHTS: Fantastic coastal vistas, beautiful Cape Breton Island scenery and their legendary hospitality, fresh seafood, whale-watching even from your bike, hiking on one of the 25 trails in Cape Breton Highlands National Park, browsing museums and galleries, bear and moose sightings

DISTANCE: 298 km (185 mi) loop

TIME NEEDED: A minimum of 5 days; ideally a week to allow for side trips

GRADE: Difficult

WHERE: The Cabot Trail is located on the northern part of Cape Breton Island; it passes through the very scenic Cape Breton Highlands National Park. Baddeck is 350 km (218 mi) east of Halifax.

WHEN: Early June to mid-October

HOW: Bring your own bike or rent from **frameworkfitness.com** out of Sydney. For a fee they will deliver to your starting point. You can also rent from Sea Spray Outdoor Adventures in Smelt Brook near Cape North.

COST: Bike rentals, accommodations (a choice of camping, B&Bs, motels and a few hotels), food, Cape Breton National Park pass

DON'T FORGET: Clothes you can layer, full rain gear including booties, bicycle pump and a repair kit

OPTIONS: Easy to do as a self-supported trip staying at B&Bs, motels, hotels or campgrounds

TOUR COMPANIES: Maritime Cycle Tours, Atlantic Canada Cycling, Eastwind Cycle, Freewheeling Adventures, Pedal and Sea Adventures

INTERESTING FACT: Back when the 80 km (50 mi) Cabot Trail was first driven in 1932, it took 10 hours. It wasn't paved until 1961.

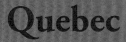

Quebec

Bathurst ●

● **Sagamook
Trail**

New
Brunswick

U.S.A.

Fredericton
●

N

Saint John
●

○ **Fundy Isles**

P.E.I. & New Brunswick Adventures

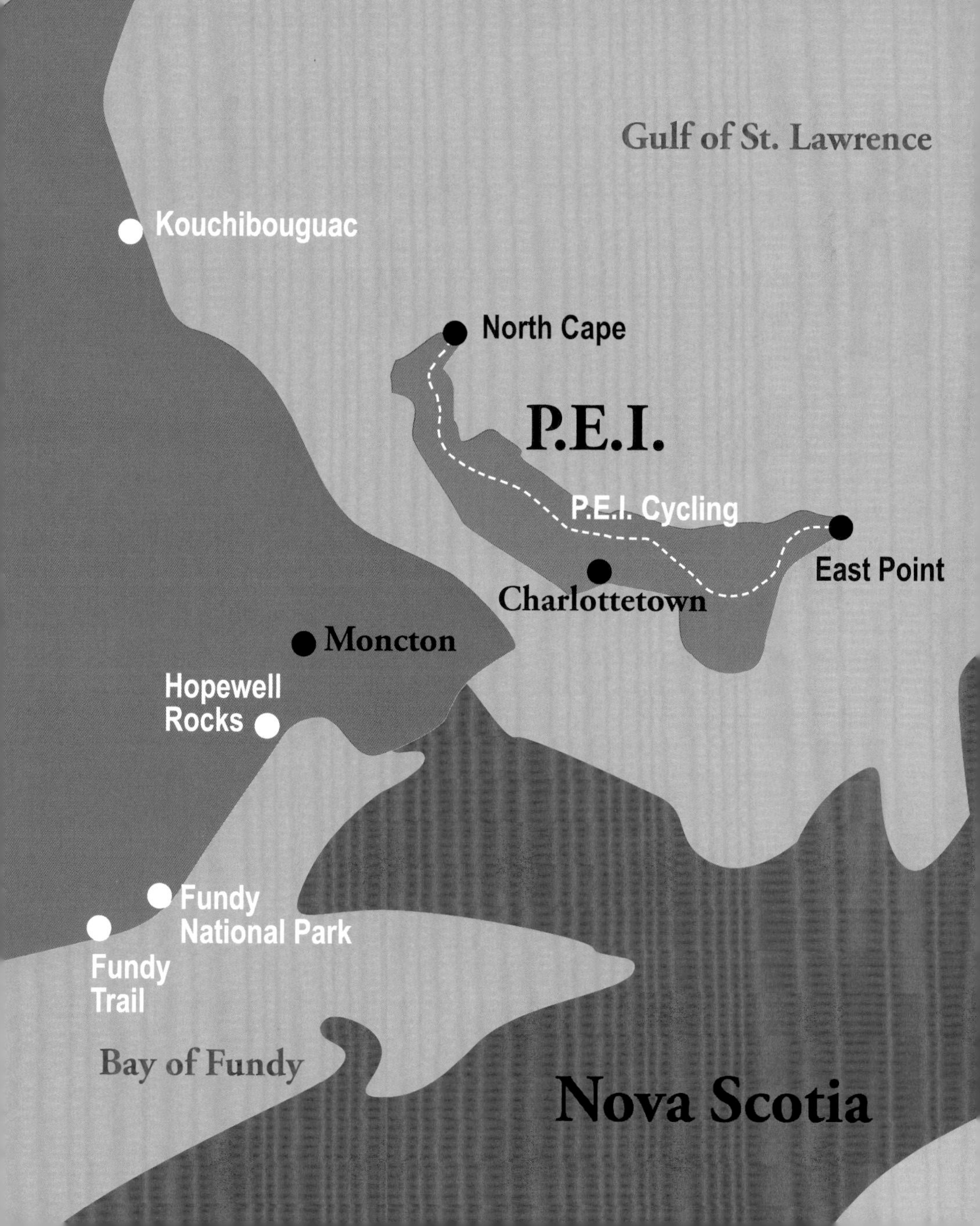

Gulf of St. Lawrence

Kouchibouguac

North Cape

P.E.I.

P.E.I. Cycling

East Point

Charlottetown

Moncton

Hopewell
Rocks

Fundy
National Park

Fundy
Trail

Bay of Fundy

Nova Scotia

Cycling the length of
Prince Edward Island
from North Cape to East Point

■■☐☐

Prince Edward Island (PEI) is Canada's smallest province, measuring only 220 km (137 mi) long by 64 km (40 mi) at its widest. With its quiet back roads, gently rolling terrain and coastal views, it's a great cycling destination for people who are new to multi-day bike trips. Scenic roads and sections of the 273 km (170 mi) Confederation Trail take you through a patchwork of farmland, and past thousands of acres of potato fields (PEI's most famous export). A real treat is the new 10 km (6 mi) multi-use trail along the Gulf Shore Parkway in Prince Edward Island National Park.

Book a shuttle before setting out for either North Cape or East Point. If you start from North Cape, visit the Wind Energy Interpretive Centre, and take the obligatory selfie in front of the historic North Cape lighthouse. With the wind at your back, it's an easy 35 km (22 mi) to Northport — a lovely spot to spend the night. From Northport, it's 84 km (52 mi) to Summerside. The roads take you through picturesque fishing villages and past rivers where you might see oyster fishermen at work. You'll cycle in sight of Malpeque Bay, world-famous for its oysters. Next up, and only 58 km (36 mi) away, is Cavendish and Prince Edward Island National Park where you'll find some lovely beaches and the Anne of Green Gables House.

From there it's a beautiful 33 km (21 mi) ride east to Brackley Beach, one of the most famous of the forty or so beaches in PEI. The swimming is pleasant, with water temperatures as warm as any you'll find off North Carolina.

The next destination, St. Peters Bay, can be accessed via highways, but take the Confederation Trail; it's flat and you'll knock off the 68 km (42 mi) in no time. Should your legs have some extra juice, cycle the very scenic section of road around St. Peters Bay to Greenwich. Lock your bike and head out for a 4.8 km (3.0 mi) walk on the trail to the Greenwich Dunes. Spectacular boardwalks, parabolic sand dunes and a beautiful beach are the reward.

It will only take a few hours to ride the final 56 km (35 mi) to the East Point lighthouse where the Northumberland Strait meets the Gulf of St. Lawrence, and the end of the tip-to-tip bike ride. But if you've got time, I'd recommend weaving your way down the coast and back around to Charlottetown, which can be comfortably done in a few days.

HIGHLIGHTS: Scenic roads, Anne of Green Gables House, PEI National Park, beaches, fishing communities, pastoral countryside, fresh seafood

DISTANCE: 334 km (208 mi) if you ride tip to tip

TIME NEEDED: 2–7 days

GRADE: Easy to moderate

WHERE: Start in North Cape via a shuttle from Charlottetown and finish at East Point.

HOW: For a self-guided trip, order a map from PEI Tourism, book accommodations and reserve a shuttle with George Larter, PEI Guide and Travel Service (1-902-393-6029).

COST: $200–225/couple for bike rental and shuttles from Charlottetown to North Cape or East Point, accommodations

WHEN: May to early October

DON'T FORGET: Bike tune-up if bringing your own, pump and patch kits; repair shops are only in Charlottetown and Summerside

OPTIONS: Start in Charlottetown to loop the outer roads that circle the province. Don't miss the views of the Northumberland Strait from the coast between Panmure Island and Wood Island.

TOUR COMPANIES: Pedal and Sea Adventures, MacQueen's Island Tours (they rent and repair bikes too), Freewheeling Adventures, Atlantic Canada Cycling, Go Wheelin', Easy Rider Tours

BEFORE YOU GO: Read *Anne of Green Gables* by Lucy Maud Montgomery.

INTERESTING FACT: No place on the island is more than 16 km (10 mi) from the ocean.

Hiking the
Mount Sagamook Trail
in Mount Carleton Provincial Park

☐ ■ ☐ ☐

Mount Carleton Provincial Park, located in a remote area of northern New Brunswick, is the largest park in the province. It encompasses a number of mountain peaks that make up the northern extension of the Appalachian Mountains. Peaks that can be accessed by hiking include Mount Carleton, the highest peak not only in the province but in the Maritimes as a whole. You might think you would get the most amazing views from that vantage point, but it's just a monotonous view of about ten million trees, many of which are being logged. There are no lake views whatsoever — and who wants to see a clear-cut?

Mount Sagamook, Mount Carleton's prettier neighbour, scores much higher, and while it may not give you the satisfaction of bagging the province's highest peak, its views are superb, untarnished and expansive. In the fall when the colours hit their prime, it's a riot of orange, red and yellow as far as the eye can see.

The trail to Mount Sagamook can be done as a loop. It's exceedingly steep at times — a bit like a StairMaster, except it's in the woods. Fortunately, the trail to the top is only 2.3 km (1.4 mi) if you hike the steeper west route (counterclockwise direction) and 3.5 km (2.2 mi) hiking up the other way. It's best to ascend via the steeper section and descend on the longer east route. But no matter how you do it, pay attention to your footing as the roots and rock, especially if wet, will conspire to trip you. Don't expect much in the way of views until you reach the signed lookouts or the summit, although the hiking is very pleasant through the open woods. On the descent, plan to be waylaid by patches of lush wild blueberries.

Mount Carleton Provincial Park sees fewer than thirty thousand people per year, so there's a good chance you'll have the trail to yourself. It's a beautiful park and one well worth exploring in depth, especially if you're a fan of wilderness camping and canoeing.

HIGHLIGHTS: Quiet trails, incredible views, 10 million trees, fall colours, birds, wildlife including moose

DISTANCE: 5.8 km (3.6 mi) as a loop plus short side trails to viewpoints

TIME NEEDED: 3–4 hours

GRADE: Moderate

WHERE: The park entrance is about 46 km (29 mi) east of Saint-Quentin, the nearest town via Highways 17, 180 and 385. All roads are potentially dangerous at dawn or dusk because of the high possibility of the sudden appearance of a moose. Logging trucks moving at high speeds on Highway 385 and large potholes make it an even more exciting road to drive.

WHEN: May 15 to September 29

HOW: Purchase a park permit and pick up a map at the park entrance.

COST: $8/vehicle entrance fee; camping is $25/night, less for wilderness camping

DON'T FORGET: Layer your clothes, as it can be cool and windy at the top.

OPTIONS: There is the option of hiking to Mount Carleton from Mount Sagamook; it's best done with a pre-arranged car shuttle. The 5.1 km (3.2 mi) trail to Mount Carleton heads off along a ridge just below the Mount Sagamook summit.

TOUR COMPANIES: None

INTERESTING FACT: There is an annual mountaintop fiddle jam on the summit of Mount Sagamook on the last Sunday in September.

Cycling in
Kouchibouguac
National Park

■ □ □ □

The drive into Kouchibouguac National Park is underwhelming. Trees line either side of the road and block any views of the coast. You might be half wondering why you've even bothered to come. But don't despair, because once you're on a bike, the charm of the 238 sq km (92 sq mi) park becomes apparent. The park is, in fact, considered to be one of the best cycling destinations in all of Atlantic Canada.

The word 'Kouchibouguac' means 'River of Long Tides' in Mi'kmaq. You will discover just what this looks like as you cycle along the river's banks. Explore salt marshes and bogs as you loop through the park on 60 km (37 mi) of trails, stop to admire fields of wildflowers and listen for birdsong in the woods.

The parking lot near Ryans, where you can rent a bike, seems like a good place to begin. From there you have a choice: either follow the coast towards the Salt Marsh, or head in the other direction along the south shore of the Kouchibouguac River. There's no right or wrong way to go, but if you follow the coast you really should plan a stop just 2 km (1.2 mi) after starting. There is a beautiful 1.2 km (0.8 mi) boardwalk that takes you to Kelly's Beach, but you must leave your bike behind. This is a great place to swim and relax — and, as such, might make a better stop towards the end of the day.

Continuing past the boardwalk, the bike path heads away from the water into the woods. Several short nature trails offer further diversions. Continue through the woods until you reach one of the many well-signed intersections. There are shortcuts back to Ryans through the interior of the park, but if you have the time and the energy, it's worth continuing across the Kouchibouguac River. Once you're on the other side of the river, you have the option to bike alongside it until it empties at the lagoon, or you can plan on a longer ride and bike a further 16.9 km (10.5 mi) to Pointe-Sapin through the woods and across the Black River. To return to Ryans, you'll have to retrace your route to the river and continue along its south shore to complete the loop.

Cycling through Kouchibouguac is an enjoyable way to spend a day . . . though you may not get very far, with all the possible diversions. Don't forget to pick up a free map at the park entrance to help you plan your day.

HIGHLIGHTS: Beautiful beaches and marshes, sheltered lagoons, boardwalks, swimming, easy bike trails, seabirds

DISTANCE: There are 60 km (37 mi) of cycling paths.

TIME NEEDED: A half day to a full day

GRADE: Easy and family-friendly

WHERE: The entrance to the park is 113 km (70 mi) north of Moncton and 57 km (35 mi) southeast of Miramichi.

HOW: Bring your own bike or rent a no-speed bike from Ryan's Rental Centre in the park. Food choices in the park are minimal, so buy picnic supplies ahead of time.

WHEN: May to mid-October

COST: Park entrance fees are $7.80/adult and $3.90/youth. Onsite bike rentals are $8/hr, $25/4 hrs and $50/day.

DON'T FORGET: Bike locks aren't provided. Bring your own if you want worry-free time on the beach.

OPTIONS: There are 10 nature trails to hike ranging from 0.9 km (0.6 mi) to 11.3 km (7.0 mi) long. Canoeing is another excellent option for exploring the park. Rent canoes at Ryans, book one of two back-country spots and then head out to explore.

TOUR COMPANIES: None

INTERESTING FACT: The park boasts the second-largest tern colony in North America.

Kayaking around
The Hopewell Rocks
in the Bay of Fundy

■□□□

If you want to experience what has been called the highest tidal paddling experience on Earth, then an easy kayaking trip on the Bay of Fundy — a UNESCO Fundy Biosphere Reserve — is in order. During each tide cycle, over a billion tons of water move in and out of the Bay of Fundy; equivalent to the flow of all the world's rivers combined.

One of the best places on the Bay of Fundy to see this phenomenon is at the Hopewell Rocks Park just an hour south of Moncton. Here the difference between high and low tide is between 10 and 14 m (33–46 ft). It's possible to walk the ocean floor at low tide among exceptionally scenic eroded rock formations called the Flower Pots, and then just a few hours later to kayak in exactly the same spot. Over those couple of hours you can watch how fast the water rises, which is — on average — between 1.2 to 1.8 m (4–6 ft) per hour.

It's feasible to launch your own kayak at the Hopewell Rocks, but most people sign up with Baymount Outdoor Adventures, which has a storefront located just a few hundred metres from the beach. The time of the kayaking trip changes every day according to the tides. On the day I went, we started as the tide was rising, and in fact just sat in the kayak and let the water float us off the beach.

The beauty of a kayak trip here is that it's perfect for first-timers and it's family-friendly. Helpful guides give you basic instruction in how to put on a spray skirt, adjust a personal flotation device, hold a paddle and adjust your rudder pedals. They also suggest that either the most experienced or the heaviest of each twosome be the one to sit in the back of each double kayak and steer.

When we finally got on the water, it was an easy paddle down to the first of the rock formations. The real fun of the trip for me was maneuvering the kayak through the tight passages around the rock formations while trying not to shear off the rudder. Exploring the insides of caves was also interesting, but not something I'd want to do under conditions with big waves.

We were able to paddle as far down as scenic Shepody Bay, which is only possible on days when the wind isn't blowing hard. This is a trip done not for exercise but for the excitement of seeing the Bay of Fundy's tides in action. Everyone I spoke with — especially the newly minted kayakers — was thrilled with the experience. Just one word of caution: don't wear white. The water is muddy, the land is muddy, and whites and mud do not mix well.

HIGHLIGHTS: Rugged coastal scenery, Flower Pot rock formations, highest tides in the world, interesting experience to see the difference between low and high tide, bird life

DISTANCE: A few kilometres each way

TIME NEEDED: A few hours. The start time changes daily depending on the tides.

GRADE: Easy and family-friendly

WHERE: Located on the Bay of Fundy just 30 minutes south of Moncton

HOW: Make a reservation with Baymount Adventures, especially in the height of the summer.

WHEN: Early June to early September

COST: Admission to Hopewell Rocks is $9/adult and $6.75/child. Kayaking is approximately $50/adult and $40/child depending on which tour you take. Paddling is free if you have your own kayak, but you must speak with park personnel about where to launch.

TOUR COMPANIES: Baymount Adventures

INTERESTING FACT: Every summer — usually sometime in August — the Bay of Fundy serves as a refuelling stop for approximately two million migratory birds on their way to South America from Canada's Arctic. The vast majority of the birds are semipalmated sandpipers, but other species present in abundance include the least sandpiper, the semipalmated plover, sanderlings and the piping plover.

Hiking
The Coastal Trail
in Fundy National Park

□ ■ □ □

Fundy National Park boasts over 100 km (62 mi) of hiking trails, but many are in dense woods, and that type of hiking just doesn't appeal to me. There is one trail, however — the Coastal Trail, which parallels the Bay of Fundy — which merits the five to six hours it will take you to hike it. The trailhead is easy to find, located within 100 m (330 ft) or so of the swimming pool at the east entrance to the park, just five minutes from the town of Alma.

The hike starts off steeply through a mixed forest of birch, spruce and maple. Once you reach the ridgeline, there are some lovely open woods. Through here, the hiking is totally delightful and easy. Next is a steep descent to reach the junction with the Tippen Lot Trail just before Herring Cove. It's surprisingly tough going at times, and sturdy boots definitely come in handy.

Herring Cove, accessed by a set of steps on either side of the beach, deserves some time. It's a great spot to have a picnic, but the beach also begs to be explored, especially if it's low tide. It would be quite easy to call it a day here, but assuming you're keen to hike, continue towards Matthews Head, 1.8 km (1.2 mi) away. There are a couple of exceptional vistas along this section, though the bulk of the trail is in the trees.

Once you reach Matthews Head, keep left at the next two intersections to continue to Point Wolfe, the trail's endpoint. If it's clear, you'll be able to enjoy one of the best vistas of the hike shortly after Matthews Head. It's called Squaw's Cap Look-off, and it's on the UNESCO Fundy Biosphere Amazing Places list. From this vantage point at the top of the cliff you get a real sense of the wild and rugged nature of the Fundy coastline, as well as a great view of Squaw's Cap, a rocky island just off the coast. The final part of the trail involves a steady climb and a steep descent. The trail ends not far from the covered bridge at Point Wolfe.

To return to your starting point, you have several options: if you have a second car, you can shuttle it to Point Wolfe before commencing the hike; you can hope to meet some accommodating people who might be kind enough to drive you back to the trailhead; or lastly, you can retrace your steps with one variation, heading left at the first intersection on your return and enjoying a wonderful walk through flower-filled meadows. When you reach Herring Cove Road, stay right to return to Matthews Head. From there it's all familiar territory back to the trailhead.

The Coastal Trail doesn't pack the same visual punch as the Cape Chignecto Trail (right across the Bay of Fundy on the Nova Scotia side), but if you have a day, it is worth the hike, especially if you plan some breaks at the lookouts and beaches.

HIGHLIGHTS: The Bay of Fundy, huge tidal variation, beaches, views, wildflower-filled paths, bird life

DISTANCE: 13.8 km (8.6 mi) return

TIME NEEDED: 5–6 hours

GRADE: Moderate

WHERE: The east entrance, just minutes from the town of Alma, is 81 km (50 mi) southwest of Moncton and approximately 179 km (111 mi) southeast of Fredericton.

HOW: Reservations aren't required. The hike's best done on a clear day for the views.

WHEN: Mid-May to late October

COST: The park entry fee is $7.80/adult, $3.90/youth.

DON'T FORGET: Grab a map at the entrance to the park. Don't forget water, food and sturdy hiking shoes.

OPTIONS: The Fundy Footpath starts in Fundy National Park and runs north out of the park for a total of 50 km (31 mi). It's a strenuous 3–4 day coastal trek.

TOUR COMPANIES: None

INTERESTING FACT: Seven hiking trails link up to form the Fundy Circuit, a 48 km (30 mi) loop in Fundy National Park. Allow 3 days to backpack it.

Cycling
The Fundy Trail Parkway
near Fundy National Park

□ □ ■ □

If you're looking for great views, coastal wilderness and a challenging bike ride on the New Brunswick side of the Bay of Fundy, make your way to the Fundy Trail Parkway, a 16 km (10 mi) coastal road commencing 10 km (6 mi) east of the village of St. Martins. There are plans to extend the parkway by another 49 km (31 mi) to the border of Fundy National Park in 2017, but at the time of writing only the Fundy Footpath Trail continues from the end of the Parkway, and it's not suitable for cycling.

Before heading out on your bike, stock up in St. Martins, since the only other place to get food is at the Interpretive Centre, 11 km (7 mi) and many steep climbs away. You have a choice of biking on the road or on a trail shared with hikers. The trail is tougher than the road, though both have short sections with grades approaching 17 percent. The trail has the advantage of keeping you close to the coast and the sublime views. Parts of it are mossy and a tad slippery, so be careful on the steep downhill sections. Both the trail and the road begin gently, but in no time you're into the hills and it stays that way for the duration. But there are a lot of great downhill sections, especially on the return. Be sure to take advantage of the numerous lookouts.

Factor in time for side trips. Fuller Falls, accessed via a rickety set of cable-ladder stairs, is a beautiful waterfall that makes it onto the list of Fundy Biosphere Reserve Amazing Places. The same goes for the Big Salmon River: here you'll find a suspension bridge and one of the major access points to the Fundy Footpath. If you want a break from your bike, the Flower Pot Rock and Bradshaw Footpaths are worth investigating too.

The Fundy Trail, on bike or on foot, offers an unspoiled look at the natural beauty of the Bay of Fundy.

HIGHLIGHTS: Fuller Falls (a Fundy Biosphere Reserve Amazing Place), towering coastal cliffs, Big Salmon River, pristine beaches, suspension bridge, Interpretive Centre

DISTANCE: 16 km (10 mi) each way

TIME NEEDED: A half to a full day depending on how far you cycle and how many side stops you make

GRADE: Difficult

WHERE: The Fundy Trail is located approximately 10 km (6 mi) east of the village of St. Martins. It's accessible from both Moncton (130 km/81 mi) and Saint John (57 km/35 mi).

WHEN: Mid-May until mid-October, though it's still accessible on bikes, foot, skis and snowshoes after the gates have closed for the season

HOW: Bring your own bike or rent one at the entrance for $11/hour. Be warned: they aren't very well maintained.

COST: $5.50/adult, $4.50/senior and $3.50/child (12 and under)

DON'T FORGET: A patch kit, energy bars, water and rain gear

OPTIONS: Stay overnight at the Hearst Family Lodge (of William Randolph Hearst publishing fame), located on the Big Salmon River. Or take a 4-hour guided interpretive hike to the Hearst Lodge, where lunch is served. Make reservations by visiting the Fundy Trail Parkway website.

TOUR COMPANIES: None

INTERESTING FACT: The Big Salmon River was an important area for logging, fishing and shipbuilding until the 1950s.

Cycling
The Fundy Isles
in southern New Brunswick

□ ■ □ □

If you look at a map of New Brunswick, you'll notice the Fundy Isles off the southwest coast. Three of the islands in particular are worthy of a bike trip: Deer and Campobello, which can easily be done together, and Grand Manan. The biggest issue is the ferry schedule and the fact that the ferry terminals are 27 km (17 mi) apart. You would need to cycle on the Trans-Canada Highway to do a seamless trip between them. If you have a car and a bike rack, then it's certainly easier.

Pick up a map once you're on a ferry. All the islands have one main road, and the fun, I think, lies in exploring the side roads of each of these unique places. Deer Island, the smallest of the three, relies on fishing and aquaculture, and to a lesser degree, tourism. Don't miss a visit to Old Sow, the largest whirlpool in the western hemisphere, which can be seen from shore about three hours before high tide.

The fishing industry is also important to Grand Manan. The largest of the three islands, it does a good job with activities for visitors, including kayaking and whale-watching. Appreciate its rugged beauty from the many clifftop trails, leaving your bike at any one of the trailheads to check out the magnificent views. Other highlights of the island include the Swallowtail and Southwest Head Lighthouses, Hole in the Wall, and the fishing villages of Seal Cove and Dark Harbour.

Campobello Island feels very different, mainly because of its long history with the United States and the fact that it's connected by a short bridge to Lubec, Maine. You can tour the sprawling summer home of former US president Franklin D. Roosevelt and cycle on quiet trails through Roosevelt Campobello International Park. Include a ride to the northern tip of the island to see the beautiful Head Harbour Lighthouse — just don't get stranded by the tides!

Cycling the Fundy Isles is a great way to engage the senses and experience the landscape. Don't be in a rush to leave; stay a night or two on each island.

HIGHLIGHTS: Coastal scenery, lighthouses, Roosevelt homestead, pastoral scenery, whale-watching, birding

DISTANCE: Highly variable depending on how much exploring you do on each island

TIME NEEDED: 3–5 days, depending on how many islands you cycle

GRADE: Moderate

WHERE: Grand Manan is 225 km (140 mi) southwest of Moncton and 70 km (43 mi) west of Saint John by ferry. Campobello Island is northwest of Grand Manan Island; Deer Island is 4 km (2.5 mi) northwest of Campobello Island.

WHEN: May to early October

HOW: The ferry to Grand Manan Island is from Blacks Harbour. The ferry to Deer Island leaves from Letete, 27 km (17 mi) west of Blacks Harbour. For Campobello Island, take the ferry from the south end of Deer Island. There are no ferries between Grand Manan Island and the other islands.

COST: Budget for ferries, bike rentals, food and accommodation. Many camping and B&B options

DON'T FORGET: Know your ferry schedule. Miss one and you may end up waiting for hours.

OPTIONS: Kayaking will give you a very different perspective of the islands.

TOUR COMPANIES: Eastwind Cycle, Maritime Cycle Tours. Also, Adventure High on Grand Manan Island, Seascape Kayak Tours on Deer Island, and Campobello Island Outdoor Adventures on Campobello Island; all three rent bikes.

INTERESTING FACT: Grand Manan Island is the dulse capital of the world. The edible seaweed is hand-picked at low tide, then sun-dried and exported worldwide.

N

Hudson Bay

Quebec
Adventures

Rouyn-Noranda

Ontario

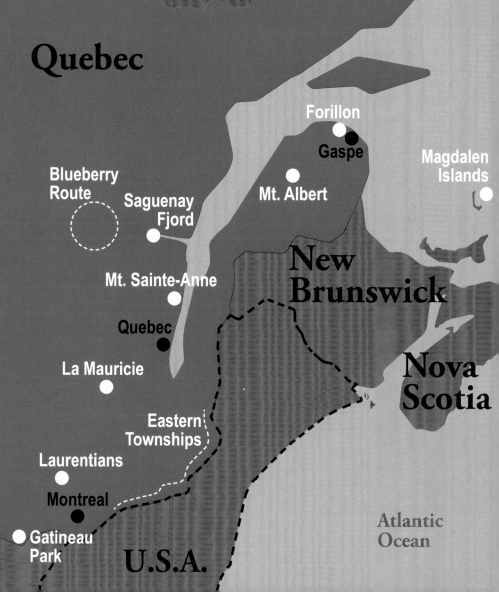

Labrador

Quebec

Forillon

Gaspe

Magdalen
Islands

Blueberry
Route

Saguenay
Fjord

Mt. Albert

Mt. Sainte-Anne

New
Brunswick

Quebec

La Mauricie

Nova
Scotia

Eastern
Townships

Laurentians

Montreal

Atlantic
Ocean

Gatineau
Park

U.S.A.

Paddling the lakes of
La Mauricie National Park
near Shawinigan

■■□□

Canada's twenty-third national park lies roughly halfway between Montreal and Quebec City in the Laurentian foothills. Its 536 sq km (207 sq mi) protect a chunk of the billion-year-old scenic Canadian Shield. You'll find that the landscape of mixed forest dotted with a hundred and fifty lakes and rivers is perfect for paddling. In the fall, the foliage display is truly one of the most spectacular in Canada.

There are two main launch points for a paddling trip: Lac Wapizagonke and Lac Édouard. These are a great option for new paddlers and families. Both offer easy paddling as long as the winds don't blow up, and there are campsites within a short distance of each launch site. Starting from these locations also provides opportunities for extended wilderness trips for those prepared for some portaging.

If you start on Lac Wapizagonke, which is 17 km (10.6 mi) long, you can do a circular route with either seven or nine portages, depending on how much time you have and how many lakes you want to visit. Portages range in length from 0.4 km (0.3 mi) to 2.4 km (1.5 mi). For the very energetic, there is also the 4.7 km (2.9 mi) one-way portage to Lac Houle. There's no camping once you get there, though.

Paddling possibilities out of Lac Édouard are numerous as well. If you paddle north through a string of long, narrow lakes and a minimum of four portages, you can explore some of the least visited and most inaccessible areas of the park. You can also paddle south and head for Lac à la Pêche, although five portages in just over a kilometre are required for that trip.

Make sure you don't leave the park without seeing more of stunning Lac Wapizagonke. Beautiful outcroppings and plenty of bird life adorn its long, narrow length. It's also the site of red ochre rock paintings that attest to the five-thousand-year presence of the Atikamekw, a branch of the Algonquin Nation.

As you paddle, look out for the prolific wildlife that live and thrive in La Mauricie. There are healthy populations of forty mammal species, including approximately 125 black bears and two packs of Eastern wolves, as well as moose, beavers, coyotes and red foxes.

What La Mauricie lacks in grandeur, it makes up with peaceful, contemplative adventure that soothes the soul. The swimming is sublime, too.

HIGHLIGHTS: Beautiful lakes, swimming, beaches, easy canoeing perfect for first-timers, chance to do a multi-day loop, outstanding fall colours, wildlife

DISTANCE: Highly variable

TIME NEEDED: A few hours to several days

GRADE: Easy and family-friendly; moderate with portages

WHERE: The park is about 180 km (112 mi) west of Quebec City and 200 km (124 mi) northeast of Montreal. Shawinigan is only 15 km (9 mi) away from the eastern entrance.

HOW: Bring your own canoe or rent from Location Canot right beside the lakes. You can reserve online at **locationcanot.com**.

WHEN: May to mid-October

COST: $7.80/adult/day, $3.90/youth/day, $15.70/night for canoe camping, $24.50/night for canoe camping with firewood, $9.80 daily fishing fee

DON'T FORGET: Sunscreen, sun hat, bathing suit and towel. Lakes are beautiful for swimming and comfortably warm by July.

OPTIONS: If you don't want to canoe, consider hiking one of the 14 trails ranging in length from 0.3 km to 17 km (0.2–10.6 mi).

TOUR COMPANIES: None at this time

INTERESTING FACT: Sixteen private hunting and fishing clubs operated in what is now La Mauricie National Park between 1883 and 1970.

Cycling
The Green Route
through the Eastern Townships

□ ■ ■ □

Quebec's Eastern Townships, located in the foothills of the Appalachian Mountains south of the St. Lawrence River and north of Vermont, can be reached in short order by driving from Montreal. The townships are a superb place to explore on a bike. A combination of mostly quiet back roads and dedicated bike paths that are part of Quebec's famous Green Route criss-cross the landscape and make exploring safe and easy. The landscape is a blend of rolling farmland, forests, vineyards, orchards and small villages, including many of the members of the Most Beautiful Villages of Quebec association.

The Green Route itself traverses the area for a total of 225 km (140 mi) and could be biked over a long weekend. If you go self-supported with a couple of panniers, you have the flexibility to stay in some of the small towns before returning to your starting point. Magog — a pretty town located on the Green Route on Lake Memphremagog — is a great base, for it allows you to cycle two different out-and-back sections of the Green Route: either head west for Granby via Mont-Orford National Park or east to Danville via North Hatley and Sherbrooke.

There are plenty of other worthwhile loops to ride. If you enjoy wine, don't miss the 31 km (19 mi) wine route that starts and ends in Dunham. It takes in two beautiful villages: Frelighsburg and Stanbridge East. It's also possible to do a difficult 78 km (49 mi) loop ride through the hilly but beautiful ski country near Sutton. Or cycle both sides of Lake Memphremagog and include a side trip to Saint Benoît-du-Lac Abbey, famous for its apple cider and homemade cheeses. If you choose to continue south, a visit to Beebe Plain and Stanstead on the US–Canada border is in order. Don't miss the lakeside towns of Ayer's Cliff and North Hatley on Lake Massawippi, either; both are known for their antiques and laid-back vibes.

There are all manner of accommodation choices in the Eastern Townships, from camping to a large number of B&Bs to small hotels and even five-star Relais and Châteaux properties.

You can't help but focus on the food in the area, especially with the appetite you work up cycling. Restaurants are generally excellent and boast an ever-increasing focus on a large assortment of locally produced food. This area is famous for its cheeses, apples, pâtés, Brome Lake duck and a wide variety of maple products.

Cycling the Eastern Townships is an exceptional way to experience the countryside and the culture.

HIGHLIGHTS: Scenic wine country, outstanding cuisine, quiet cycling along the Green Route, some of Quebec's most beautiful villages, fall colours

DISTANCE: Variable, depending on how much time you have

TIME NEEDED: 3–7 days

GRADE: Moderate to difficult

WHERE: 100–125 km (62–78 mi) east of Montreal, depending on whether you start in Lac-Brome or Magog

HOW: Rent bikes at Ski Vélo in Magog and VéloGare in Granby, or bring your own.

WHEN: May to mid-October. Fall colours are best in display from late September to mid-October.

COST: Budget for getting to the Eastern Townships, bike rentals, meals and accommodation. There is a bus to Granby and Magog from Montreal.

DON'T FORGET: Order free maps ahead of time at **easterntownships.org**.

OPTIONS: Taxi-Vélo-Rando is a bike taxi for bikers. Call 1-877-766-8356. It's $45 for the first 30 km (20 mi) and $1.70/km (0.6 mi) thereafter.

TOUR COMPANIES: Randonnée Tours, Great Explorations, Gabriola Island Cycle and Kayak, Freewheeling Adventures

INTERESTING FACT: There are now approximately 20 wineries in the Eastern Townships, along a signed and drivable 130 km (81 mi) wine route.

Cross-country skiing
The Laurentians
in southern Quebec

■■■□

Superlative cross-country skiing awaits anyone who visits the Laurentians. The number of opportunities for cross-country skiing is mind-boggling: you can choose to backcountry ski in Mont-Tremblant National Park, ski the old rail bed known as Le P'tit Train du Nord, or choose from at least a dozen ski areas that offer groomed track-set trails.

With limited time, I skied the trails at Ski de fond Mont-Tremblant, located within spitting distance of the downhill resort bearing the same name. The skiing was excellent. Not only was the snow superb — which it usually is here; in fact, more than anywhere else in the Laurentians — but the trails are well groomed and signage is very good, except on one of the backcountry trails. The biggest takeaway from skiing here is how pretty the area is. Rolling hills, big vistas, beautiful mixed forests and a certain joie de vivre — that last perhaps because of the wide range of ages and the number of families skiing — all combine to provide an outstanding experience. If I lived nearby I would be a frequent visitor.

There are a number of loops you can do, ranging from short half-day loops to a delightful 25 km (16 mi) set of trails that takes you through a wide range of terrain. Naturally, that's the one my husband and I opted for. Starting from the ticket office, we skied off, first through a plantation-like forest and then along the river on undulating hills. From there we chose to investigate the backcountry trails, which I highly recommend for their solitude and beauty. But the bulk of the skiing took place on flat trails that circled Lac Ouimet. Only one major climb was required, towards the end of the day. Interestingly, at the top of the hill, there is a bell. Ring it if you're heading downhill to announce your presence to the uphill skiers and prevent collisions.

On our route we came across three warming huts. One was bursting at the seams with people; its proximity to the start of the trails ensured that we didn't stop. Another was an open-air structure with a warming fire and plenty of black-capped chickadees looking for seed handouts. The last one, Refuge Forget, was located within a few kilometres of the end of the trail; it would be useful to anyone skiing the northern loops of the ski area.

Needless to say, a day of skiing only gives you a taste of the area. I know I left wishing I'd had more time. Should you find yourself anywhere near Montreal or Ottawa in the winter, don't miss a chance to ski and explore the Laurentians.

HIGHLIGHTS: Fantastic range of ski hills, beautiful Laurentian Mountain scenery, pretty villages

DISTANCE: Highly variable, depending on how energetic you are

TIME NEEDED: At least a half day; up to a week if you want to explore multiple ski areas

GRADE: Easy to difficult

WHERE: The Laurentian region is located between Mont-Tremblant and Saint-Jérôme, though the Laurentian Mountains cover a much larger area. Saint-Jérôme is just 60 km (37 mi) northwest of Montreal, so most of the region is within an hour's drive of the city, traffic permitting.

HOW: Reservations are only required for backcountry huts. Cars should have snow tires.

WHEN: December to March

COST: Depending on where you ski. At Ski de fond Mont-Tremblant, it's $18.50/adult/day and $8.50/child or youth/day.

DON'T FORGET: A thermos of hot drinks and many layers of warm clothes. Pick up a map of the trails once you're at the ski resorts.

OPTIONS: Choose to backcountry ski on over 100 km (62 mi) of trails in Mont-Tremblant National Park. To prolong the experience, book a hut for a night or two through Sépaq at **sepaq.com/reservation/**

TOUR COMPANIES: None

INTERESTING FACT: The rocks that make up the Laurentian Mountains date to the Precambrian period and are more than one billion years old.

Cross-country skiing
Gatineau Park
in the Outaouais Region

■■■□

Gatineau Park, located within twenty minutes of downtown Ottawa, protects 361 sq km (139 sq mi) of the Canadian Shield. In winter, the park becomes a playground — primarily for residents of the National Capital Region, as they make up over 75 percent of the visitors. The reason: wonderful cross-country skiing on over fifty trails stretching from Gatineau to Wakefield.

The trails range in difficulty from beginner to expert. Classic skiers have 200 km (124 mi) of trails to choose from, while skate-skiers must share roughly 100 km (62 mi) of trails with the classic skiers. For those of you who love the wilder areas, you have 45 km (28 mi) of backcountry trails to explore.

There are fifteen starting points within Gatineau Park. It's worth stopping to chat with the staff at the Gatineau Park Visitor Centre to get their advice on local conditions and suggestions on where to ski, especially if you're new to the area. Pick up a map as well.

On very cold days, choose one of the trails with a warming hut. There are ten of them scattered around the park, and some are worthwhile as destinations in and of themselves. If you're a strong skier, make an effort to visit the beautiful Herridge Shelter; it's got a long history. Its first inhabitants were a family from Ireland. Eventually, it was sold to a politician named William Duncan Herridge, a friend of Prime Minister Bennett. It became a shelter in the park in the early 1980s, and is now recognized as a Federal Heritage Building. Healey Hut, less than a kilometre away, is also a ski-worthy destination and an equally beautiful building. One more that might be worthwhile is Western Hut, as it has a spectacular view of the Ottawa River.

You'll find that the trails take you through a real mix of terrain. The rock outcrops here are some of the oldest in Canada, dating back three billion years. If you stray from the easy trails, you can expect a lot of rolling hills. Most trails take you into the woods, where up to fifty tree species can be seen. Other trails, like those in the Wakefield area, head out through open fields with expansive views.

Gatineau Park is an exceptional place to ski or snowshoe. It's great for families, but it's got something for everyone. And if you're into Loppets, don't miss the mid-February annual Gatineau Loppet, which has distances available for all abilities.

HIGHLIGHTS: Rolling terrain, lakes, open woods, beautiful warming huts in historic buildings, well-groomed trails

DISTANCE: Highly variable and entirely at your whim

TIME NEEDED: One day at least, but there are 200 km (124 mi) of ski trails

GRADE: Easy to difficult, depending on the trail and distance you cover

WHERE: The Gatineau Park Visitor Centre is located in Chelsea at 33 Scott Street. Chelsea is 19 km (12 mi) north of Ottawa.

HOW: Bring your own skis or rent from Greg Christie's Ski & Cycle Works in Chelsea, or Sport Échange Outaouais in Gatineau.

WHEN: Mid-December until mid-March

COST: $15/adult/day; $11/day for students, seniors and youth; free for children under 12. Buy passes at the Visitor Centre or a kiosk at one of the 14 cross-country ski starting points. The kiosks are cash only. Interestingly, you can ski for free by borrowing a park pass with your library card at libraries in Ottawa, Gatineau and the Outaouais region.

DON'T FORGET: Waxing kit, warm drinks, layered clothing

OPTIONS: Ski into a yurt, four-season tent or cabin and spend the night. Reservations open at 9:00 a.m. on November 1 every year. You can do it online at **reservations. gatineaupark.ca**, by phone to 1-819-827-2020 or 1-866-456-3016 or in person at the Visitor Centre. Baggage and water delivery is extra. There are also 55 km (34 mi) of snowshoeing trails available in the park.

TOUR COMPANIES: None

INTERESTING FACT: In 1905, Canada's first geodetic survey marker was installed at the top of King Mountain in Gatineau Park.

Cycling
The Blueberry Route
around Lac Saint-Jean

□ ■ □ □

Quebec has done a superb job of creating a network of over 4,500 km (2,800 mi) of bike paths called the Green Route (La Route Verte) through scenic parts of the province. A section of the Green Route, the Blueberry Route — so called because of the blueberries that thrived there after a huge forest fire created ideal growing conditions — takes you 256 km (159 mi) around Lac Saint-Jean, a massive lake located a few hundred kilometres north of Quebec City. It can be comfortably cycled over three to four days. Start anywhere and cycle in either direction. On a three-day trip you can expect to cycle 94 km (58 mi), 92 km (57 mi) and 70 km (43 mi) respectively. Although the distances might seem high, the route is mostly flat, with wind being the biggest issue.

Highlights along the way include rolling farmland with fields of bright yellow canola begging to be photographed; Point-Taillon National Park with its lovely lakeside trails and sandy beaches; numerous small villages dominated by beautiful churches and spectacular waterfalls. Lac Saint-Jean isn't always in sight, but it's never far away. The passenger- and bike-only ferry ride to Peribonka, accessible from the beach at the 20 km (12.4 mi) mark in the national park, offers a scenic alternative to cycling and shaves 10 km (6 mi) off the distance.

It's easy to cycle this route independently, but you can also take advantage of companies that move your luggage for you, or you can even join a tour. Route-finding is rarely an issue, and volunteer roving ambassadors are there to help with any problems you might encounter. Parking is also easy and free in municipalities along the route.

Start in the town of Alma, a city built on aluminum, paper and water. This unlovely industrial town is actually a good place to begin, as there's lots of parking and Équinox Aventure has a bike rental facility here. Points of interest along the route include family-run cheese-making operations (many of which offer free tastings), tours and picnic areas. Look for fresh, squeaky cheese curds everywhere, even at gas stations. In Saint Félicien, there's a zoo where you're the one behind the bars and the animals roam freely. Val-Jalbert is home to a spectacular waterfall worthy of a side trip.

The Blueberry Route offers a safe way to see the countryside by bike. The route is a mix of dedicated bike paths, paved shoulders and designated roads that mostly take you through quiet neighbourhoods. On the highways, shoulders are wide and drivers are extremely courteous. Cycling the Blueberry Route is a great way for families and friends to share the outdoors and discover a scenic part of Quebec.

HIGHLIGHTS: Point-Taillon National Park, waterfalls, canola fields, family cheese-making operations, pretty Quebec villages, Lac Saint-Jean, French culture

DISTANCE: Cycle the whole 256 km (159 mi) or choose a section of the route.

TIME NEEDED: 3–4 days to do the whole route, even more if you want to make a lot of side trips

GRADE: Moderate

WHERE: Alma, a very common starting point, is 227 km (141 mi) north of Quebec City.

WHEN: Late April until late October, though it's officially open from May 15 to October 15

HOW: Bring a bike and park for free in all municipalities. In Alma, a guarded, paid parking area is available at the Dam-en-Terre complex. Luggage-moving services are offered by Gilles Girard Luggage

Shuttles starting June 15 and by Équinox Aventures starting June 1.

COST: The trail is free. Extras include bike rentals, luggage moving, food and accommodations. The Peribonka ferry is $6 pp.

DON'T FORGET: A bike repair kit, a bathing suit for the beaches in Point-Taillon National Park

OPTIONS: Cycle an additional 72 km (45 mi) one way on the Horst de Kénogami, another section of the Green Route that takes you from Lac Saint-Jean and drops you at the Saguenay River near Jonquière.

TOUR COMPANIES: Équinox Aventure, Atlantic Canada Cycling, Freewheeling Adventures

INTERESTING FACT: The Blueberry Route is extremely popular with locals and Quebecers. In 2012, the Blueberry Route hosted an astonishing 223,820 cyclists, with only 7 percent from out of province.

Kayaking
The Saguenay Fjord
in the Saguenay–Lac Saint-Jean Area

■■■□

The Saguenay Fjord was formed at the end of the last ice age, more than ten thousand years ago. Most of its 103 km (64 mi) length lies in Saguenay Fjord National Park in the Saguenay–Lac-Saint-Jean area of Quebec, just a few hours' drive east of Quebec City, before it empties into the St. Lawrence River at Tadoussac. This excellent kayaking destination, both for those interested in a multiple-day trip and for novices who just want a taste of the fjord experience, offers a chance to paddle below beautiful cliffs — some almost a thousand feet high — and to explore beaches and observe wildlife. Curious harbour seals will inspect you from a distance, the cry of the loon might just lull you to sleep at night, and if you're very lucky you might see beluga whales.

The small towns on either side of the fjord, tour boats, and hydro lines strung across some of the narrower sections mean you're never far from signs of humanity. But the scenery is exceptional, and there aren't many places on the planet where you have such a good chance of kayaking with beluga whales. La Baie-Sainte-Marguerite sees a great number of beluga whales in summer, probably because the sloped, sandy bottom is an ideal place for giving birth and teaching young belugas to hunt. I've been told that under whitecap conditions, it's easy to confuse waves with whales and vice versa.

If you're organizing your own trip, you'll find campsites conveniently situated along the length of the fjord at intervals of a day's paddle. And because the fjord is narrow — just 1.2 to 4.4 km (0.8–2.7 mi) wide — it's easy to explore both sides of it. But if the wind blows up, which it does frequently and without warning, it can make paddling both difficult and dangerous.

The Saguenay Fjord, though always close to civilization, still feels unspoiled. Kayaking is one of the best ways to experience it.

HIGHLIGHTS: Fjord scenery, seals, possible beluga and minke whale sightings, peregrine falcons (there are 10 nests along the length of the fjord), the rare possibility of a Greenland shark sighting

DISTANCE: Entirely up to you

TIME NEEDED: Half a day to 5 days

GRADE: Easy to difficult, depending on the wind

WHERE: The fjord is 2.5 to 4 hours northwest of Quebec City, depending on where you start. Launch from L'Anse-de-Roche, Baie-Éternité, La Baie, L'Anse-Saint-Jean, Sainte-Rose-du-Nord, Tadoussac, L'Anse Saint-Étienne or Saint-Fulgence

HOW: Possible to do on your own, but you need to be a strong paddler. You must pre-book campsites as if you were travelling towards Tadoussac.

WHEN: Mid-May to late September. High tides make paddling dangerous in October and November.

COST: About $58/3 hours for a guided trip, $589 for a guided 3-day trip with food and campsites. Park fees are $6.50/adult/day, $3/child/day and camping fees are $29/night.

DON'T FORGET: Paddling gloves, a sunhat that won't blow off, weather radio

OPTIONS: The ultimate trip would start at the inland end of the fjord and end 5 days later in Tadoussac, with a return by boat to the start of the trip.

TOUR COMPANIES: Fjord en Kayak, Azimut Aventure, OrganisAction

INTERESTING FACT: Beluga, minke, blue and fin whales can be found at the mouth of the Saguenay River.

Hiking to the summit of
Mont Albert
in the Chic-Chocs

☐☐■☐

Mont Albert is one of the twenty-five hiker-friendly peaks over 1,000 m (3,281 ft) high in the Chic-Chocs, a narrow mountain range forming the northern extension of the Appalachians. It's located inland on Quebec's Gaspé Peninsula in Gaspésie National Park. The trail to the super-sized plateau at the top of Mont Albert is open from June 24 until September 30.

The trailhead is located a short walk away from the Visitor's Centre. The 17 km (11 mi) loop hike can be done in any direction, but I recommend hiking up the short, steep section and returning via the longer route because it keeps you above the tree line and offers expansive views for hours. At the beginning, it's so steep it feels like you're on a StairMaster missing its off switch, and for most of the 5 km (3 mi) hike up a 885 m (2,900 ft) rise, there are no views to speak of expect for the odd peekaboo. But a wonderful surprise unfolds as you climb the last few hundred metres. Abruptly leaving the trees, you enter a landscape of lichen-covered rock interspersed with hardy alpine flowers, stunted spruce trees — and sublime views!

The plateau is extraordinary; 'massive' barely begins to describe it. It's 13 km (8 mi) across, over 20 sq km (7.7 sq mi) and home to the two summits of Albert North (1,070 m or 3,511 ft) and Albert South (1,151 m or 3,776 ft). Most of the plateau is boggy and essentially impossible to hike if you're human, but it's perfect if you're one of the woodland caribou that hang out there. There are numerous benches scattered around the summit, as well as a small hut that provides shelter should the weather turn nasty. In summer, beware of thunderstorms and be prepared to descend quickly.

Heading down, first cross the easy sections of boardwalk put in place to prevent you from disappearing into the bog. Next, the challenging descent begins. Initially, it's a steep hike down a rocky trail winding around the mountain. After that, there's a long section of huge boulders where one misstep could result in a twisted ankle or knee. It's not until you're on the home stretch in the last kilometre that the hiking gets easy.

It's a hard but rewarding hike, even without a caribou sighting, but it should only be attempted by seasoned and prepared hikers.

HIGHLIGHTS: Magical 360-degree vistas on the massive summit, tundra, waterfalls, possible caribou sightings

DISTANCE: 17.4 km (10.8 mi) loop

TIME NEEDED: 6–8 hours

GRADE: Difficult

WHERE: Located in the Gaspésie National Park, 40 km (25 mi) south of the town of Sainte-Anne-des-Monts and 530 km (329 mi) east of Quebec City.

WHEN: First week of June until September 30, though it varies year by year

COST: $6.50/adult for a daily park pass

DON'T FORGET: Hiking poles for the descent, rain gear, water

OPTIONS: Choose the shorter and easier 8.3 km (5.2 mi) family-friendly Mont Jacques-Cartier trail.

TOUR COMPANIES: None

INTERESTING FACT: The first recorded ascent of the mountain was made by geologist Alexander Murray on August 26, 1845.

Hiking
Les Graves
in Forillon National Park

■ □ □ □

Forillon National Park sits at the eastern tip of the Gaspé Peninsula, sandwiched between the Gulf of St. Lawrence and Gaspé Bay. The park's diverse landscape is made up of forests and small lakes, with rugged cliffs rising above cobble beaches and tiny coves on two of the park's three sides. If it's a clear day, the coastal views are impressive and you stand a good chance of seeing marine wildlife including seals, whales and seabirds. Although a variety of mammals inhabit the park, including moose, black bears, beavers, coyotes, ermines, snowshoe hares, minks and lynxes, the best I could do was a few porcupines in the vicinity of the lighthouse.

The park offers eight hikes ranging from an easy 0.6 km (0.4 mi) trail to a challenging 17.6 km (10.9 mi) wilderness hike. I chose the coastal Les Graves for a four-hour, 15.2 km (9.4 mi) out-and-back hike. I could have started at Mont Saint-Alban and added 4 km (2.5 mi) to the day, or just done the 8 km (5.0 mi) hike to the lighthouse. The energetic hiker can also add a 7.8 km (4.8 mi) loop that also begins at Mont Saint-Alban and heads up to an observation tower where there are views of the sea and cliffs. Add three hours if you hike this loop at either the beginning or end of Les Graves. For a picnic, choose one of the beaches or wait until you reach the lighthouse and snag a picnic table with a view of the rugged 95 m (312 ft) cliffs. The lighthouse can be reached from either a coastal road or a less taxing forested inland trail. Nearby is the zero marker for the Canadian portion of the International Appalachian Trail.

Les Graves is an outstanding hike and very family-friendly because it offers so many diversions. In Grand-Cave, which was a fishing village in the late nineteenth and early twentieth centuries, guides in period costume demonstrate what daily life looked like back then. After Grand-Cave, the trail meanders along grassy paths and through meadows bursting with wildflowers, interspersed with pretty cobble beaches and spectacular views of eroding cliffs. Be on the alert for great blue herons, gulls, double-breasted cormorants, terns, black-legged kittiwakes, razorbills, black guillemots and sandpipers.

Sweeping views, beaches and wildflowers are the hallmarks of this trail. Aim to hike it in the summer when it's at its most beautiful.

HIGHLIGHTS: Cobble beaches, prolific wildflowers, coastal views, dramatic cliffs, Cape Gaspé lighthouse, restored homestead and farm of Anse-Blanchette in Grand-Cave, seabirds

DISTANCE: 8–19 km (5–12 mi) return

TIME NEEDED: A half to a full day

GRADE: Easy and family-friendly

WHERE: The town of Gaspé is only a 40-minute drive from the park. From Quebec City, it's a beautiful 10-hour drive on the Trans-Canada Highway.

WHEN: Mid-June to mid-October, though summer is best for the wildflowers. The Visitor Centre is open from June 2 to September 2, but the trails are open until the road barriers are put in place, which is usually sometime in November or December.

COST: $7.80/adult, $6.80/senior and $3.90/youth (16 and younger)

DON'T FORGET: Food, water, binoculars

OPTIONS: Choose from 7 other hikes in the park across a range of difficulty.

TOUR COMPANIES: None

INTERESTING FACT: Over 700 species of local flora can be found in the park, including purple mountain and tufted saxifrage, plants usually found in the Arctic.

Cycling
The Magdalen Islands
in the Gulf of St. Lawrence

□ ■ □ □

The Magdalen Islands are an archipelago of more than a dozen almost treeless islands linked by kilometres of sand dunes as far as the eye can see. Plunked down in the Gulf of St. Lawrence, they take up a mere 206 sq km (80 sq mi), so there's a good chance you've never heard of them. Although French is the first language for most of their thirteen thousand inhabitants, many of whom are either Acadians or descendants of shipwreck survivors, English is widely understood.

My first view of these magical islands was from the deck of a ferry bound for Cap-aux-Meules on Île du Cap-aux-Meules, an island of red cliffs with a smattering of rainbow-coloured houses overlooking the sea. Other than the ferry from Prince Edward Island or a cruise ship from Montreal, the islands are accessible only via flights from one of three cities in Quebec. The difficulty in accessing the islands seems only to add to their charm.

The Magdalen Islands are home to a section of the Green Route, Quebec's famous network of cycling trails. Mind you, on these islands there is only one main road — Highway 199 — so it's hard, if not impossible, to get lost. In theory, you could cycle from Havre-Aubert to Grande-Entrée and back in a day, but that would be a 150 km (93 mi) return and sure wouldn't leave you with much time to explore. The Magdalen Islands deserve to be discovered at a more leisurely pace. With more than 300 km (186 mi) of beaches, so many activities such as cave swimming and windsurfing to try and plenty of restaurants offering fresh seafood and local specialties, it's highly likely that you'll want to slow down and savour the experience.

Although you could choose any section of the main road to cycle, you can also have fun exploring all the back roads and side trails — on Île du Cap-aux-Meules, for example. Laundry blowing in the breeze, houses painted every colour of the rainbow, lighthouses and fantastic red rock cliffs are just some of the delights you'll encounter.

Be prepared for near-constant wind, however. On particularly blowy days, you might want to delay your ride. Otherwise, hook up with Autobus les Sillons and get a shuttle so you can cycle with the wind at your back.

I think you'll find it hard not to succumb to the charm of the Magdalen Islands.

HIGHLIGHTS: Beaches, red cliffs, pretty coastline, great culture, excellent food, friendly locals, loads of optional activities

DISTANCE: Highly variable, but it's possible to cycle from Havre-Aubert to Grande-Entrée, a one-way distance of roughly 75 km (47 mi). Or cycle 54 km (34 mi) from Fatima on Île du Cap-aux-Meules to Grande-Entrée, one way.

TIME NEEDED: 1–3 days

GRADE: Moderate

WHERE: The Magdalen Islands are located approximately 105 km (65 mi) north of Prince Edward Island (PEI). They are accessible via a 5-hour ferry ride from PEI or a short flight from either Montreal, Quebec City or Gaspé.

WHEN: April to early October

HOW: Grab a map on the ferry or from a bike store. There's only one main road.

COST: Free if you bring a bike. Otherwise, you can rent a bike on Île du Cap-aux-Meules at Véli-Vélo or Le Pédalier.

DON'T FORGET: There are long distances between towns. Bring a bike pump, water and a wind-proof jacket.

OPTIONS: To do a one-way bike ride, it's possible to hire a shuttle (Autobus les Sillons) from mid-June until the end of September.

TOUR COMPANIES: Freewheeling Adventures

INTERESTING FACT: Houses are painted every colour of the rainbow partially to brighten dreary winter days but also to serve as markers for boats at sea.

Cross-country skiing at
The Mont Sainte-Anne
Cross-Country Ski Centre

■■■■

If you live outside of the Quebec City area, chances are you associate Mont Sainte-Anne with its wonderful downhill ski resort. But just 7 km (4.4 mi) up the road, beyond the tiny village of Saint-Ferréol-les-Neiges, lie 200 km (124.3 mi) of phenomenally well-groomed and track-set classic and skating ski trails.

There are a lot of factors that make Mont Sainte-Anne a delight to cross-country ski. The snow falls early here and stays late. In a good year it can snow over 400 cm (13.1 ft). Then throw in the fact that the sheer choice of trails is fantastic. The Mont Sainte-Anne Cross-Country Ski Centre bills itself as the resort with the largest number of cross-country ski trails in all of Canada.

The range of trails cuts across all levels of difficulty. A little under a quarter of the trails are easy, 42 percent are moderate and 3 percent are classified as very difficult. Most of the trails start from the main chalet adjacent to the parking lot. Easy loops ranging in length from 3.7 km (2.3 mi) to 13 km (8.1 mi) are great for families. There are a couple of moderate loops, including one dedicated to skate-skiing only, and several very difficult ones including a 21 km (13.0 mi) trail that takes you deep up into the hills.

The Mont Sainte-Anne ski area is also very beautiful. Many of the trails take you through mixed woods of birch, maple, pine and spruce, and they're open enough to only rarely feel oppressively dark. If you're lucky enough to make it to the Refuge Saint-Anselme, one of five warming huts scattered across the resort, you will be rewarded with expansive views of the back side of the Mont Sainte-Anne downhill ski resort, as well as peekaboo views of the distant St. Lawrence River.

Wildlife abounds in this part of the world, as evidenced by the huge number of animal tracks. Moose sightings are common, especially off of trail #24, one of the most difficult ones. In fact, a warning sign at the start of all the trails advises you to be on the lookout for moose. They aren't likely to cede the trail, so be prepared to retrace your steps. Consider yourself lucky if you see more than the tracks of wolves, foxes, lynxes, deer or rabbits.

Delightful cross-country skiing on trails that are rarely flat, with the option of solitude, is the treat waiting for you if you can swing a visit to Mont Sainte-Anne.

HIGHLIGHTS: Lots of snow with excellent grooming, beautiful warming cabins, high probability of seeing a moose, expansive views, lots of variety in the trails, mixed forest

DISTANCE: Highly variable. There are 200 km (124.3 mi) to ski if you were to complete all the loops.

TIME NEEDED: At least a full day, but there are enough trails for many days of exploring

GRADE: Easy to very difficult

WHERE: The parking area is located 7 km (4.4 mi) up the road from the Mont Sainte-Anne Ski Resort in Beaupré, which is approximately 44 km (27.3 mi) northeast of Quebec City.

HOW: The trails are open Monday to Friday from 9:00 a.m. to 4:00 p.m; on Saturday and Sunday, the trails open at 8:30 a.m.

WHEN: Opens sometime in November, depending on the year, and closes on the first weekend in April

COST: $26/day/adult, $20/youth, $55/family; rates decrease if you buy consecutive day passes (5/6 days is $100).

DON'T FORGET: This part of Canada can get very cold in winter, so dress warmly and in layers. Carry a copy of a map with you, especially if you're heading out on the most difficult trails.

OPTIONS: There are 37 km (23.0 mi) of dedicated snowshoeing trails. Tickets are $11/adult.

TOUR COMPANIES: None

INTERESTING FACT: The 'black' trails — the most difficult — were specifically designed for the first major international Nordic race to be held in Canada: the World Junior Nordic Championships in 1979.

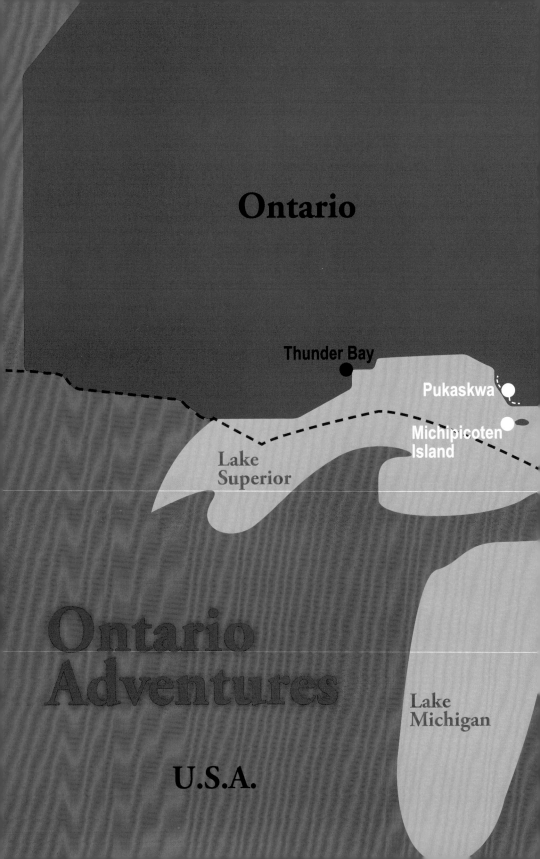

Ontario

Thunder Bay

Pukaskwa

Michipicoten
Island

Lake
Superior

Ontario
Adventures

Lake
Michigan

U.S.A.

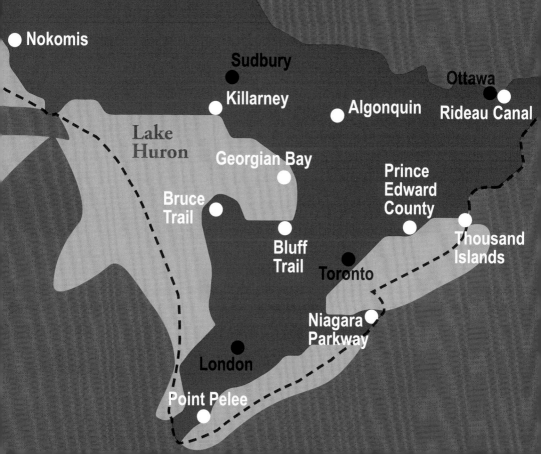

James
Bay

N

Quebec

Nokomis

Sudbury

Killarney

Algonquin

Ottawa

Rideau Canal

Lake
Huron

Georgian Bay

Prince
Edward
County

Bruce
Trail

Thousand
Islands

Bluff
Trail

Toronto

Niagara
Parkway

London

Point Pelee

Cycling
The Niagara Parkway
to Niagara Falls

■ ☐ ☐ ☐

Starting from the town of Niagara-on-the-Lake, the Niagara River Recreation Trail is packed with attractions: quiet riverside paths, museums, world-class wineries, orchards and thundering waterfalls. While still in town, wine lovers can pick up a map from the Chamber of Commerce to help plan a wineries tour for their return ride, and history buffs can stop at Fort George, a British base during the War of 1812 and a National Historic Site today.

Follow the trail out of town, enjoying the views across the Niagara River to the United States, and ogle all the lovely homes en route to picturesque Queenston. For a picnic lunch and a delicious sampling from the famous Niagara Fruit Belt, keep an eye out for Kurtz Orchards and Walker's Country Market. Over the next few kilometres, watch for museums: the RiverBrink Art Museum with its focus on historical Canadian art; the Mackenzie Printery and Newspaper Museum in the restored home of publisher William Lyon Mackenzie, which showcases five hundred years of printing technology; and the Laura Secord Homestead, where you can learn how she made the courageous 32 km (20 mi) walk to warn the British of a surprise American attack during the War of 1812.

Next is a climb up the Niagara Escarpment, a short, steep hill that many cyclists choose to walk. Once at the top, continue on the paved trail past the Butterfly Conservatory, the Floral Clock and the Sir Adam Beck Hydroelectric Generating Station, where you'll want to gawk down at the power of the Niagara River. The paved trail ends after this, but the shoulder of the road is good until Niagara Falls. Over the next 4 km (2.5 mi), you'll pass two more bridges to the US: the Whirlpool Rapids Bridge and the Rainbow Bridge. About a kilometre (0.6 mi) from Niagara Falls, the traffic makes cycling dicey. Experienced cyclists should exercise extreme caution and families should consider dismounting to walk along the side of the road, which still offers plenty to see. Even though the carnival atmosphere around Niagara Falls may be a tad off-putting, the falls are still a sight to behold, especially when you consider that the three falls that make up Niagara Falls have the highest flow rate of any waterfall in the world! For a different perspective, try a Maid of the Mist tour below the falls.

To return to Niagara-on-the-Lake, cycle back the way you came or take an alternate route using the winery map. Just be forewarned that some of the side roads are unpaved and dusty.

Highlights: Niagara Falls and the Niagara River, wineries, orchards, history

Distance: 25 km (15.5 mi) each way between Niagara-on-the-Lake and Niagara Falls

Time needed: A half day to a full day

Grade: Easy and family-friendly

Where: On the Niagara River Recreation Parkway between Niagara-on-the-Lake and Niagara Falls. It's a 90-minute drive from Toronto, and only 45 minutes — with a cooperative border guard — from Buffalo, New York.

How: Bring your own bike or rent from Zoom Leisure in either Niagara-on-the-Lake or Niagara Falls.

When: Mid-April until late October; summer is hot and humid, September is usually lovely.

Cost: Free unless you rent a bike

Don't forget: A bike lock — and a corkscrew if you have a picnic with wine

Options: Continue on to Fort Erie, a further 29 km (18 mi) away on mostly dedicated bike paths. Explore the side roads and visit wineries.

Tour companies: Zoom Leisure, Niagara Wine Tours International

Interesting fact: The Niagara River flows from Lake Erie to Lake Ontario and forms a section of the border between Ontario and New York State.

Hiking
The Trails
of Point Pelee National Park

■ □ □ □

You don't have to be a fanatical birder to enjoy a visit to Point Pelee National Park, though an interest in birds and reptiles could certainly make any hike you do more meaningful. Canada's second-smallest national park — located at the crossroads of major migration routes for not only birds but also butterflies, bats and dragonflies, and with just 15 sq km (6 sq mi) of space — offers a variety of loop trails that lead you through five unique Carolinian habitats. Look for dry forest, wet forest, swamp, cedar savannah, marsh and rock beach, habitats that make up less than one quarter of one percent of Canada's total land mass but boast more rare species of plants and animals than anywhere else in the country.

It's easy to hike all the trails in the park in a day by combining loops, but there are lots of diversions depending on which trail you choose. The highlight for many will be the walk to the end of a narrow spit of land, the southernmost tip of mainland Canada. The latitude here is equivalent to the northern border of California. From the tip, beaches spread up either side of the 10 km (6 mi) sand spit, beckoning you to lounge rather than hike.

Assuming you're keen to continue, try some of the wooded trails where in spring the trilliums abound and birdsong is loud. The birds are around, but unless you've got a good pair of binoculars you won't see many of them. An exception to that is the wild turkey. It's hardly exotic, but I loved coming across these birds with attitude.

The 1 km (0.6 mi) Marsh Boardwalk is one of the must-do hikes. It's popular with families, as it allows you to get close to cattails, lily pads, turtles, frogs and birds. Taking the time to paddle through the marshy areas would be a fabulous way to further explore the park.

Don't miss the 1.2 km (0.8 mi) DeLaurier Homestead and Trail. Although short in length, it takes you through ten thousand years of Point Pelee history, from the First Peoples through to homesteaders, fishermen, farmers and finally to cottagers.

Despite its diminutive size, Point Pelee sees three hundred thousand visitors a year. Go not just for the hiking but for the chance to see nature in action. Try to visit during the major bird migration in early May; if you've ever seen the movie *The Big Year* you will appreciate the thrill of seeing so many species of bird at one time. And if you can't catch the birds, catch the monarch butterfly migration in September instead.

There really is something for everyone in this small gem of a park.

HIGHLIGHTS: Birds, birdsong, boardwalk, walk to the most southernmost tip of mainland Canada, swimming, beaches, paddling, biking, fall monarch butterfly migration

DISTANCE: Variable. Seven trails offer hikes from 1 to 4 km (0.6–2.5 mi) in length, but it's easy to tie many loops together to create a 12–14 km (7.5–8.7 mi) hike.

TIME NEEDED: Half a day to a day, unless you're a very keen birder

GRADE: Easy and family-friendly

WHERE: 355 km (221 mi) southwest of Toronto and 50 km (31 mi) southeast of Windsor. The closest town is Leamington.

WHEN: Open year-round, but check the Parks Canada website for current operating hours.

COST: $7.80/adult from April to October, $6.05/adult from November until March

DON'T FORGET: Currents and undertows at the tip are very dangerous. Do not swim or even wade here. Check yourself for ticks, especially after walking through shrubs and grassy areas. Learn what poison ivy looks like so you can avoid it.

OPTIONS: Rent a canoe at the Cattail Café and explore the ponds near the boardwalk — from June 1 until September 2 only.

TOUR COMPANIES: None. Don't miss the Festival of Birds during the first few weeks of May, though. Sign up for a free two-hour hike with experienced birders.

INTERESTING FACT: There are over 700 species of flowering and non-flowering plant, some of which are found only in this area.

Backpacking
The Bruce Trail
in Bruce Peninsula National Park

□ ■ ■ □

The most scenic section of the 894 km (556 mi) Bruce Trail — Canada's longest marked hiking trail — is the 21 km (13.1 mi) section that jogs through Bruce Peninsula National Park, a UNESCO World Biosphere Reserve and one of the last remaining chunks of natural habitat in southern Ontario. Expect to see exceptional clifftop scenery, rugged trails, caves, crystal-clear Caribbean-bright water, ancient cedar trees, rare orchids and white stone beaches.

Although you can see the best the park has to offer in a day trip, the best way to discover it is a two- to three-day backpacking trip from the Crane Lake Trailhead to the Cyprus Lake Trailhead. You'll need to arrange a shuttle to take you back from this one-way hike. It starts with an easy amble through mixed woods for 8.2 km (5.1 mi) until you reach Georgian Bay and the steep side trail to High Dump, one of the two beautiful backcountry campsites on the trail. This will take fit hikers about four hours, but if you plan to continue to the next campsite (Stormhaven) on the same day, allow another five and a half hours to complete the very demanding final 9.3 km (5.8 mi). From High Dump past Stormhaven through to Overhanging Point is both the most rugged and most beautiful section of the entire Bruce Trail. Looking down to crashing waves from atop the cliffs is awe-inspiring . . . and a little scary, for those with vertigo.

Allow plenty of time to explore both Indian Head Cove and the Grotto, both about a ninety-minute hike west of the Stormhaven campsite. These two spots, just ten minutes apart, are the most interesting on the trail and are both easily accessible to day hikers. At Indian Cove, the colour of the water, white rocks and eroded spires will take your breath away. The Grotto, a big cave on the shore carved by waves over thousands of years, is beautiful from any angle. Pick your way down the rocky cliff to the mouth of the cave, where on sunny days you can see a dazzling underwater tunnel.

Another point of interest is the fantastic lookout of Overhanging Rock, but the trail to get there from the Grotto is tough and filled with uneven, sharply pointed rocks and big tree roots. From there, you can return to the Cyprus Lake Trailhead via the easy Marr Lake Trail, or hike another 17.5 km (10.9 mi) to Tobermory, the official end of the Bruce Trail.

No matter how much time you choose to spend in the park, you can't help but come away inspired by the rugged beauty of the area.

HIGHLIGHTS: Turquoise water and rocky beaches, the Grotto, clifftop views, some of the oldest trees in Canada, wildflowers, orchids, wildlife

DISTANCE: Varies, depending on whether you do a loop or an out-and-back hike. It's 21 km (13.1 mi) from the Crane Head Trailhead to Overhanging Point, about a kilometre away from the Cyrus Lake Trailhead.

TIME NEEDED: 1–3 days

GRADE: Moderate to difficult, depending on which section you hike

WHERE: At the tip of the Bruce Peninsula, 100 km (62 mi) north of Owen Sound, 289 km (180 mi) north of Toronto

WHEN: Late April to October

HOW: Book a Stormhaven or High Dump campsite at main office in Bruce Peninsula National Park or call 1-519-596-2263

May to October. Bring exact change or a credit card. There are nine campsites at each. Reserve well in advance for July through September.

COST: $11.70/vehicle/day, $9.80/backcountry reservation, $9.80/night for a backcountry campsite, $23.50/unserviced campsite at Cyprus Lake

DON'T FORGET: Bear spray, waterproof bag to hang food, bug repellent, hiking shoes, hiking poles

OPTIONS: Park highlights can be seen in an overnight return hike from Cyprus Lake Trailhead to Stormhaven.

TOUR COMPANIES: None, but there is a summer weekend bus from Toronto to the park. Reserve at **parkbus.ca**.

INTERESTING FACT: Approximately 43 orchid species are found in the park. Admire but don't pick. Visit the Bruce Trail Conservancy online at **brucetrail.org**.

Hiking
The Bluff Trail
in Awenda Provincial Park

■ □ □ □

If you or your family are in need of a nature fix, head to Awenda Provincial Park, just two hours north of Toronto. Awenda boasts the largest stand of old-growth deciduous forest in Canada, with sugar maples that are reportedly 260 years old. The park also offers 5.5 km (3.4 mi) of natural shoreline along the Georgian Bay that's in much the same shape that it was five hundred years ago, with a mix of sand dunes and rugged elements and nary a cottage in sight.

In the park, you'll find 29 km (18 mi) of trails including the circular 13 km (8 mi) Bluff Trail. The Bluff Trail itself is hardly what you would call a 'wilderness' trail. It's simply an easy walking trail linking campsites through beautiful woods. At times the trail parallels the road. Don't let that deter you, though. The woods are truly magnificent in spring and fall. In spring, lime-green foliage combined with an understory of red, white and painted trilliums will quite literally take your breath away. Return in the fall and it will have the same effect: this park puts on one of the best autumnal colour shows anywhere in Ontario.

The well signed Bluff Trail has little elevation change. It will probably take you under four hours, even with stops. There are additional trails you can hike from it, including the circular 5 km (3.1 mi) Wendat Trail, which takes you around Kettle Lake, an area that's great for wildlife viewing. You could also add on the 0.5 km (0.3 mi) Nipissing Trail. It takes you from the top of the Nipissing Bluff — the primary glacial feature in Awenda — down to the Beach Trail, where it's possible to add another 4 km (2.5 mi) of hiking and make a full day of it.

There isn't much in the way of views on the Bluff Trail, despite its name. You only get peekaboo glimpses of Georgian Bay and Giant's Tomb Island along the bluff portion of the trail, after the trees have leafed out. Listen for birdsong: over two hundred species of bird have been sighted in the park, including an array of warblers. In spring the birdsong is pure delight.

The Bluff Trail doesn't offer a mind-blowing, wilderness sort of experience. What it does offer is quiet beauty in an area that's been taken over by big box stores and cottages. A walk in the park — especially in the early season when it's quiet — will take you back in time and provide a glimpse of what this part of the province once looked like. You will be glad you did this hike.

HIGHLIGHTS: Breathtaking trillium-filled forest in spring, spectacular fall colours, excellent birding, cross-country skiing in winter, Georgian Bay beaches

DISTANCE: 13 km (8 mi) round trip

TIME NEEDED: 3–5 hours

GRADE: Easy and family-friendly

WHERE: Located at the edge of the Pene-tanguishene Peninsula on Georgian Bay, 164 km (102 mi) north of Toronto

WHEN: April to October for hiking; winter months for cross-country skiing

HOW: It's possible to do just a section of the Bluff Trail.

COST: $14/day/vehicle

DON'T FORGET: Binoculars. There is cell phone coverage in this park.

OPTIONS: Camping in the park is an option. There are a total of 333 camping sites in 6 campgrounds, many suitable for RV hookups.

TOUR COMPANIES: None

INTERESTING FACT: The park is home to 7 species of bird, 2 types of mammal and 9 reptile species that are threatened, endangered or of special concern.

Kayaking around
Franklin Island
in Georgian Bay

■■■□

The magnificent Georgian Bay wilderness, home to thirty thousand windswept granite islands scoured by glaciers in the last ice age, makes a superb kayaking destination. Its rugged beauty, so expertly painted by the Group of Seven, is the backdrop for the duration of any trip.

Georgian Bay, sometimes called the sixth Great Lake, covers close to 15,000 sq km (5,792 sq mi), about 80 percent of the size of Lake Ontario. As such, it is capable of generating its own weather, waves and currents. It's justly famous for its winds that blow up out of nowhere, making calm water gnarly and dangerous in a matter of minutes.

The hardest decision you'll have to make is what part of Georgian Bay to explore. Time and your paddling ability figure prominently into the equation, as does any forecast with wind warnings. You can launch anywhere between Snug Harbour and Killarney to access the myriad of islands and islets, but always have a fall-back plan in place; there are islands, particularly the distant outer islands, where you can get wind-bound for days.

If you're a novice to intermediate paddler, one of the easier three-day kayaking trips is a circumnavigation of Franklin Island. Accessible with a launch from Snug Harbour, the island offers quintessential Georgian Bay scenery: twisted, folded and cooked metamorphic rocks; wind-twisted and gnarled white pines; flat slabs of crystalline rock perfect for sunbathing; beaches for swimming; and fresh blueberries to pick in season. There are loads of camping sites and privacy should never be an issue. The actual circumnavigation of Franklin Island should take no more than four or five hours at a relaxed place.

Experienced paddlers might want to use Franklin Island as a stopping point on the way to or from the Mink Islands. These islands see fewer paddlers but offer plenty of opportunities for exploration. In particular, look for the wreckage of the steamship *Seattle*, which sank 300 m (984 ft) off Green Island in 1903. Adventurous paddlers can continue farther and explore the McCoy group of islands.

Georgian Bay is a magical area and the ideal destination for a dose of rugged wilderness.

HIGHLIGHTS: Windswept rock islands, white pines, pristine waters, sandy beaches, excellent swimming, Group of Seven scenery, bonfires, blueberry picking

DISTANCE: It's 13 km (8 mi) to circumnavigate Franklin Island. The Mink Group is a 5 km (3 mi) open-water crossing from Franklin Island. From there you can access the McCoy Islands.

TIME NEEDED: 3–7 days or more

GRADE: Easy to difficult, depending on the winds and the weather

WHERE: Launch for Franklin Islands from Snug Harbour, located 275 km (171 mi) north of Toronto via Highway 400, Highway 559 and Snug Harbour Road.

HOW: Bring your own kayak, rent from White Squall or Killarney Outfitters, or join a tour.

WHEN: Late May to late September

COST: Franklin Island is Crown land, so camping is free.

DON'T FORGET: Marine charts, weather radio and extra food. Sudden winds can change paddling conditions in minutes. Watch out for rattlesnakes.

OPTIONS: Other route possibilities: start in Killarney and head for Phillip Edward Island and the Fox and Chicken Islands; launch from Key River Marina and head for the Bustard Islands; or leave from Britt and head to the Churchill Islands.

TOUR COMPANIES: Wolf Den Expeditions, White Squall, Voyageur Quest, Wilderness Adventures, Black Feather Wilderness Adventure Company, Wild Woman Expeditions, Killarney Outfitters

INTERESTING FACT: In 1822, Admiral Henry Wolsey Bayfield of the British Royal Navy named Georgian Bay after King George IV.

Canoeing the lakes of
Killarney Provincial Park
in central Ontario

■■■□

Called one of the crown jewels of the Ontario park system, Killarney Provincial Park presents a striking wilderness landscape of pink granite rocks and towering jack pines dominated by white quartzite ridges and the hills that make up the La Cloche Range. Add in over fifty exceptionally clear, sapphire-blue lakes and you've got a paddling destination made in heaven.

The 645 sq km (249 sq mi) park came into being in 1964 thanks to the lobbying efforts of several of the Group of Seven artists, particularly A.Y. Jackson and Franklin Carmichael, who painted the landscape to great effect. In fact, a recent book — *In the Footsteps of the Group of Seven*, by Jim and Sue Waddington — documents the exact locations in Killarney Park where the Group of Seven painted.

The park's location on the north shore of Georgian Bay puts it in striking distance for weekend paddlers from southern Ontario, even more so now that **parkbus.ca** offers service on some weekends from Toronto to the main launch site on George Lake.

The debate will be where to paddle in the park. There are a number of books written on the subject — *A Paddler's Guide to Killarney and the French River* by Kevin Callan is one example — but it's also possible to plan your own route by spending some time looking at a map. How many days do you have and how many portages are you interested in doing are the first questions you need to ask yourself. Don't forget that a loop trip is almost always more rewarding than retracing your footsteps. It's worth checking out the map on Killarney Outfitters' website. It's particularly helpful in providing the approximate time required for each portage, as well as useful information about water levels and campsites.

Although it's been a few years since I've canoed in Killarney, it's a trip that has stood the test of time, chiefly because the landscape is unique and very beautiful, and because the lakes are so spectacularly clear.

Highlights: Wildlife, fantastic swimming, blueberries in season, fall colours, solitude

Distance: Varies

Time needed: At least a weekend

Grade: Easy to difficult, depending on distance and number of portages

Where: Park entrance is 90 km (56 mi) southwest of Sudbury and 400 km (249 mi) north of Toronto via Highways 69 and 637. Access western part of park on Highway 6, halfway between Little Current and Espanola.

How: Reserve up to five months ahead. Call 1-888-668-7275 or 1-519-826-5290. Killarney Outfitters offers paid shuttle service and canoe rentals in park. For the park's west section, rent canoes from Widgawa Lodge.

When: Mid-May to mid-October. Bugs can be awful in June.

Cost: Backcountry camping fees: $10.50/adult/night, $8.40/senior/night, $4.50/child or youth/night. Reservation, deposit, cancellation, and change fees in effect. Parking is included with camping, but one-day vehicle permit is $14.

Don't forget: Waterproof tent and gear as thunderstorms are common, bug spray

Options: Ten hiking trails, including the beautiful and tough 78 km (48.5 mi) La Cloche Silhouette Trail

Tour companies: Wild Women Expeditions, Dog Paddling Adventures

Interesting fact: Killarney is home to the threatened Eastern Massasauga Rattlesnake found on the islands and shore of Georgian Bay and in rocky upland areas in summer.

Hiking
The Nokomis Trail
in Lake Superior Provincial Park

□■□□

The Nokomis Trail is the perfect half-day hike for people who are either staying in Lake Superior Provincial Park or are driving through on the Trans-Canada Highway and want more than just a stroll on the beach. The trail follows the Old Woman River Valley, which forms an interesting divide between forest and lowlands. North of the Old Woman River Valley, the boreal forest is predominant, and to the south is the deciduous Great Lakes–St. Lawrence Forest which is broken by boreal lowlands. In the fall, trees change colour on one side and remain green on the other.

The trail travels over ancient ankle-breaking cobblestone beaches, which are fragments of an old lake bed. Exercise caution when it's wet, as these moss- and lichen-covered rocks can get very slick. Also keep your eyes open for the Pukaskwa Pit. Native people believe this circular depression to be a spiritual site. About thirty minutes into the hike, there is a steep climb up to the first of many viewpoints. Look to the 200 m (656 ft) cliff face over Lake Superior to see if you can find Nokomis, grandmother of the Ojibway demigod Nanabozho, or 'Old Woman of the Wind,' as she is also known. (I needed some help to locate her profile in the cliff face.) From this viewpoint you can also look down to the river, where black bears can sometimes be seen along the edge. Finally, turn your gaze southwards to the hills, which in the fall display a stunning palette of colours.

From here on, most of the climbing is over. Continue past beautiful outcrops of granite to reach one overlook after another. At the high point, the view is simply superb, and on a clear day the chilly water of Lake Superior looks deceptively inviting, but in fact it's almost too cold to swim in without a wetsuit.

To complete the hike, descend on a well-marked trail through red and jack pine trees, past beautiful lichen-covered rock outcrops to a trail that runs parallel to the highway. Look both ways before crossing the highway and heading for the beach, which is a perfect place to end the hike with a picnic.

This hike offers some of the best views in Lake Superior Provincial Park.

HIGHLIGHTS: Boreal forest, beautiful views over Old Woman River Valley and Old Woman Bay, lichens, fall colours, wildlife

DISTANCE: 5 km (3 mi) loop

TIME NEEDED: 2–3 hours

GRADE: Moderate

WHERE: 880 km (547 mi) northwest of Toronto, 200 km (124 mi) north of Sault Ste. Marie, 27 km (17 mi) south of Wawa

HOW: No park permit is required, just the parking fee.

WHEN: May to mid-October

COST: $5.25/2 hours of parking, $7.50/4 hours of parking

DON'T FORGET: Binoculars, water, bathing suit if you love cold water

OPTIONS: If you have the time, hike the nearby Towab Trail. It follows the Agawa River up to Agawa Falls; in fall the colours are superb. You'll need 10 to 12 hours; it's doable as a long day hike, but better as an overnight backpacking trip.

TOUR COMPANIES: None

INTERESTING FACT: The cliffs around Old Woman Bay are a prime nesting area for peregrine falcons. Six nests have been used since 1998.

Kayaking around
Michipicoten Island
in Lake Superior

☐ ■ ■ ☐

My neighbour, an eighty-one-year-old retired BC Ferries captain, looks at me incredulously when I tell him where I'm going. "You're kayaking on Lake Superior? You can't be serious. Do you realize it's more dangerous than the North Atlantic?"

Our group of four (plus guide) didn't think it would be that risky, and it wasn't, but timing is everything when you're dealing with Lake Superior. It's the biggest lake in the world by surface area, the deepest of the Great Lakes (407 m or 1,335 ft at the deepest point), and the average water temperature even in August is a frigid 14°C (58°F). The lake is capable of making its own weather system and has a bad reputation for sinking ships.

July and August are the best months to kayak. The weather is more predictable and there are fewer storms. All the same, come prepared for all types of weather conditions, including thick fog. Definitely wait for fog to lift — unless you are with a guide and they think it's okay. Also build in a day or two for wind; there's no point going out in bad conditions just to stick to a schedule.

On a six-day paddle around Michipicoten Island, you'll have a chance to explore a rocky coastline broken by quiet coves and beaches, an abandoned fishing village and a bay filled with shipwrecks. The water lapping some of the beaches looks as seductive as any you'll see in the Caribbean. If you're a tough nut, you might be able to swim for a few minutes, but that's about all, unless you bring a wetsuit.

You won't see another soul for days around this remote and mysterious island, nor hear the whine of a motorboat engine or see planes fly overhead. With no interruptions from the modern world you'll find yourself getting into a simple rhythm of kayak, eat, rest, read, sleep.

There are a lot of animals on the island — one day we glimpsed a rare albino woodland caribou. You can see caribou walking the beach at dawn and dusk. Beavers are also plentiful and there's enough bird life to keep a novice birder happy. Rock hounds will have fun poking about the colourful beaches for hours.

This is a superb trip for the adventurous kayaker who wants to paddle where few have travelled.

HIGHLIGHTS: Rugged coastline, caribou sightings, shipwrecks, an abandoned fishing village, beautiful rocky beaches, sense of isolation, lighthouses

DISTANCE: 70 km (44 miles) to circumnavigate the island

TIME NEEDED: 6–7 days, plus a few extra days if you elect to do the 18 km (11 mi) crossing from Bonner Head to the mainland and back to Michipicoten Bay

GRADE: Moderate to difficult, depending on wind and water conditions. You should be a strong intermediate paddler. This is no place for beginners.

WHERE: 60 km (37 mi) from Michipicoten Bay to the East End Lighthouse on Michipicoten Island

WHEN: July until mid-August

HOW: You'll need a water taxi to get to Michipicoten Island. Call Keith McCuaig at 1-807-229-0193 to organize one, or email him at **mccuaigmarine@shaw.ca.** He can give you current pricing.

COST: Approximately $1,500 for a guided week-long tour

DON'T FORGET: A map and compass, wetsuit if interested in swimming, extra food

OPTIONS: Book a boat over from the mainland and do the tour yourself if you have the paddling skills.

TOUR COMPANIES: Naturally Superior Adventures

INTERESTING FACT: The island once boasted a producing copper mine. It's long since been abandoned.

Backpacking
The Coastal Trail
in Pukaskwa National Park

□□■□

The Coastal Trail in Pukaskwa National Park is one tough hike. The trail weaves along the shore of Lake Superior, a lake that behaves like a hormonal teenager. One minute it's glassy calm and the next it's throwing a temper tantrum and kicking up waves that can swallow ships. It's a lake you can't help but respect, especially considering it's the largest in the world by surface area. It's bloody cold, too, averaging 4.4°C (40°F). But it's also incredibly beautiful, and the reward at the end of every hard hiking day is a lakefront campsite on a beach that's likely to be deserted and have sublime views.

The Coastal Trail is typically done as a one-way hike. You can start at either end, but if you begin at the outlying North Swallow River, every step is in the direction of the parking lot — and safety. This way, there is no need to coordinate your finish time with the arrival of a boat, which, depending on the weather, may or may not show up. Campsites must be prebooked. Don't overestimate your abilities or hiking speed; count on covering 2 km/h (1.2 mph) or less. The trail is tougher at the far end and easiest on the hike out from the White River Suspension Bridge. If it's rainy, progress will be excruciatingly slow, as the slabs of granite are super slick when wet.

The hike is incredibly diverse. Every day is surprisingly different, though all have some common elements including steep ascents and descents, narrow gorges and uneven ankle-breaking rock fields, as well as countless sections of granite slabs. Be prepared for three days of very rugged hiking between North Swallow River and Oiseau Bay. From Oiseau Bay to Hattie Cove it's still tough, but slightly less rugged. The trail is usually easy to follow. Difficulties arise in route-finding when exiting a stretch of beach, though the parks people continue to make improvements.

If you're lucky enough to hike this trail in the fall, you will be treated to a blueberry bonanza. But with blueberries you get bears, so be on high alert and make lots of noise. Bear boxes are available at all campsites.

Bugs can also be a problem, especially early in the season. Blackflies, mosquitoes, horseflies and deer flies are quite capable of driving you mad. Forget bug jackets and bug dope at your peril if you're hiking at any time between early May and late August.

Despite the challenges, the Coastal Trail is one of the premier backpacking trips in Canada. Be one of the few to enjoy one of the largest sections of undeveloped shoreline on the Great Lakes.

HIGHLIGHTS: Beautiful beach camping, variety of hiking terrain, Lake Superior shoreline, sunsets, blueberries, solitude

DISTANCE: 60 km (37 mi) plus a boat shuttle

TIME NEEDED: 4 nights and 5 days at a minimum

GRADE: Difficult

WHERE: Pukaskwa National Park is located off Highway 17 between Thunder Bay, 689 km (428 mi) to the west, and Sault Ste. Marie, 402 km (250 mi) to the east. From Toronto it's about a 12-hour drive.

HOW: You can book beginning March 15 by calling 1-807-229-0801, ext. 242.

WHEN: From May 1 to September 30

COST: $5.40 pp/night national park fee, $9.80 pp/night backcountry fee. The boat shuttle is extra and varies according to the price of gas. Budget $650 for up to 12 people plus dogs.

DON'T FORGET: Allow time either the night before or the morning of your departure for a 15–20-minute pre-trip talk given by a national parks ranger. Purchase last-minute supplies in the town of Marathon, 30 minutes from the park entrance. Pack hiking poles. Invest in top-of-the-line footwear.

OPTIONS: If money is tight but time isn't, hike out and back. Allow 10 days.

TOUR COMPANIES: Naturally Superior Adventures. Call Keith McCuaig at 1-807-229-0193 to organize a boat shuttle, or email him at **mccuaigmarine@shaw.ca**.

INTERESTING FACT: The new suspension bridge over the White River gorge is designed to last 75 years. It's anchored 11 m (36 ft) into the bedrock.

Canoeing
The Lakes
of Algonquin Provincial Park

■■☐☐

Ontario's Alqonquin Park is a premier wilderness canoeing destination that gets more popular with every passing year. Part of its appeal lies in its proximity to the Toronto–Ottawa corridor. It's also huge: half again the size of Prince Edward Island. There is something for every type of paddler, from easy-to-access lakes with busy campsites to challenging paddling and solitude.

There is literally a lifetime of paddling and exploring to do in the park. Over 2,400 lakes and 1,200 km (745 mi) of rivers are linked through 2,000 km (1,243 mi) of canoe routes. But the park isn't just about the lakes. Algonquin Park boasts one of the largest stretches of continuous forest in the southern part of Ontario. It's a magnificent spot in the fall when the maple trees are ablaze with colour, and it's almost as pretty in spring with its fresh growth in a palette of greens, a feast for colour-deprived winter eyes.

The biggest challenge lies in picking a canoe route to suit your skill level. Nearly two thousand backcountry campsites are at your disposal via twenty-nine designated access points around the periphery of the park, with the more developed section of park accessible from Highway 60.

But where do you even begin?

If you're planning to do a self-guided canoe trip, you need to purchase the *Canoe Routes Map of Algonquin Park*. Decide how much time you have and where you'd like to start. How many portages do you want to do? If you have your own canoe, you can start at any of the designated access points. If you don't own a canoe, it's a whole lot easier and quicker to rent one from an outfitter along Highway 60 and choose a nearby access point from there. Consider that the bigger lakes may not require many — if any — portages, but they can be more challenging to paddle in bad weather.

From what little I saw over a quiet long weekend in May, the Algonquin Park canoe experience gets into your blood. You want to see more, experience more, enjoy the call of the loon one more time. You might even start to crave paddling, for it can be soothing as well as challenging. And the campsites are so beautiful you might never want to leave.

Chances are, if you venture into the park, it won't be just once . . . unless it's in June and you get eaten alive by the bugs. Next time I'll go in September, when the colours are peaking and there's hardly a bug or a living soul around.

HIGHLIGHTS: Beautiful lakes, rocky out-croppings, spectacular tent sites, wildlife, swimming, fishing, cooking by fire, wolves howling, fall colours

DISTANCE: Varies; on longer trips plan to average 10–20 km/day (6–12 mi/day).

TIME NEEDED: One day to several weeks

GRADE: Easy to moderate

WHERE: 300 km (186 mi) north of Toronto and 250 km (155 mi) east of Ottawa

HOW: Reserve up to 5 months ahead. Call 1-888-668-7275 for backcountry sites; know the lake name before you call. From Toronto, check **parkbus.ca** for bus schedule.

WHEN: May to October; June can be very buggy.

COST: $11.80 pp/night for adults, $5.09 pp/night for youth. Reservation fee is $13/group. Camping includes parking, otherwise $16/vehicle/day; backcountry deposit is $50, difference from permit cost is payable or refunded.

DON'T FORGET: The map — because it shows all the backcountry canoe routes, portages and campsites

OPTIONS: There are 3 backpacking trails with a choice of loops ranging from 6 to 88 km (4–55 mi) in length. Historic ranger cabins can be rented, some accessed by road and others only by water.

TOUR COMPANIES: Wolf Den Expeditions, Voyageur Quest. Call of the Wild Adventures Consultants. Algonquin Outfitters rents canoes and camping equipment.

INTERESTING FACT: A 2012 survey counted 3,642 moose, 2,000 black bears and 300 wolves in the park.

Cross-country skiing
The Leaf Lake Ski Trails
in Algonquin Provincial Park

□ ■ ■ □

Algonquin in winter is a very special place and very much underrated. It's exceptionally beautiful, particularly on a blue-sky day after a fresh snowfall when conifers can be seen drooping with heavy loads of snow and frozen lakes offer up an unbroken expanse of pristine and untouched wilderness. There are no crowds to speak of, either. You're more likely to run into a moose or a wolf than a human — a slight exaggeration, but only slight. The cross-country skiing is sublime.

There are three sets of cross-country ski trails within the park to choose from. For the best of the lot, head for the Leaf Lake area, just a few minutes' drive from the East Gate and the site of 32 km (20 mi) of lovingly groomed and track-set trails. The trouble will lie in choosing which of the multiple loops to do.

The loops are of varying length and difficulty, with the easier and shorter loops close to the trailhead. They are perfect for families. Two of the most scenic loops require more stamina and skill. The 13 km (8 mi) Pinetree Loop has been called the premiere ski trail in all of southern Ontario. It offers plenty of hills, so expect to climb a lot, but you'll be rewarded with some fun downhill stretches. Plan to stop at the Pinetree Cabin for lunch. Park rangers will likely have a fire warming it by the time you arrive, as they do for the other two cabins in the area. The view from this cabin is magnificent. Also, you can scatter some birdseed on the railings and then watch as a dozen or more blue jays show up in short order. Pine martens are frequent visitors here as well.

The 5 km (3 mi) Fraser Lake Loop is another of the more difficult trails, but the views from the high point offer quintessential Algonquin Park scenery and make the climb up entirely worthwhile. Thistle Cabin, located at the southern junction of the Fraser and Thistle Lake loops, is another convenient place to warm up.

Signage on the trails here is the best I've seen anywhere I've skied. Every intersection has a map and a location arrow so you should never be left wondering where you are. You can pick up maps at the park entrance, too.

In the near future, there's a good chance that an additional 15 km (9 mi) of trails will be added to the Leaf Lake area. It's already a very special place to ski; more trails will only increase its appeal.

HIGHLIGHTS: Beautiful open deciduous woods, ridge and valley terrain, chance of seeing moose, wolves and pine martens, lookouts and big views, multiple warming cabins, solitude

DISTANCE: Variable, since multiple loops are possible. Try to include the 13.2 km (8.2 mi) Pinetree Loop.

TIME NEEDED: At least a full day; more if you want to ski all possible loops

GRADE: Moderate to difficult

WHERE: The trailhead for the Leaf Lake Ski Trails is located 6.5 km (4.1 mi) west of Whitney off Highway 60, 230 km (143 mi) from Ottawa and 54.5 km (33.9 mi) east of Algonquin Park's West Gate.

WHEN: Usually from November until late March

HOW: Bring your own cross-country ski gear or rent from Algonquin Outfitters at Oxtongue Lake (10 minutes away from the West Gate).

COST: $16/car

DON'T FORGET: Water, hot drinks, warm clothes, repair gear for skis including a basket and ski tip

OPTIONS: Other trails in the park include the Fen Lake Ski Trail and the Minnesing Trails at kilometre 23. You can book one of seven yurts at the Mew Lake Campground via **ontarioparks.com**.

TOUR COMPANIES: None

INTERESTING FACT: There have been 272 bird species recorded in the park, but only between 25 and 30 of those winter over.

Skating
The Rideau Canal
in Ottawa

■ ☐ ☐ ☐

The 202 km (126 mi) Rideau Canal, built as a supply route between Montreal and Kingston, was constructed over six years and completed in 1832. But it wasn't until the winter of 1970–1971 that the canal was opened to skaters. It is the largest naturally frozen ice rink in the world, with a skating surface equivalent to ninety Olympic hockey rinks — enough to earn it a spot in the Guinness Book of World Records (British Columbia's Whiteway is the world's longest ice skating trail).

The Rideau Canal has been a huge tourist and local attraction for years. During the annual Winterlude Festival in February, up to six hundred thousand people have attended over the course of the eighteen-day event. And in a typical season, the canal sees over one million skater visits. To add to its appeal, the canal was designated a UNESCO World Heritage Site in 2007 in recognition of its design, construction and role in Canadian history.

The canal isn't just for tourists. Locals embraced the canal from the start. Growing up in Ottawa, I knew people who skated to work and to school. It still happens. I don't think you can beat a commute on skates, especially on smooth-as-glass, freshly flooded ice.

The canal is a place for people of all ages. You might see toddlers taking their first steps on ice, tweens getting a taste of freedom or young couples out skating hand in hand. And of course there are families, and the odd weekend warrior out to break distance or speed records.

The average skating season is just fifty days long, though in 1971–1972 the season lasted a record ninety-five days. If you're thinking of a winter visit to Ottawa, it's well worth including a stopover on the canal. Just keep in mind that Ottawa can be bitterly cold in the winter, so dress warmly. Fortunately, there are a number of warming huts along the route, as well as places to buy hot drinks and beavertails. If you don't know what a beavertail is, all the more reason to go.

This is truly one of the great winter outings in the National Capital Region.

HIGHLIGHTS: Pretty scenery along the route, people-watching, camaraderie, fresh air, great workout, Winterlude, beavertails

DISTANCE: 7.8 km (4.8 mi) one way

TIME NEEDED: It takes between 90 minutes and 3 hours to skate up and down the entire length of the canal, but many people just skate a short section.

GRADE: Easy and family-friendly

WHERE: The skating section of the Rideau Canal starts at the National Arts Centre in downtown Ottawa, and continues past Dow's Lake to Hartwell's Locks. Rent skates by the Mackenzie King Bridge, at Fifth Avenue, and in the Dow's Lake Pavilion.

HOW: The best parking options are in the Dow's Lake area, south of the Bronson Bridge and downtown around the National Arts Centre. There is free parking at the World Exchange Plaza on the weekends.

WHEN: It depends on the year, but generally early January until late February. The canal is open 24 hours a day but first aid is not available after 10:00 or 11:00 p.m.

COST: Free to skate. Skate rentals, boot lockers and parking are extra.

DON'T FORGET: Hockey sticks, bicycles, dogs and other pets are not allowed on the ice. You can check the ice conditions before you go on the Rideau Canal Skateway website. A first aid station is located on the ice by Fifth Avenue; a team of 50 skate patrollers, dressed in neon yellow, work to keep the skateway safe.

TOUR COMPANIES: None

INTERESTING FACT: Along the length of the Rideau Canal you'll find 47 locks, 16 lakes, two rivers and one dam at Jones Falls.

World's Largest Skating Rink!
La plus grande patinoire du monde!

Kayaking
The Admiralty Islands
in Thousand Islands National Park

■■□□

Gananoque, a charming town located in the well-travelled Ottawa–Montreal–Toronto corridor, is one of the gateways to the Thousand Islands, an archipelago consisting of 1,864 islands sandwiched between Canada and the United States on the St. Lawrence River. Although many enjoy a cruise through the Thousand Islands, paddling provides a more intimate experience. And the kayaking is superb — perfect for everyone from novice to expert. Just pick the route that's right for you.

Rocky granite islands reminiscent of the Georgian Bay area, windswept pines and super clear water — thanks to the invasion of zebra mussels — greet you. While I was there in May, there was non-stop birdsong, a feature of the islands due to their location in the Frontenac Arch Biosphere. In fact, it is the second-most biodiverse area in all of Canada. Over 250 species of birds, 53 mammals, 17 different amphibians, 15 types of snake and 98 species of fish have been observed.

Only twenty-one islands are part of Thousand Islands National Park. The level of protection varies by island. Some don't allow you to do more than use a toilet, whereas others like McDonald and Grenadier Island have a greater human presence. Two groups of islands — the Admiralty and Lake Fleet — are accessible from Gananoque. Other islands that make up the national park are better accessed via Kingston, Rockport, Mallorytown and Ivy Lea.

Along with the easy kayaking through the Admiralty Islands, there is also a chance to get a taste of Canadian history.

- Thwartway Island is a place where soldiers from World War II recuperated from shell shock — post-traumatic stress disorder, as we currently call it. When the camp closed, the island was overtaken by forest and now boasts the largest intact ecosystem of them all.

- Half Moon Bay at the southeastern corner of Bostwick Island merits a stop. On Sundays in July and August, afternoon church services are held. The pulpit is made of rock and the surrounding cliffs of the quiet bay form an amphitheatre that to this day holds spiritual significance for First Nations people.

- On Gull Rock, a tiny speck of an island, be sure to see the rusted-out moorings left over from the days when massive rafts made of white pine and white oak were floated down to Montreal for shipment to Europe.

Don't miss the opportunity to explore the accessible wilderness if you're in the area.

HIGHLIGHTS: Warm water for summer swimming, beautiful islands, history, bird life, rocky landscape, biodiversity, interesting geology

DISTANCE: Highly variable

TIME NEEDED: Minimum of a half day, up to 3–4 days

GRADE: Easy, but moderate if the weather turns and the wind picks up

WHERE: Gananoque is on the St. Lawrence River 150 km (93 mi) south of Ottawa, 300 km (186 mi) east of Toronto and 200 km (124 mi) west of Montreal.

HOW: Bring your own kayak, or rent one in Gananoque and launch from the docks behind 1000 Islands Kayaking at the historic Pumphouse on the waterfront. To reserve, phone 1-613-329-6265.

WHEN: Early May to October

COST: Kayak rental prices start at $35/3 hours for a single. Camping permits are $15.70/night/tent and are on a first-come basis, but you can reserve ahead of time on Beau Rivage, Mulcaster and Camelot Islands beginning in early April. Visit the online Parks Canada Campground Reservation Service.

DON'T FORGET: Watch for storms, which can arise quickly. Check yourself for blacklegged ticks. Cellphone coverage is generally good.

OPTIONS: A guided tour is a great way to safely explore the area, especially if you're new to kayaking.

TOUR COMPANIES: 1000 Islands Kayaking

INTERESTING FACT: An island must meet three criteria to be considered one of the Thousand Islands. It must have an area greater than one square foot, it must remain above the water level year round, and it must support at least one living tree.

Cycling
The Back Roads
of Prince Edward County

■■□□

Prince Edward County offers a pastoral landscape of gently rolling hills criss-crossed by uncrowded roads, making it an excellent cycling destination. Located almost equidistant between Ottawa and Toronto, the county borders the north shore of Lake Ontario on the Bay of Quinte.

Prince Edward County is much more than just farm country. Within the county, you can find two wildlife preserves, fourteen conservation areas, three provincial parks and some of the largest freshwater sand dunes in the world. Historic towns filled with beautiful old stone buildings, thirty-plus wineries with grapes grown on the same magic rock formation found in France's famous Côte d'Or region of Burgundy, beautiful golden sand beaches and both an Arts Trail showcasing local artists and galleries and a Taste Trail leading you to some of the hottest artisanal food producers ensure that there are plenty of places to explore on a bike.

It's best to pick up a $2 bike map at the bike shop the minute you arrive in the area. The map indicates six routes between 30 km (19 mi) and 66 km (41 mi) in length and covers all the best sections of the county. Pick a destination, whether it's a gallery, winery, restaurant or beach, and pick your way there on a series of interconnected back roads. There are lots of choices and roads and exploring is half the fun. Two roads to avoid because of the traffic are Highway 33 and Highway 62, but all others are fair game.

A favourite bike ride of mine took me from Picton past Lake on the Mountain Provincial Park and along beautiful back roads with views of the Adolphus Reach section of Lake Ontario. The farther east I travelled, the quieter the road got. There were some fun stops to make, including the Fifth Town Artisan Cheese Co., Waupoos Estates Winery — where one can sample ice wine infused with local maple syrup — and the Country Cider Company. Returning to Picton was a breeze with the option of several north-south crossroads before returning via Highway 8.

The county's charms have been appreciated by the locals for years, but with increased media coverage, tourists are showing up in greater and greater numbers. You'll find enough roads to cycle to keep you busy for at least a long weekend.

HIGHLIGHTS: Quiet back roads, wineries, birding, sandy beaches, the Arts Trail, the Taste Trail

DISTANCE: Highly variable depending on what side trips you want to take

TIME NEEDED: 1–3 days

GRADE: Easy, but moderate on the hills

WHERE: Prince Edward County is located halfway between Toronto and Ottawa, about 40 km (25 mi) south of Belleville.

HOW: Reserve a bike or bring your own. Rent a bike from Bloomfield Bicycle Co. in Bloomfield.

WHEN: Late April to mid-October

COST: Free if you have your own bike. Otherwise, allow for bike rentals and possible accommodation costs.

DON'T FORGET: Carry a bike pump and a patch kit. In summer, take along a bathing suit and a towel. A corkscrew might come in handy for an impromptu picnic.

TOUR COMPANIES: None

INTERESTING FACT: Chain hotels are non-existent, but you will find around 95 B&Bs catering to visitors.

The Prairies
Adventures

Saskatchewan

Alberta

Churchill River

Nut Point Trail

Boreal Trail

Grey Owl's
Cabin

Prince Albert

N

Regina

Grasslands

Nunavut

Hudson
Bay

Manitoba

Ontario

Gorge Creek
Trail

● Hecla Island

Spirit Sands   **Winnipeg**
●   ●   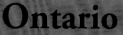● Whiteshell
                ●
          The Forks

Hiking
The Spirit Sands
in Spruce Woods Provincial Park

■ □ □ □

Spruce Woods Provincial Park is home to the only sand dunes in Manitoba. Known as the Spirit Sands, they are located just two hours from Winnipeg in the southern part of the province where the boreal forest meets the Assiniboine River. The dunes, which rise to a height of 30 m (98 ft), are a great place to hike, play, wander and photograph, especially in summer when the wildflowers make an appearance. Just beware of the copious amounts of poison ivy that line the forested trails and stairways.

There are two approaches to the sand dunes: a flat, easy trail, or one that requires a bit of stair-climbing. Climb, if you can, for the excellent views of the area. If you were a bird, the Spirit Sands would look like a medicine wheel from the air. As you reach the dunes by way of the East Gate, sometimes referred to as the 'Place of Beginnings,' be aware that you are walking on land considered hallowed by generations of First Nations. Be respectful.

You can easily hike all of the Spirit Sands trails in a few hours, but take your time to admire the cacti and wildflowers. Look for the western hognose snake and Manitoba's only lizard, the northern prairie skink. Bird life is also excellent.

After the sands, continue on the 1.9 km (1.2 mi) connector trail to visit the Devil's Punch Bowl, a blue-green crater-shaped lake fed by underground springs. Extensive stairways lead you over the boggy bits and up the sandy banks. Take advantage of well-placed benches to sit and revel in the scene. Before returning to the parking lot, follow the trail to the Assiniboine River. Signage explains the history of the people who used the river. Look for the pictures of a paddlewheel steamer and imagine a 1,650 km (1,025 mi) journey back in 1879. The river is also part of the Assiniboine River Canoe Route.

It's a unique area, and well worth exploring.

HIGHLIGHTS: Sand dunes, bird life, wildflowers, Assiniboine River, Devil's Punch Bowl

DISTANCE: Depending on what combination of trails you hike, up to 10.1 km (6.3 mi). Shorter loops are available.

TIME NEEDED: 2–3 hours

GRADE: Easy and family friendly

WHERE: Spruce Woods Provincial Park is 180 km (112 mi) west of Winnipeg and 77 km (48 mi) southeast of Brandon.

HOW: Show up.

WHEN: May till October. You can cross-country ski here in the winter.

COST: $5/vehicle for a daily park pass

DON'T FORGET: Water, sunscreen and a sunhat. Long pants for poison ivy protection. Be bear-aware.

OPTIONS: For a longer trip, try backpacking the 40 km (25 mi) Newfoundland Trail or hike a section of the Trans-Canada Trail, which runs through the park. For the non-hikers there are covered-wagon rides offered through the area as well.

TOUR COMPANIES: None

INTERESTING FACT: Ernest Thompson Seton, one of the European settlers who came to live in the area in the 1880s, was so inspired by the beauty of the sand hills that he eventually became a renowned authority on wildlife and Manitoba's first naturalist.

Hiking
The Gorge Creek Trail
in Riding Mountain National Park

□ ■ □ □

The Gorge Creek Trail, considered one of the best trails in the park, surprises with its range of ecosystems and stellar views of the plains. The hike takes you up and down the Manitoba Escarpment, a steep slope which marks the edge of glacial Lake Agassiz — an immense lake that was larger than all of the Great Lakes combined when it formed at the end of the last glacial period. The gorge itself, which formed after thousands of years of erosion, moves through aspen and hazel forests before descending through old oak forests and ending up at the Birch Picnic Area in a leafy setting of white birch and Manitoba maple.

This is an out-and-back hike, so there's no way to avoid hiking up and down the escarpment unless you want to do a car shuttle. To start the hike with a descent, begin at the western trailhead. For the first kilometre, as the trail meanders through dense woods with the occasional sunny patch of wildflowers, you might wonder why you're bothering with the hike. But once the path starts to descend, it gets interesting, especially when you emerge from the forest. The views of the plains, including the town of McCreary, are unparalleled. But so are the forest views, which under wet conditions look more like the rainforests of Costa Rica than the woods of Manitoba.

The descent can be very steep at times, and slippery when muddy. Well-maintained stairs have been placed in some of the steepest sections, but watch your footing nonetheless. Numerous bridges make stream crossings a breeze.

There's a chance you might see a black bear, a moose or a wolf, judging by the scat in evidence. Also be careful walking or sitting on benches through a 2–3 km (1.2–1.9 mi) section of trail that is rife with poison ivy. Long pants are a must, as is a thorough wash with soap and water afterwards of anything that has come into contact with poison ivy.

HIGHLIGHTS: Scenic overviews, Manitoba Escarpment, birding, variety of vegetation, wildflowers

DISTANCE: 12.8 km (8.0 mi) return with an elevation gain and loss of 300 m (984 ft)

TIME NEEDED: 3.5 to 5 hours depending on your pace

GRADE: Moderate

WHERE: The Visitor Centre in Wasagaming beside Clear Lake is 265 km (165 mi) northwest of Winnipeg via Highways 10, 16 and 1; Brandon is 95 km (59 mi) to the south via Highway 10. The western trailhead is on the north side of the road, immediately across from the South Escarpment Trail, approximately 27 km (17 mi) east of Wasagaming. It's accessed via Highway 19, a dirt road. The eastern trailhead can be found just inside the East Gate at the Birches Picnic Site.

HOW: Start at either the western trailhead at Dead Ox Creek or the eastern one at the Birches Picnic site.

WHEN: May through till late October

COST: $7.80/adult/day, $3.90/child/day

DON'T FORGET: Long pants because of poison ivy, hiking poles, water, bear spray

OPTIONS: There are other backcountry trails in the park ranging in length from 1.9 to 38.5 km (1.2–23.9 mi) one way. Be prepared to share the trail with bikes and horses.

TOUR COMPANIES: None

INTERESTING FACT: Grey Owl and Anahero, along with their pet beavers Rawhide and Jellyroll, lived here for six months in 1931. Unfortunately, the lake levels were too shallow for the beavers to overwinter, so a permanent move was made to Prince Albert National Park.

Hiking the trails of
Hecla Island
in Hecla/Grindstone Provincial Park

■ □ □ □

Hecla Island in Lake Winnipeg has not always been a recreation destination. For a long time, it was home to a successful freshwater fishing industry. But with the depressing combination of a decline in the fisheries and the subsequent exodus of islanders in search of work, the remaining community banded together to petition the Manitoba government to turn the island into a park in order to create a tourism-based economy. Now part of Hecla/Grindstone Provincial Park, the island has plenty to offer the hiker, biker, kayaker, birder or history buff. And in winter, it's a great place for cross-country skiing. Located ninety minutes north of the city of Winnipeg, Hecla Island is accessible via a short causeway that was opened in 1975. With marshes lining either side of the causeway, the entrance to the island is undeniably pretty.

For a small landmass, Hecla Island has a lot of hiking trails. The Grassy Narrows Marsh Trails are accessed from a few kilometres inland. Five different trails — some on boardwalk — offer 25 km (15.5 mi) of hiking, providing it hasn't been a rainy summer. As I write, some of the trails are underwater, but even if the trails are closed the birding is still first-rate.

The Black Wolf Trail was another reason for my visit, but it too was mostly underwater. Under normal circumstances, the trail takes you on a tour of the most untouched areas of the park. With over 22 km (14 mi) of possible hiking or biking trails, you can explore a diverse landscape that includes marsh, lake and boreal forest, and even the possibility of sighting a pack of black wolves.

Fortunately, there are several trails at the north end of the island that remain open under high-water conditions. One of the best is the Lighthouse Trail, a 3 km (1.9 mi) trail that takes you out to the lighthouse at Gull Harbour. Built to warn boats of the small land spit, it's been automated since 1961. The trail is an easy walk, with prolific bird life and great views of nearby Black Island and the Hecla Island shoreline. The 5.5 km (3.4 mi) Harbour Trail is another good one for island views. For a look at some local history and an old limestone quarry, hike the 10 km (6.2 mi) West Quarry Trail found in the northwest corner of the island.

HIGHLIGHTS: Beaches, birding hotspot, boardwalks, lighthouses, wildlife, Icelandic history

DISTANCE: Highly variable depending on which trails you choose to hike

TIME NEEDED: A half day to a whole day

GRADE: Easy and family-friendly

WHERE: Hecla Island is located approximately 170 km (106 mi) north of Winnipeg via Highway 8.

HOW: Pick up a map of the park so you can plan your day.

WHEN: Mid-June until October

COST: The park entrance fee is $5 for the day. There are three free weekends in the summer.

DON'T FORGET: Binoculars, water sandals, bathing suit

OPTIONS: Rent a kayak from Gull Harbour Marina or bring your own so you can explore the nearby islands.

TOUR COMPANIES: None

INTERESTING FACT: Hecla Island is named after Mount Hecla, one of Iceland's most active volcanoes. It was because of volcanic eruptions that many people left Iceland and came to the island for a fresh start.

Canoeing the
Caddy Lake Rock Tunnels
in Whiteshell Provincial Park

■□□□

Some of Canada's great paddling rivers are located in Manitoba, but most are quite remote. Fortunately, an accessible alternative can be found in Caddy Lake, which is located in Whiteshell Provincial Park just ninety minutes east of Winnipeg. It is part of the Whiteshell River System and is the launch site for day trips to the Caddy Lake Tunnels and a 169 km (105 mi) loop trip that takes the better part of a week to paddle.

The Caddy Lake Tunnels offer a unique canoeing experience that you'll find nowhere else in Canada. Two of them were blasted through solid granite to provide channels for waterways obstructed by the building of the Canadian Pacific and Canadian National Railway lines. The first one is located about 2.4 km (1.5 mi) from the Green Bay Resort launch site. It's not a difficult paddle if the wind cooperates, but if it doesn't, be prepared to dig in to keep your canoe moving forward. When the water level is very high, especially in the second tunnel, you'll have to portage the canoe over the railway tracks. Another option under moderately high water conditions is to put the paddle away and power your way through the tunnel by hand, pulling yourself along by grabbing rocks along the sides or the top of the tunnel.

The first Caddy Lake Tunnel takes you to South Cross Lake. After you paddle past a few cottages, wilderness takes over. Look for deer, beavers, muskrats and black bears down by the water. Overhead, there's a good chance you'll see a bald eagle soaring, and loons can be heard even during the day. If the wind blows up — which it's apt to do — paddle in the lee of one of the many small headlands. There are a few campsites available on a first-come basis where you can stop for lunch or a break.

If you continue all the way to the second tunnel, about 4.8 km (3 mi) away, then you're in for some fun. To reach it, you must paddle through a long channel lined on either side with beautiful grasses. Pass through the tunnel into North Cross Lake, which seems to beckon you to swim. If you still have time, continue to Sailing Lake via a short lift-over portage (faster than a typical portage; a lift-over doesn't require unloading the whole canoe) before going back the way you came.

There's a good chance you'll wish you had the time to explore further. One day in this beautiful area is not nearly enough.

HIGHLIGHTS: Rock tunnels, Canadian Shield landscape, swimming, bird and animal life

DISTANCE: Variable, but up to a 16 km (10 mi) return trip if you paddle to the second tunnel

TIME NEEDED: At least a half day and up to a week for the loop trip

GRADE: Easy, if the wind cooperates

WHERE: The launch at Green Bay Resort is located 168 km (104 mi) east of Winnipeg in Whiteshell Provincial Park.

HOW: Rent a canoe by the hour, day or week on the south shore of Caddy Lake from GBR Service and Marine Rentals or Caddy Lake Resort.

WHEN: June to mid-October

COST: Canoe rentals are in the range of $40/day or $185/week.

DON'T FORGET: Rain gear, bug-proof jacket in season, bathing suit

OPTIONS: Do a 3-day canoe trip to Big Whiteshell Lake or a week-long circle trip that includes Crowduck and Mantario Lakes.

TOUR COMPANIES: Wild Harmony Canoe Adventures

INTERESTING FACT: Wild rice has been harvested in the Whiteshell Provincial Park area for thousands of years. It is the only cereal native to Canada.

Cross-country skiing
The Backcountry Trails
in Whiteshell Provincial Park

■■□□

Whiteshell Provincial Park has been called the jewel of Manitoba's parks, probably because of its location in the rugged Precambrian Shield. This is an area of rock outcrop dotted with rivers and lakes. The park, located roughly 150 km (93 mi) east of Winnipeg, shares its eastern border with the Manitoba–Ontario provincial boundary line. Most of its 2,729 sq km (1,054 sq mi) area sits north of the Trans-Canada Highway.

The park is a fantastic destination for cross-country skiing. Although there are a large number of trails, two in particular stand out: the Alf Hole–Goose Sanctuary Loop and the Pine Points Rapid Trail. They are about a thirty-minute drive apart and both can be comfortably skied in a day.

The 7 km (4.3 mi) Alf Hole–Goose Sanctuary Loop, accessed near the small hamlet of Rennie, takes you into what feels like real wilderness — at least once you're away from the snowmobile trail. I think this trail is best skied in a counter-clockwise direction. Ski through rolling countryside lightly forested with black spruce, white spruce and balsam fir until you reach Goose Pond, which is more lake than pond. There's a warming hut here, and the view across the snow-covered lake is beautiful. To continue, take the trail from behind the hut, re-cross the snowmobile track and in short order you'll be back where you started.

The Pine Points Rapid Trail, just north of Betula Lake, is quieter than Alf Hole. It can be done as a loop, too. If you ski it in a clockwise direction, the first 2.4 km (1.5 mi) to Pine Point Rapids are uncomplicated. For a stretch, it's arrow-straight through the trees on an old road that ends at a set of impressive rapids. There's a warming hut here, should you need it. It's easy to see why this is such a popular place in the summer and fall. Even in the winter it's pretty, especially with the rapids still running. It's worth checking them out from various angles, but don't trust the ice at the edge.

If you want to complete the loop, continue alongside the Whiteshell River for about half a kilometre. Then, head into the woods on a trail that at times is hard to follow. Ultimately, it deposits you on the track you started on, about half a kilometre from the parking lot. It's slower going through the woods as there are a number of downed trees, but at a leisurely pace it's possible to do the loop in ninety minutes.

HIGHLIGHTS: Pine Point Rapids, wildlife including deer and wolves, sense of wilderness in the Canadian Shield

DISTANCE: 7 km (4.3 mi) for Alf Hole, 5.2 km (3.2 mi) for Pine Point Rapids

TIME NEEDED: 1 day

GRADE: Easy to moderate

WHERE: 150 km (93 mi) east of Winnipeg in Whiteshell Provincial Park

HOW: Get a map from the Whiteshell Provincial Park Office or download a version from the web.

WHEN: Late December until March

COST: $4 for the required backcountry pass. Many of the Canadian Tire and Walmart stores in the Winnipeg area sell the pass. The Parks office sells passes too, but it's closed on weekends. In Falcon Lake, you can purchase passes at Falcon Beach Auto or Lumber Building Supplies.

DON'T FORGET: Warm clothes, extra food, hot drinks, emergency supplies for winter driving (leave these in the car) including a shovel and blankets

NOTE: Cell service is good at Falcon Lake and West Hawk Lakes, but is minimal in all other areas of the park.

OPTIONS: Rent cross-country skis at MEC in Winnipeg.

TOUR COMPANIES: None. Do it on your own.

INTERESTING FACT: The park gets its name in part from the cowry shells used in ceremonies by the Ojibway, Midewiwin and Anishinaabe peoples.

Skating
The Forks
in Winnipeg

■□□□

Until British Columbia's Whiteway bumped it out of first place, the Forks in Winnipeg was the world's longest natural outdoor rink. Close to downtown Winnipeg, the Forks sit at the junction of the Red and Assiniboine Rivers. Every year the river is cleared of snow and flooded with river water to create a skating rink that, although the length varies from year to year, can be up to 11 km (6.8 mi) long.

If it's cold — as in -20°C (-4°F) sort of cold — then chances are you'll be sharing the rink with only a few other hardy souls. But if the wind disappears and the temperatures stay above -20°C (-4°F), the Forks can see up to thirty thousand people over a single weekend. I was told that the Red River is usually the coldest section to skate because it's less protected and the wind can howl right down the length of it. When it's really cold, choose the tree-lined Assiniboine River.

Try to time a visit to the Forks near the end of January to coincide with when the warming huts are open to the public. Not just any old warming huts, these were built from winning designs submitted by architects from around the world. The competition, first dreamed up by a group of Winnipeg architects over beer, has now become an annual event. The three 2013 winners were chosen by a blind jury from a hundred international entries.

The beauty of the Forks is you don't even have to be a skater. There's a snow-covered trail alongside the ice for hikers, skiers and snowshoers to travel, so everyone can get out and enjoy the fresh air. In addition, there are two rinks where you can watch hockey or broomball. And if you have young kids, or are new to skating, then you can try out the small man-made ice rink just outside the Forks Market.

Skating the Forks is a great way to appreciate the city of Winnipeg in winter, especially on one of its famous blue-sky winter days.

HIGHLIGHTS: Long sections of ice to yourself, beautiful setting, great winter workout

DISTANCE: The length varies from year to year but up to 11 km (6.8 mi) of skating is possible on a combination of the Red and Assiniboine Rivers.

TIME NEEDED: 1–3 hours

GRADE: Easy and family-friendly

WHERE: Downtown Winnipeg at the junction of the Red and Assiniboine Rivers. Parking is available at the Forks Market.

HOW: Bring your own skates or rent them at the Forks Market.

WHEN: Varies from year to year, but the ice is usually open from late December until late February or early March

COST: Free. Adult skate rentals $4.50, kids $2.50. Lockers $2

HOURS: The ice is open 24/7; skate rentals at the Forks Market only from 10 a.m. to 10 p.m.

DON'T FORGET: Warm clothes, especially something to cover your face

OPTIONS: After skating, warm up with a hot drink from the adjacent Forks Market. Try a piece of the divine Saskatoon berry-rhubarb pie from the Tall Grass Prairie Bread Company.

TOUR COMPANIES: None

INTERESTING FACT: The Assiniboine River is a tributary of the Red River, which flows north and eventually empties into Lake Winnipeg.

Hiking
The Front-Country Trails
in Grasslands National Park

■□□□

Saskatchewan's Grasslands National Park may not have the popular appeal of some of the spectacular mountain and ocean adventures in this book, but this quiet, expansive landscape, best explored on foot, does deserve a trip. The park provides both front-country and backcountry hiking experiences. But the backcountry ones are for the truly adventurous only, as none of the trails are marked and would require a GPS, map and compass. Check in at the Visitor Centre for up-to-date information as well as detailed maps and trail descriptions.

Three front-country hikes — all accessible from side roads leading off from Highway 4 south of the town of Val Marie — are recommended. They include the 70 Mile Butte Trail, the Two Trees Trail and the Riverwalk Trail. If you spend three to four hours walking these trails, you'll get a real sense of the lonesome breadth of the land on the one hand and the diversity of the prairie ecosystem on the other. But you have to look closely.

The 70 Mile Butte Trail, which is nowhere near seventy miles long, includes a climb to the highest point in the park. Big, sweeping vistas, striking badlands and more types of prairie grasses than you probably knew existed greet you on this loop hike. You can't help but be surprised at the sheer variability of texture and the subtleties in colour of grasses, rocks and lichens.

The other two hikes start from the same trailhead but head off in opposite directions. The Riverwalk Trail takes you along the banks of the Frenchman River, whereas the Two Trees Trail leads you up into rolling hills with impressive views of the Frenchmen River Valley.

All three hikes offer the chance to see wildlife. Look for white-tailed and mule deer, pronghorn antelopes and lone coyotes. Watch for snakes, including the threatened eastern yellow-bellied racer — which can move up to 70 km/h (43 mph) — or the venomous prairie rattlesnake. Birds are plentiful too, especially the Lark Bunting and Baird's Sparrow. You may also see raptors, owls, ducks and pheasants.

If you love solitude and the wind as your constant companion, you will appreciate these lonely, wild spaces while learning to value the understated pleasures of the grasslands.

HIGHLIGHTS: Wildlife including bison, black-tailed prairie dogs, mule and white-tailed deer, pronghorn antelopes, American badgers and coyotes; badland topography, native prairie ecosystem, big skies, some of the darkest skies in Canada for stargazing

DISTANCE: The Riverwalk Trail is 2 km (1.2 mi), the Two Trees Trail is 3.5 km (2.2 mi), and the 70 Mile Butte Trail is 5 km (3.1 mi).

TIME NEEDED: At least 4 hours to do the three hikes

GRADE: Easy and family-friendly

WHERE: Southwestern Saskatchewan near the Montana border. The West Block can be accessed via Highways 4 and 18 near Val Marie.

WHEN: May to October

COST: There are no entry fees.

DON'T FORGET: Fill up your car well before you get near the park. Gas stations are few and far between.

SAFETY ISSUES: Check yourself for ticks. Watch for rattlesnakes. Stay at least 100 m (300 ft) away from bison.

OPTIONS: Don't miss the Ecotour, an 80 km (50 mi) round-trip, self-guided driving adventure that starts and ends in Val Marie. Check out the signed stops and learn more about the history of the area. This road allows you to see the endangered black-tailed prairie dog, and there's a good chance to see bison, too.

TOUR COMPANIES: None

INTERESTING FACT: Less than one quarter of the original mixed-grass prairie in Canada remains in its natural state. It is this habitat that is so important for burrowing owls.

Backpacking
The Boreal Trail
in Meadow Lake Provincial Park

■■■□

The 120 km (75 mi) Boreal Trail is Saskatchewan's only long-distance backpacking trail. Located in Meadow Lake Provincial Park in the west-central part of the province, the trail showcases the beauty of the boreal forest. Not only will you be awed by the huge swaths of aspen interspersed with bands of pine and spruce trees, but you'll see prime examples of the area's glacial past. Wander up and down eskers — long, sinuous ridges of sand and gravel — and past numerous kettle lakes that are perfect for swimming in the summer. Walk old roads and listen to a multitude of birdsongs. But always stay alert for wild animals. There is plenty of evidence of their presence.

The Boreal Trail runs across the park in an east-west direction, linking eight front-country campgrounds with nine beautifully situated backcountry campsites, all of which come equipped with a bear locker, a composting toilet and a fire pit. Although the Boreal Trail can be done as an epic backpacking trip, it can also be explored via a series of day hikes. Review the map to decide which section of the trail to hike. Longer sections may require a car shuttle or a pre-arranged drop-off; Clearwater Canoeing, for instance, can help you accomplish your goal.

The western end of the trail is located just a few hundred metres east of the intersection of Cold Lake and Cold River. There's a big sign so you'll know you're on the trail. The eastern end of the trail is more difficult to locate. You'll find it on the west side of Greig Lake, about a kilometre up a side road signed for Water's Edge Eco Lodge. Do check the Boreal Trail website before heading off, as it will tell you if any parts of the trail are closed.

Once you're on the trail it's generally very well signed. Look for trail markers approximately every kilometre or at important intersections. Sometimes the trail takes you onto the road, but plans are in place to change that. Also be aware that you may have to share some sections of trail with ATVs, but that too may change over the next few years. There are loads of well-trodden game trails that should not be mistaken for the Boreal Trail.

The Boreal Trail does not always have a wild feel to it. But as you stand on the trail and look north, appreciate the fact that there is nothing but boreal forest — no settlements or towns — between you and the tundra of the Northwest Territories, some thousand kilometres to the north.

HIGHLIGHTS: Wildlife including moose, bears, wolves and coyotes; fantastic bird life, beautiful lakes, vast stands of aspen

DISTANCE: 120 km (75 mi) to do the whole trail, but there are lots of interesting shorter sections if you prefer

TIME NEEDED: At least a day; up to a week if you hike the whole trail

GRADE: Easy to moderate depending on what section you do. As a backpacking trip it's difficult if you don't resupply along the route.

WHERE: Meadow Lake Provincial Park is 5 km (3 mi) north of Goodsoil on Highway 26, 24 km (15 mi) north of Pierceland on Highway 21 in west central Saskatchewan.

WHEN: May to October

HOW: At least two weeks prior to visiting, book a backcountry reservation by filling out forms you can find on the Meadow Lake Provincial Park website.

COST: $7/day/car entrance fee, or $25/week/car; $11/tent/night camping fee

DON'T FORGET: Bear spray, insect repellent, bathing suit and a topographical map of the trail

OPTIONS: Arrange a shuttle with Clearwater Canoeing so you can do the trail as a one-way hike.

TOUR COMPANIES: Clearwater Canoeing

INTERESTING FACT: The Boreal Trail opened in 2011, a recent addition to Canada's network of long-distance backpacking trails. Only 11 km of the trail is newly built; the rest was cobbled together with existing trails, roads and bridges.

Canoeing
The Churchill River
from Trout Lake to Missinipe

□ ■ □ □

Take a look at a detailed map of the Churchill River. You'll see a series of lakes connected by rapids and waterfalls, making it a perfect destination for paddlers with some whitewater experience. In particular, the Saskatchewan section of the 1,609 km (1,000 mi) river remains largely wild and undeveloped. It's one of Canada's most accessible northern rivers, and you can feel the history stretching back thousands of years.

When Europeans first arrived at the Churchill River, they encountered Woods Cree and the Dene people, but undoubtedly there were peoples there long before them. Pictographs scattered in nineteen locations along the river attest to their presence. If only the portage trails could talk! By 1776, the fur trade was in full swing on the Churchill, securing its importance as a major route linking the west and east. Now, with two roads in place — Highway 102 from La Ronge to Missinipe and Highway 155 to Buffalo Narrows at Churchill Lake — it's easy to gain access to the river, though some sections of it are better accessed via a float plane ride. That's particularly easy to do in Missinipe, and in fact feels almost like hailing a cab in New York City does. Planes can be made ready on very short notice.

Deciding what section of the Churchill River to canoe depends a lot on how much time you have. Contact Ric Driediger at Churchill River Canoe Outfitters for advice, or pick up one of the guidebooks outlining all the routes on the river. Give yourself a minimum of three days, but a week or more would be even better. One of the premier sections of the river is the 150 km (93 mi) stretch between Sandfly Lake and Otter Rapids. A shorter four-day section would take you from Black Bear Island Lake or Trout Lake all the way back to Missinipe. There are also some great routes out of Missinipe itself. Though they tend to be busier, the upside is that they don't require a float plane.

No matter what route you choose, you will paddle through fabulous Canadian Shield landscapes featuring some of the oldest rocks on the continent. Tree-covered islands, big vistas, campsites on rocky points and large numbers of white pelicans and bald eagles soaring overhead are the hallmarks of this paddling adventure. Every day you'll fall asleep to the call of the loon. Don't expect to see a lot of wildlife, but do expect to catch your own dinner if you're a few portages out from Missinipe.

The Churchill River will whet your appetite for more paddling on Canada's great northern rivers.

HIGHLIGHTS: Canadian Shield landscape, swimming, bird life, waterfalls and rapids, fun rapid-running, petroglyphs, fishing

DISTANCE: Highly variable depending on how much time you have, how fast you paddle and how good you are as a navigator

TIME NEEDED: A minimum of 3 days, but a week would be great

GRADE: Moderate

WHERE: Missinipe is 80 km (50 mi) north of La Ronge via a mostly dirt road. Driving time from Saskatoon is approximately 6 hours.

HOW: Either bring your own canoe or rent one in Missinipe. A float plane may be necessary depending on where you want to start on the river.

WHEN: Late May to mid-September

COST: Factor in canoe rentals and a possible float plane ride.

DON'T FORGET: Bug net, bug jacket and bug spray just in case, as well as an axe, fire-starter and extra food

OPTIONS: Do a 3-day loop on Otter, French and Ducker Lake — part of the Churchill River. Highlights include petroglyphs and 3 waterfalls.

BEFORE YOU GO: Read *Canoeing the Churchill* by Sid Robinson or *The Lonely Land* by Sigurd Olsen.

TOUR COMPANIES: Churchill River Canoe Outfitters, CanoeSki

INTERESTING FACT: The Churchill River is unique in that all the water flowing in the river is Saskatchewan-derived, with not a drop of mountain water.

Backpacking
The Nut Point Trail
in Lac La Ronge Provincial Park

□■■□

Backpacking is probably not the first thing that comes to mind when you think of northern Saskatchewan. Justly famous for its lakes and rivers, it's a first-class destination for fishing and paddling, but not for much else. There are always exceptions, though, and for this area, the Nut Point Trail in Lac La Ronge Provincial Park is it.

The 15 km (9.3 mi) trail, located just minutes from the town of La Ronge, takes you all the way down the spine of a wooded rocky peninsula to its tip, which juts out into Lac La Ronge. Classic Canadian Shield scenery — exposed bedrock and windswept pines — provide a stunning setting for your campsite and a great place to spend a few days, especially with all the excellent swimming and fishing possible from within feet of your tent. Do the trail as a backpacking trip, or you'll have a solid eight-hour day hike and no time to enjoy the scenery at the end.

The trail alternates between high, rocky ridges on exposed bedrock, where the hiking is easy and fast, and low-lying muskeg, where it's not so easy and not so fast, unless you're on a section of boardwalk. Be prepared for some route-finding issues through boggy ground after the halfway point. Most of the trail is in a mixed forest with lots of black spruce, except in the area of the 1999 Mallard fire, where new growth has replaced the swaths of hundred-year-old black spruces lost to the fire. Views of Lac La Ronge are few and far between until the very end of the trail. Granted, there are sneak peeks here and there, but you have to make it to the end to get the full reward.

From the Nut Portage at the halfway point, the trail markedly deteriorates for a couple of kilometres. It's too bad, as it wouldn't take much work to clear the deadfall. Fortunately, once you're back on the ridges again, it's clear going until you pop out at the end of the peninsula.

The trail is generally well marked, but don't expect to see any mile markers. Gauge your location in relation to your usual hiking speed. Be alert for wildlife including moose, bears, deer and elk, and carry a can of bear spray.

Despite the need for some trail maintenance, chances are the scene at the end of the trail will thrill and excite you. With expansive views, the rugged, rocky landscape will make every step and every bug bite worthwhile. Try to hike it on a weekday so you can have the campsite to yourself.

HIGHLIGHTS: Exposed bedrock like sidewalks, spectacular campsite at the end of the trail, Canadian Shield scenery, swimming, blueberries in late summer

DISTANCE: 15 km (9.3 mi) each way

TIME NEEDED: 1–2 days

GRADE: Moderate as a backpacking trip, difficult as a day hike

WHERE: La Ronge is approximately 380 km (236 mi) north of Saskatoon via Highways 11 and 2. The trailhead is just 3.5 km (2.2 mi) from the centre of La Ronge.

WHEN: May to early October

HOW: Simply head out from the parking lot. There isn't even a register to sign, but do let someone know of your plans.

COST: Free entry to the park; backcountry camping is free as well.

DON'T FORGET: Bug net, bug jacket, bathing suit

OPTIONS: Lac La Ronge — home to 1,300 islands — is a paddler's paradise, with over 30 documented canoe routes, many of which follow old fur trade routes.

TOUR COMPANIES: None

INTERESTING FACT: Lac La Ronge, the fourth-largest lake in the province, drains into the Churchill River at Nistowiak Falls.

Hiking to
Grey Owl's Cabin
in Prince Albert National Park

■□■□

Located at the southern edge of the boreal forest, the hike to Grey Owl's cabin on the shores of Ajawaan Lake offers an insight into the life of one of Canada's first naturalists. Originally a trapper, Grey Owl credited his Iroquois wife, Anahareo, with making him a conservationist. He went on to write three bestselling books and travel extensively on lecture tours to talk about his Native lifestyle and the wonders of northern Canada. Claiming to be part Apache and part Scots, Grey Owl lived with his wife in a simple cabin along with their pet beavers, Rawhide and Jelly Roll. After his death, the discovery that Grey Owl was actually born Archibald Belaney in England created a scandal which overshadowed his very real contributions as a conservationist. His cabin is well worth visiting.

There are several ways to reach Grey Owl's cabin. The shortest and easiest trip requires a boat shuttle across Kingsmere Lake followed by a 6.4 km (4 mi) round-trip hike to the cabin. You can also rent a canoe on a calm day and paddle for three hours across the lake, hike, and then paddle back. Or, instead of hiking from Kingsmere Lake to Ajawaan Lake, you can portage 600 m (1,969 ft) and approach the cabin from the water. But if you're canoeing, be prepared for a day that could turn epic if the winds blow up on Kingsmere Lake. Keen hikers can make a day of it by returning on a trail that parallels the eastern shore of Kingsmere Lake for 17 km (10.6 mi). The Canadian Shield terrain is easy to negotiate and pretty, with lots of open woods, lake views and plenty of deer. In the summer, a swim in the lake is a welcome break.

The trail can also be done as a two- to three-day backpacking trip. There are campsites at either end and three backcountry campsites along the trail. All offer bear-proof methods of storing food. Head for the Sandy Beach Campsite 12.7 km (7.9 mi) from the trailhead, spend the night and then hike to the cabin without the weight of a backpack. On the return, either camp another night or hike back to the trailhead. Avoid going in mid-July when bugs are at their peak; aim for late August or September instead.

A unique souvenir of your trip is a postcard only available to those who visit the cabin.

HIGHLIGHTS: Grey Owl's cabin, swimming in Kingsmere Lake, beautiful forest walking, deer, bird life, history

DISTANCE: 20 km (12.4 mi) to Grey Owl's cabin

TIME NEEDED: One very long day to a 2–3 days backpacking trip

GRADE: Easy as a hike from the boat shuttle; difficult as a backpacking trip

WHERE: The trailhead is located at the Kingsmere River parking lot and day use area, 33 km (21 mi) from Waskesiu via the Kingsmere Road.

HOW: Buy a park pass at the entrance for a day trip and a backcountry pass at the Visitor Centre for an overnight trip. There are 6 backcountry campsites to choose from.

WHEN: May to October. It can be *very* buggy in July.

COST: Park permit is $7.80/day/adult; backcountry camping permit is $9.80 pp/night.

DON'T FORGET: Bug spray, bug jacket, head net, extra food, bathing suit

OPTIONS: Canoe or boat to the trailhead on Kingsmere Lake and then enjoy a 6 km (3.7 mi) round-trip hike to Grey Owl's cabin.

TOUR COMPANIES: Waskesiu Marina Adventure Centre offers a shuttle to a dock close to Grey Owl's cabin for $40 pp each way.

INTERESTING FACT: Grey Owl was the first naturalist hired by Dominion Parks Canada, the precursor to today's Parks Canada. Initially, he lived in a cabin in Riding Mountain National Park, but unsuitable water conditions for the beavers forced a move to Prince Albert National Park.

Alberta
Adventures

N

British
Columbia

Pacific Ocean

Alberta

Edmonton ●

 Jasper

Maligne Canyon

Maligne Lake

Skyline Trail

Skoki Circuit

Sentinel Pass

● Banff

Calgary ●

Mt. Assiniboine

Prairie Mt.

Highwood Pass

Peter Lougheed

Dinosaur

Crypt Lake

 U.S.A.

Hiking to the summit of
Prairie Mountain
in Kananaskis Country

□ ■ ■ □

If you're looking for a great year-round workout, one that's akin to a StairMaster but with superb prairie and mountain views, include the hike to the top of Prairie Mountain, located just forty-five minutes from Calgary near Bragg Creek in Kananaskis Country. It's one of the few mountains anywhere near Calgary that can be hiked every month of the year, providing you have appropriate footwear and Mother Nature doesn't throw any curveballs in the form of thunderstorms, wind storms or blizzards.

The hike starts by the winter gates located across the highway from Elbow Falls. Directly across from the trailhead there is a small unmarked parking lot along the highway with room for about fifteen cars; otherwise, park in the large Elbow Falls lot.

There are several narrow, steep trails heading up from the highway, but the trail you want is on the north side of the road and angles steeply up from the bridge into the woods. Do not take the trail that follows the Elbow River Valley parallel to Highway 66, and keep off any small trails to prevent erosion. Once you're on it, you'll find the trail is well used and easy to navigate.

The hike starts steeply, moderates briefly, then climbs again through a section of trees, which offer the odd peekaboo view. This part of the walk will test your conditioning program . . . or lack thereof. But once you clear the trees, the grade moderates for the rest of the way. Turn right once out of the trees and stay close to the eastern escarpment until you reach the cairn at the summit, approximately a kilometre away. Don't get too close to the edge; cornices form once the snow starts to fall. The summit offers outstanding views. You can see downtown Calgary in one direction and Moose Mountain to the north as well as many other peaks.

This hike is used by locals as a spring conditioner for bigger mountains. Others climb it on Christmas or New Year's Day. Strong hikers should allow three hours to do the 7.6 km (4.7 mi) return hike. Slower hikers could take upwards of five hours. It's a quick descent in the winter, as the snow makes it easy to descend, but it's rocky and more difficult the rest of the year.

The popularity of the Prairie Mountain makes it likely you'll meet many people going up and coming down on almost every day of the year.

HIGHLIGHTS: Spectacular mountain views, Calgary city views, great workout, year-round accessibility

DISTANCE: 7.6 km (4.7 mi) return with 726 m (2,381 ft) of elevation gain

TIME NEEDED: 3–5 hours

GRADE: Moderate to difficult

WHERE: 22 km (13.7 mi) west of Bragg Creek via Highway 66 across from the Elbow Falls parking lot. From Calgary it's about 67 km (42 mi) to the trailhead.

HOW: Go prepared with the 10 essentials (see page xviii). Although popular, it is still a mountain environment.

WHEN: Year-round, providing weather conditions are favourable

COST: Free park access. No parking fees

DON'T FORGET: Wind-proof jacket for the summit. In winter, take gaiters and Yactrax or something similar with good gripping power on snow and ice. Bring poles if your knees are bad. This is a dog-friendly hike.

OPTIONS: Climb Moose Mountain to the north — a 15 km (9.3 mi) return hike — but only in the summer or fall.

TOUR COMPANIES: None

INTERESTING FACT: Kananaskis Country, with a land mass almost four times the size of Hong Kong, is a park system west of Calgary boasting over 4,000 sq km (1,544 sq mi) in the foothills and front ranges of the Canadian Rockies.

Cycling
Highwood Pass
in Kananaskis Country

If you're a cyclist, you're going to love the ride up Highwood Pass in Kananaskis Country. Ideally, you want to find the one perfect day in late May or early June when the snow is gone, the sun is shining and there's not a car to be seen. This ride is spectacular from start to finish, but even more so before June 15, when you have the freedom to cycle anywhere you want on the road because cars aren't allowed. Even after the 15th, the road traffic is light to the end of June.

You can begin at one of the two winter gates. By car, they are over two hours apart, so the possibility of a car shuttle is not very practical — not early in the season, at least. Most people do an out-and-back ride.

There are three options:

• Start at the winter gate by King Creek on the west side and cycle 17 km (11 mi) up Highway 40 on a moderate grade, steep for the last 5 km (3 mi). Enjoy a fun, fast return.

• Start at the Highwood Junction winter gate on the east side and cycle 37 km (23 mi) up to 2,206 m (7,238 ft) Highwood Pass. The grade is mostly gentle to moderate until you reach Peter Lougheed Provincial Park, 4 km (2.5 mi) from the pass. Then it ramps up to a 7 percent grade. Return the way you came.

• Start at either winter gate and do a full out-and-back ride. This will definitely test your conditioning program, given that it is a 108 km (67 mi) round trip with a total elevation gain of 1,267 m (4,157 ft).

The shoulder is wide, so even if you must share the road with cars, you will never feel squeezed for space. There's also a rumble strip for most of the length of the road, which makes it even safer. The road is even swept in the spring to get rid of gravel build-up.

There are numerous recreation areas where you can pull over, especially on the section between Highwood Junction and Highwood Pass, for washrooms and picnic tables. Do go prepared. You are in a mountain environment for the entire ride. The pass is notoriously cold and windy, so you'll likely need a jacket. In summer, during peak berry season, stay tuned for grizzly bears as this is a favourite area for them.

HIGHLIGHTS: Mountain views, car-free highways until June 15, elk, deer, moose, big-horned sheep, bears

DISTANCE: 37 km (23 mi) to Highwood Pass from Highwood Junction gate; 17 km (11 mi) to Highwood Pass from King Creek gate. Elevation gain of 700 m (2,297 ft) from Highwood Junction gate and 536 m (1,759 ft) from King Creek gate

TIME NEEDED: 3–7 hours, depending on how far out and back you ride

GRADE: Moderate to difficult

WHERE: There are two start points: For the King Creek Trailhead, drive 50 km (31 mi) south on Highway 40 from the intersection with Trans-Canada Highway; park by winter gates. The Highwood Junction gate is 45 km (28 mi) west of Longview via Highway 541; Longview is 80 km (50 mi) southwest of Calgary.

HOW: Park at either entrance for an out-and-back ride. For a one-way ride after June 15, have someone drive to meet you at the far trailhead.

WHEN: Late May to October, depending on how long snow stays in spring

COST: Free unless you rent a bike

DON'T FORGET: Warm clothes, rain gear, gloves, repair kit, water, energy bars, bear spray

OPTIONS: From Highwood Pass, lock your bike and do the easy 3.6 km (2.2 mi) Ptarmigan Cirque hike which is famous for summer wildflowers.

TOUR COMPANIES: None, but the Gran Fondo runs a supported ride in the summer

INTERESTING FACT: Highwood Pass is the highest paved road in Canada.

Cross-country skiing
The Trail System
in Peter Lougheed Provincial Park

■■□□

Peter Lougheed Provincial Park is home to some of the best Nordic skiing in western Canada. An extensive trail system with over 75 km (46 mi) of mostly beginner to intermediate trails caters to people of all ages and abilities. Snow conditions can vary widely across the trails, though, so it's always worthwhile to stop and chat with the rangers at the Barrier Lake Visitor Information Centre on the way to the park. They can direct you to the best snow and should be able to provide a grooming report as well.

Ten parking lots, starting at the Pocaterra Day Use Area and heading south, provide access to the trails. As a general rule of thumb, the farther south you go, the more difficult the trail. The most difficult trails are also generally ones where a lot of climbing or descending is involved. In my opinion, they are also where you get the best views: extensive vistas of snow-covered mountain peaks, the Kananaskis Lakes and the gorgeous Kananaskis Valley. If that's what you like, head to either the Lookout or Blueberry Hill and enjoy some fun, fast downhill on the return.

No matter where you ski in the park, you'll find it to be peaceful. Never do you hear the whine of a snowmobile motor. Apart from the wind or the gurgle of a winter stream, the only thing you're likely to hear is a squawk from a gray jay keen on sharing your lunch.

There are only a couple of warming huts: the Pocaterra Warming Hut and the Visitor Information Centre in the park. Should you choose to ski the trails to the south, ensure you have lots of extra clothes and high-energy food as the weather can change dramatically and it's no place to get stranded.

If you're looking for a great workout or a peaceful backcountry ski outing in an alpine setting, a visit to this park is certainly worth the ninety-minute drive from Calgary.

HIGHLIGHTS: A wide variety of trails to suit all abilities, well-groomed trails, beautiful alpine scenery, peaceful setting

DISTANCE: There are 98 km (61 mi) of trails to choose from.

TIME NEEDED: A half day to a full day

GRADE: Easy to moderate

WHERE: The park is approximately 138 km (86 mi) southwest of Calgary via the Trans-Canada Highway and Highway 40. There are 10 parking lots scattered over 13 km (8 mi) along the Kananaskis Lakes Trail.

HOW: Call the Barrier Lake Visitor Information Centre at 1-403-678-0760 or stop in to pick up a map and get an up-to-date ski report. Look for it on the west side of the road as you drive south.

WHEN: Late November until mid-April, depending on the snow year

COST: Free

DON'T FORGET: Bring your own skis, as there is nowhere to rent. Take extra clothing and a thermos of something hot to drink. Duct tape can useful if you have equipment failures. A snow shovel might be necessary to dig your car out. Dogs are not allowed.

OPTIONS: If the driving is bad, go only as far at the Ribbon Creek area — approximately 10 km (6 mi) past the Barrier Lake Visitor Information Centre near Nakiska Mountain Resort — and explore the multitude of trails in there.

TOUR COMPANIES: None

INTERESTING FACT: Dan Gardner, one of the team behind the design of the cross-country ski trails for the 1988 Calgary Winter Olympics, played an important role in designing and building the trails in Peter Lougheed Provincial Park.

Hiking
The Crypt Lake Trail
in Waterton Lakes National Park

□ ■ □ □

"No one has ever died on the exposed section," declared our boat guide en route to the Crypt Lake Trail. Would you find those words reassuring as you headed out to test your mettle on what has been called the 'Indiana Jones adventure' of the Canadian Rockies?

Crypt Lake is by no means the prettiest hike in the Rockies, or even in Waterton Lakes National Park for that matter. But it does offer a variety of experiences that you're not likely to find on any other hike in Canada.

The hike starts with a scenic fifteen-minute boat ride. This is when it first strikes you that you won't be alone on the trail. For some, that will be a positive thing, since this is bear country after all. But if you're looking for a solitary experience, you won't find it hiking to Crypt Lake, unless it's a weekday in September.

Hiking Crypt Lake is really about going for the thrill of crossing a narrow scree slope with drop-offs: climbing an eight-foot ladder, getting low and wiggling through a 20 m (60 ft) tunnel, and then scaring the living daylights out of yourself as you inch along the narrow rocky trail with a steel cable handhold on one side and a drop-off on the other. Once you're through the cable section, you can breathe a big sigh of relief. Or stop crying, at least, since you will have to return the same way you came if you ever want to eat a hot meal again.

The route up to Crypt Lake is easy to follow. On the way you'll pass three waterfalls: Twin Falls, Burnt Rock Falls and the wonderful Crypt Falls. You have the option of visiting Hell Roaring Falls via a spur trail near the beginning of the hike, but that will add to your overall mileage. Plan on at least two and a half hours to hike each way. Even if you're a fast hiker, you may have to factor in waiting for people to pass through the cabled section on your return.

Crypt Lake itself is a treat. Beaches line part of the lake, and because you'll likely have some time before you have to head back for the return boat trip, it's a perfect place to lie out in the sun and relax. Alternatively, take the thirty-minute walk around the lake, the far end of which is on the United States–Canada border.

HIGHLIGHTS: Beautiful alpine lake, wide range of experiences on the hike including a ladder, a tunnel and chains, boat ride, waterfalls, vistas, wildlife

DISTANCE: 17.4 km (10.8 mi) round trip with 690 m (2,263 ft) of elevation gain

TIME NEEDED: 5–7 hours

GRADE: Moderate

WHERE: Waterton Lakes National Park is in southern Alberta, approximately 280 km (174 mi) south of Calgary.

HOW: Book a passage with the Waterton Shoreline Inter-Nation Cruise Co. You must reserve both the morning and the afternoon boat rides. In peak season, the last boat leaves at 5:30 p.m. You can buy the tickets down on the dock on the morning you plan to hike.

WHEN: As early as late May, depending on the year, through to mid-October.

COST: A national parks day pass is $7.80/adult and $5.80/adult in the shoulder season. The boat ride is $20/adult and $10/child (4–12 years).

DON'T FORGET: Reserve a seat on the boat, bring bear spray, dress in layers

OPTIONS: Make a side trip to Hell Roaring Falls (add 0.5 km/0.3 mi) and/or walk around Crypt Lake (add 1.8 km/1.1 mi).

TOUR COMPANIES: None

INTERESTING FACT: The Waterton–Glacier International Peace Park, created in 1932, is the world's first international peace park. Now there are over 170 of them worldwide.

Backpacking to
Magog Lake
in Mount Assiniboine Provincial Park

■ ❑ ■ ❑

You must visit Mount Assiniboine Provincial Park for its mind-blowing mountain scenery that competes with the best in Canada, if not the world. Impressive Mount Assiniboine dominates the landscape, but it's not the only reason to visit. Numerous mountain peaks, a host of dramatic blue-hued lakes, and meadows brimming with summer wildflowers are the reward for any visitor — be it someone who has arrived by helicopter or a backpacker who has hiked over 25 km (15 mi) from either the Mount Shark or Sunshine Trailheads. The park is located in British Columbia, but accessed from two different points in Alberta (see the WHERE section).

Most backpackers hike into the Lake Magog Campground via Bryant Creek and Assiniboine Pass from the Mount Shark Trailhead. It's a 27.5 km (17. 1 mi) slog with unremarkable views for the most part, but it's well marked and the elevation gain is less than via Wonder Pass. On Friday, Sunday and Wednesday be prepared for considerable helicopter traffic for several hours when guests fly into the lodge.

If you plan to return to the Mount Shark Trailhead, hike over Wonder Pass and enjoy terrific views of Marvel Lake. Some people break up the trip on the way in by staying overnight in the simple but dry, three-room Bryant Creek Shelter. As it's in Banff National Park, you will need a park pass to spend the night, and you must reserve a space ahead of time.

The prettier access, though a more challenging one, is via a 27.5 km (17.1 mi) hike that starts at Sunshine Meadows. It takes you over Citadel Pass through the Valley of the Rocks, past Og Lake and on to the Lake Magog Campground. Be prepared for only a few places to fill water bottles in the Valley of the Rocks, and consider breaking up this trip with a stay at the Og Lake Campground.

Once you've made it up to Lake Magog, there is a lot of exploring to do. For the finest views in the park, hike to the summit of Nub Peak via an airy ridge from the Nublet — where the views are also magnificent. If you don't plan to return via Wonder Pass, then explore the area around the pass as part of a day hike. Windy Ridge is the other must-do hike. Not only are the views into Yoho and Kootenay National Parks excellent, summer wildflower displays on the way up are magnificent.

Don't rush a visit to the Mount Assiniboine area. You'll shortchange yourself if you allow any fewer than three days.

HIGHLIGHTS: Outstanding mountain scenery, alpine meadows, glaciers, mountain lakes

DISTANCE: Varies depending on the trailheads and hikes you choose. It's 55 km (34 mi) with an elevation gain of 395 m (1,296 ft) just to hike in and out.

TIME NEEDED: 3–5 days

GRADE: Difficult as a backpacking trip, but easy hiking options if you fly in and out

WHERE: The park is about 35 km (22 mi) southeast of Banff as the crow flies. The Mount Shark Trailhead is 38 km (24 mi) south of Canmore; the Sunshine Trailhead is accessed via Sunshine Village, 18 km (11 mi) west of Banff.

HOW: No reservations needed to camp at Lake Magog. Reserve Naiset Huts through Assiniboine Lodge. To hike in via the Sunshine Trailhead book a bus seat through **sunshinemeadowsbanff.com**.

WHEN: July to mid-September

COST: $10 pp/night at the Magog Campground; $20 pp/night in the Naiset Huts. Check the Assiniboine Lodge website for current pricing. One-way helicopter flights are $150.

DON'T FORGET: Warm clothes as it can snow at any time, gaiters, hiking poles, rain gear, bear spray

OPTIONS: Arrange car shuttle to hike in from Sunshine Trailhead and out over Wonder Pass to finish at the Mount Shark Trailhead.

TOUR COMPANIES: Yamnuska Mountain Adventures, White Mountain Adventures

INTERESTING FACT: Mount Assiniboine is known as the Matterhorn of North America. The summit is 1,525 m (5,003 ft) above Lake Magog.

Hiking to
Sentinel Pass
in Banff National Park

□■□□

The hike to Sentinel Pass is sublime. It's truly one of the most impressive day hikes in all of Banff National Park. The only downside to the hike is that it's very popular, so solitude isn't necessarily available. It's also required by law that you hike as a tight group of four between July 12 and October 8. The trail traverses prime grizzly bear habitat, but fortunately, there's never been a documented bear attack on a group of four or more.

The hike begins just past Moraine Lake Lodge. The trail to Sentinel Pass is well marked, but to start up it, you need to show the parks personnel that you have your group of four. If you don't, be prepared to wait until someone else comes along. The first few kilometres take you steeply up a series of switchbacks. Climb 352 m (1,155 ft) in 2.5 km (1.6 mi) to reach Larch Valley and a beautiful meadow. In late September, this area is a riot of yellow with all the larch trees changing colour. As you enter the meadow, look around. The views over to the Valley of the Ten Peaks are gorgeous.

Continue north to reach Sentinel Pass. In less than fifteen minutes you'll come to three tiny lakes referred to as Minnestimma Lakes. The trail slips between the lakes, and the craggy, austere environment that makes up Sentinel Pass can be seen ahead. Continue to climb 175 m (574 ft) up a talus field on another series of switchbacks to top out at the pass. At 2,611 m (8,566 ft), it's the highest point reached by a maintained trail in the Rockies. At the pass, you can't help but be awestruck at the views in every direction you look.

Mount Temple is on your right as you approach the pass, Pinnacle Mountain on your left. Paradise Valley unfolds on the other side of the pass while the Valley of the Ten Peaks fills your line of vision if you look back the way you've come. And all around the pass are pinnacles of rock like the Grand Sentinel — a favourite of rock climbers.

Retrace your steps to return. If you still have some energy it's well worth continuing on the flat trail to the far end of Moraine Lake to get an altogether different perspective of the Valley of the Ten Peaks.

Except for the steep section in the trees, be prepared to be wowed every foot of the way. It's a hike that makes you feel happy to be alive.

HIGHLIGHTS: Pretty meadows, phenomenal mountain scenery, Valley of the Ten Peaks, yellow larches in the fall

DISTANCE: 11.6 km (7.2 mi) return and an elevation gain of 726 m (2,382 ft)

TIME NEEDED: 4–5 hours

GRADE: Moderate

WHERE: Start at the Moraine Lake Trailhead, accessed via Lake Louise and Moraine Lake Roads. Turn left off of Lake Louise Road onto Moraine Lake Road and follow it for 12.5 km (7.8 mi) until you reach a massive parking lot. It's roughly 180 km (112 mi) from Calgary to the Village of Lake Louise.

HOW: Join others to make a party of four, as required by law, at the trailhead. You must stay together for the duration of the hike.

WHEN: July to early October

COST: You must have a Banff National Parks pass displayed on your vehicle. It's $9.80/adult/day. Youth are $4.90/day.

DON'T FORGET: Bear spray, bear bangers. Carry an ice axe and know how to use it if you're hiking before mid-July. Get to the parking lot early to avoid the crowds, especially during the larch-viewing season, or head out in the mid-afternoon if there's plenty of daylight left.

OPTIONS: Continue from Sentinel Pass into Paradise Valley, but arrange a car shuttle ahead of time as the Paradise Creek and Moraine Lake parking lots are approximately 9.7 km (6.0 mi) apart.

TOUR COMPANIES: None

INTERESTING FACT: In 1969, and again in 1979, the back side of Canada's twenty-dollar bill sported a picture of the Valley of the Ten Peaks.

Backpacking
The Skoki Circuit
in Banff National Park

□ ■ □ □

The Skoki Circuit is a super-accessible backpacking loop through first-rate alpine scenery which includes gorgeous turquoise lakes, pretty meadows and the grey austerity of the Slate Mountains. Much of the hiking is above the tree line so views are particularly rewarding, especially those from the top of Deception Pass. Many hikers on the trail spend the night at Skoki Lodge, while others vie for the limited campsite space, so chances are you won't find solitude.

The start of this otherwise enjoyable hike is an unappealing 4 km (2.5 mi) slog up a steep ski road. Then it's into the woods for another 3 km (1.9 mi). It's not until you've hiked 7 km (4.3 mi) that the views open up and the wildflower-dotted subalpine meadows appear. Around the Halfway Hut, keep a close eye out for grizzlies. We missed the sight of a grizzly frolicking in the stream by five minutes.

Next up is the aptly named Boulder Pass. At the top of it sits beautiful Ptarmigan Lake. It's a stunning place to linger on a sunny day. The final 4.5 km (2.8 mi) to the Baker Lake Campground is sublime hiking, with nothing but mountain vistas for as far as the eye can see. The campground, located at the far end of the lake, is one of the most popular on the Skoki Circuit. Although the setting is extraordinarily pretty, the campground is showing signs of heavy use and is not as pristine as might be desired. Hopefully, the park will soon put some effort into repairing tent sites and cleaning outhouses.

On day two, leave your tent up and hike a 15 km (9.3 mi) loop that includes Skoki Lodge and Deception Pass. The loop from Baker Lake to Skoki Lodge via Jones Pass is an easy one. Two side trips are possible: a 4.6 km (2.8 mi) return hike to the Red Deer Lakes and a worthwhile 5.8 km (3.6 mi) return hike to Merlin Lake. From Skoki Lodge, where it's possible to enjoy afternoon tea, it's 3 km (1.9 mi) up to the top of Deception Pass. This section affords the viewer some of the prettiest scenery on the loop. From the top of Deception Pass, at an elevation of 2,470 m (8,104 ft), it takes about an hour to hike back to the Baker Lake Campground. Hike out the following morning.

Despite the worn campsite, the trip is outstanding for its alpine lake and mountain scenery.

HIGHLIGHTS: Beautiful alpine lakes, wild-flower-dotted alpine meadows, expansive mountain views, the Slate Range Mountains, wildlife including grizzly bears, wolves and moose

DISTANCE: 41.4 km (25.7 mi) to the Baker Lake Campground, including a loop hike over Deception Pass on the second day; mileage for extra side trips not included

TIME NEEDED: 3 days to do the circuit, plus more time for additional day hikes

GRADE: Moderate

WHERE: Start at the Fish Creek parking area just below Lake Louise Ski Resort, about 185 km (115 mi) west of Calgary.

HOW: Book Baker Lake campsite reservations up to 3 months in advance by calling the Banff Visitor Centre at 1-403-762-1556. You can also try your luck showing up at the Banff or Lake Louise Park office in person, but you may be disappointed on a busy summer weekend.

WHEN: July to mid-September

COST: $9.80 pp/night backcountry pass, $9.80 pp/day national park fee, $11.70 reservation fee

DON'T FORGET: Bear spray and bear bangers, bug dope (deer flies can be awful), water filter

OPTIONS: Consider camping at the Hidden Lake, Merlin Meadows or Red Deer Lakes Campgrounds; or book a stay at Skoki Lodge and start exploring from there.

TOUR COMPANIES: Yamnuska Mountain Adventures

INTERESTING FACT: Built in 1931, Skoki Lodge is a Canadian National Historic Site.

Backpacking to
Abbot Pass Hut
in Banff National Park

☐☐☐■

The second-highest permanent structure in Canada, Abbot Pass Hut sits at an altitude of 2,925 m (9,598 ft). It's primarily used in the summer months, as the avalanche risk is too high to reach it safely in the winter. Hardcore mountaineers hoping to climb nearby Mount Lefroy or Mount Victoria are frequent visitors, but there are plenty of hikers too, either experienced or just keen to try a route a little outside their comfort zone. The views from the hut — and from the outhouse, for that matter — are outstanding. Built from local stone and materials packed in by horses in 1922, it stands as a monument to the Swiss guides who first ventured into the Rocky Mountains in 1899 under the sponsorship of the Canadian Pacific Railway. It sleeps twenty-four people, dorm-style. The hut comes furnished with mattresses, cooking gear, tables, benches and even a guitar. Cooking is done on propane stoves and wood is used to heat the place.

Getting to Abbot Pass Hut takes you through some of Canada's most beautiful alpine scenery. Turquoise Lake O'Hara is the starting point. From here it's an easy 3.3 km (2.1 mi) of hiking beside the lake and up some benches to reach Lake Oesa, itself a captivating sight. The elevation gain to that point is only 240 m (787 ft). The tougher hiking lies ahead.

From Lake Oesa, head for the scree slopes to the north. The hiking through here is still easy, even as you ascend a series of ledges. It's the final 600 m (1,969 ft) that get gnarly. It's time to put on the helmets when you look up and see nothing but boulders and scree.

The trick to a safe hike in Abbot Pass is to avoid getting hit by rocks. That means that as a hiker, you must concentrate on your foot placement to avoid dislodging anything of any size. Be aware of who is above and below you at all times. Keep your group together and stick to the middle of the couloir. Most of the serious injuries occur because of rock-fall off the mountains, so move into the centre of the couloir as soon as you safely can. I found the middle section of the climb to be the most intimidating. Medium-sized boulders were quite loose, so you had the sensation of taking one step forward, two steps back.

The actual hike up to Abbot Pass Hut from Lake Oesa will take strong hikers about ninety minutes. Others could easily spend hours. But trust me, as you come over the lip at the top, it's an intoxicating feeling to look down a few thousand feet to Lake Oesa on the south side and to the Plain of the Six Glaciers at the bottom of the Victoria Glacier on the north side.

HIGHLIGHTS: Lake O'Hara scenery, grand mountain scenery, precarious mountain pass, starry nights, glaciers, historic hut, great sense of accomplishment

DISTANCE: From the Lake O'Hara Trailhead it's 3.3 km (2.1 mi) to Lake Oesa and roughly another 1.5 km (0.9 mi) from there to the hut. The elevation gain from Lake O'Hara is 900 m (2,953 ft).

TIME NEEDED: Two days, though it only takes 3–6 hours to hike from Lake O'Hara to the Abbot Pass Hut.

GRADE: Very difficult

WHERE: On the boundary between Banff and Yoho National Parks, which also marks the British Columbia–Alberta border

GETTING THERE: The turnoff to the signed parking lot for Lake O'Hara is about 200 km (124 mi) west of Calgary and 21 km (13 mi) west of Lake Louise off the Trans-Canada Highway, just across the Alberta–BC border on the BC side.

HOW: Reserve the hut ahead of time at **alpineclubofcanada.ca.** Then, 90 days before your date, book a bus ride to take you from the parking lot up the 11 km (6.8 mi) road to Lake O'Hara. Phone 1-250-343-6433 to make the bus reservation. Return reservations are not required. Book a Yamnuska mountain guide if you want the security of their expertise.

WHEN: July, August or September

COST: It's $22/night for Alpine Club of Canada members, and $32/night for non-members.

DON'T FORGET: Food, sleeping bags, warm clothes, helmet, trekking pole(s), toilet paper

TOUR COMPANIES: Yamnuska Mountain Adventures can guide you up.

INTERESTING FACT: In 1992, the hut was designated a National Historic Site.

Cycling from
Banff to Jasper
in Banff and Jasper National Parks

□ □ ■ □

The 290 km (180 mi) bike ride between Banff and Jasper is one of the most impressive mountain rides in the world. The route runs parallel to the Continental Divide, so you're always looking at mountains. For the experienced cyclist, it offers challenging hills and epic downhill rides. It's not just the scenery and spectacular mountains that this route is famous for, either. Sightings of black and grizzly bears, elk, mountain goats and bighorn sheep are common. Fences and overpasses keep the wildlife at bay between Banff and Lake Louise, but once you reach the Icefields Parkway those structures disappear. Keep your camera and a can of bear spray ready.

The cycling is all done on highways: the Trans-Canada Highway between Banff and Lake Louise, and the Icefields Parkway from Lake Louise all the way through to Jasper. Fortunately, big trucks are banned on the Icefields Parkway. The roads do offer wide shoulders, but they can get busy around Banff, Lake Louise, the Columbia Icefield and Jasper. Elsewhere, they're reasonably quiet, especially on weekdays. It's possible to take Highway 1A — also called the Bow Valley Parkway — between Banff and Lake Louise if you want a quieter route for that section. I don't think it's as pretty, but there is more wildlife and it provides the option of a side trip to Johnston Canyon.

The route is bookended by the two famous mountain towns of Banff and Jasper. You can start in either place, though most cyclists and touring companies seem to start in Banff. There are loads of accommodation options ranging from camping through to five-star hotels. Book in advance, as beds and campgrounds fill up quickly. Going north from Banff, you reach Lake Louise in only 55 km (34 mi). It's worth stopping here for an extra day for the incredible hiking. In particular, Lake Agnes and the Plain of Six Glaciers are not far and offer mountain teahouses with stunning views for refuelling.

From Lake Louise it's an uphill cycle to reach Bow Pass, the highest point on the Icefields Parkway, and the Peyto Lake viewpoint. Continuing north, descend to Saskatchewan River Crossing where three rivers converge, then climb to the Columbia Icefields. It's a good place to spend the night and will allow the option of touring the glacier. North of the Columbia Icefield, you'll see Sunwapta Mountain and the Endless Chain Ridge. The rest of the bike tour takes you alongside the Sunwapta and Athabasca Rivers into Jasper.

Plan to be challenged by this very scenic and often difficult bike tour.

HIGHLIGHTS: Stunning panoramas for the entire ride, Banff and Jasper National Parks, Waputik Icefields, Peyto Lake, Athabasca Glacier and the Columbia Icefields Centre, Mistaya Canyon, Sunwapta Pass, Bow Pass, wildlife

DISTANCE: 290 km (175 mi) each way

TIME NEEDED: 4–5 days

GRADE: Difficult

WHERE: The Banff–Jasper corridor is accessible via Calgary, located 125 km (80 mi) to the east. Edmonton is also a possibility; it's 360 km (215 mi) east of Jasper.

HOW: Most people start in Banff, but the prevailing winds might actually make it easier to start in Jasper. Bring your own bike or rent one from Snowtips-Bactrax Ski and Bike Rental in Banff or from Freewheel Cycle Jasper.

WHEN: June to early October, depending on the year

COST: Highly variable, depending on whether you do it with a tour company or on your own. Factor in bike rentals and either campground or hotel/motel stays for 3–4 nights plus food and transportation back to your start point. Brewster transports bikes between towns and it's free, but they have to be in a box and it depends on how much space is left on the bus.

DON'T FORGET: Rain gear, warm clothes for the descents, bear spray. Avoid a trip during the Banff–Jasper Relay held every June. Don't bike at dusk or after dark, when many of the animals come to life and you're harder to see.

TOUR COMPANIES: Rocky Mountain Cycle Tours, Freewheeling Adventures, Great Explorations, Backroads, Mountain Madness, Bicycle Adventures

INTERESTING FACT: In June, daylight lasts for 16.5 hours here.

Hiking
The Maligne Canyon Icewalk
in Jasper National Park

■☐☐☐

As we strap ice cleats onto our insulated waterproof boots, I consider what lies ahead. Is the Maligne Canyon Icewalk going to live up to the hype or is it just another overrated tourist attraction?

Maligne Canyon in winter turns out to be pure magic. Over the ninety minutes or so it takes to hike to the furthest accessible reaches of the canyon, we get a lesson in geology and admire icicles the size of grown men; squirm head-first into a cave we would have missed without a guide; and slip behind a frozen waterfall to look out through the layers of ice. It's an otherworldly view.

Lying in what is known as karst terrain, Maligne Canyon is characterized by an extensive underground system of caves and fissures formed in limestone rock. The water in the Maligne River comes in part from nearby Medicine Lake, which is fed by rainwater and glacier- and snow melt. It drains from the bottom like a bathtub into a network of caves and fissures, some of which reaches the Maligne River. Stretches of the river are also fed by springs that never freeze because the water rises out of the ground at 4°C (39°F).

In summer the river level is much higher, as evidenced by the line of moss showing a high-water mark well above head height. When winter comes, the river freezes. As winter progresses, the water under the ice drops, leaving a big gap between the ice and the lowering water surface. This ice can be quite thick and can create long bridges that are strong enough to walk on. Ice cleats help enormously, but it can still be slippery. It would be a bad idea to head to the canyon without a pair, and could put you at risk for a serious fall and injury.

As you hike up the canyon, you pass one beautiful icefall after another. The finish is at the biggest icefall of all, where you're likely to find ice climbers, especially on a weekend. Visit the icewalk between mid-December and mid-April for a frozen experience like no other.

HIGHLIGHTS: Ice caves, beautiful ice formations, frozen waterfalls, ice climbers, incredible setting, interesting geology, wildlife

DISTANCE: 4 km (2.5 mi) return

TIME NEEDED: 3 hours

GRADE: Easy and family-friendly

WHERE: 7.6 km (4.7 mi) from downtown Jasper off Maligne Road

HOW: You can do it on your own if you have waterproof boots and ice cleats. It's fun, informative and safe if you go with a guided tour.

WHEN: December to mid-April, depending on the year

COST: Approximately $59/adult, $29.00/child

DON'T FORGET: Warm clothes and your camera

OPTIONS: Three tours a day — at 9:00 a.m., 1:00 p.m. and in the evening — run even in the dead of winter.

TOUR COMPANIES: Maligne Adventures and Jasper Adventure Centre

INTERESTING FACT: Scientists put a harmless dye in Medicine Lake to see how long it took to drain. In the summer it reached the Maligne River in 12 hours. In winter, with the Maligne River's flow curtailed by dropping temperatures, the dye took 88 hours to flow underground.

Kayaking or canoeing
Maligne Lake
in Jasper National Park

□■□□

Within days of moving to Calgary, I had a chance conversation with an electrician who'd dropped by my house to give me a quote on some work. He told me about kayaking Maligne Lake, and I immediately knew I had to visit.

Maligne Lake is take-your-breath-away gorgeous. Photos don't do it justice. For starters, the lake is turquoise in colour, similar to Lake Louise but on a grander scale, and it's ringed by mountains. Throw in a few glaciers for drama, add Spirit Island — one of the most photographed spots in the world — and top it all off with wildlife including bear, moose, elk and deer, and you have something really special.

Just getting to Maligne Lake from the town of Jasper is part of the experience. The Maligne Lake Road takes you through a wildlife corridor, and although it's only 48 km (30 mi) between the town and the lake, it will likely take an hour with all the stops you'll make to admire the animals. Factor that into your launch time.

Ideally you should be on the water before 9:00 a.m., but that can be a challenge depending on where you're coming from. Maligne Lake is big — the largest natural lake in the Rockies, as a matter of fact — so wind can be a problem, especially sudden winds that whip up out of nowhere. Plan to paddle close to shore as much as possible. Keep a close eye on the weather when and if you do cross the lake. Your paddling ability needs to factor into your campsite choice. The Fisherman's Bay Campground is 13 km (8 mi) from the launch site and can take anywhere from three to six hours to reach. The Coronet Creek Campground sits at the far end of the lake, almost 22 km (14 mi) from the launch site. Allow five to nine hours to reach it.

Despite the distance, there are some major advantages to choosing the Coronet Creek Campground. The scenery is more dramatic at the far end of the lake, the annoying tour boats are gone — left behind once you pass Spirit Island — and for hikers, there's an option to hike the 16 km (9.9 mi) Henry McLeod Trail, which takes you up into grand, glacier-rich country. You do need to be a strong paddler to attempt it all in a day. Another option — keeping in mind that you can stay no more than four nights in total on the lake — is to paddle to Fisherman's Bay for one night, then head down to Coronet Creek for one to two nights and then back to Fisherman's Bay for a final night before departing.

No matter where you camp, you will be astounded by the scenery and the beauty of the lake. Go prepared for anything Mother Nature might throw your way, though, including snow on any day of the year and hypothermia-inducing waters.

HIGHLIGHTS: Mountain scenery, starry nights, glaciers, Spirit Lake, turquoise water, beautiful hiking, birds, possible moose, black and grizzly bear sightings

DISTANCE: 13 km (8.1 mi) to Fisherman's Bay, 21.3 km (13.2 mi) to Coronet Creek Campground

TIME NEEDED: 2–4 days

GRADE: Moderate

WHERE: 48 km (29.8 mi) southeast of the Jasper Townsite in Jasper National Park via the Maligne Lake Road

WHEN: Late June to early September

HOW: Reserve campsites 90 days ahead; call 1-780-852-6177. For weekend trips, call as soon as phone lines open at 8:00 a.m. MST. Two-night limit at each campsite and no more than 6 people/group. Bring your own canoe, kayak or boat (no more than 3-HP engine). On-site rentals from **malignelake.com** are expensive.

COST: $9.80 pp/night and $11.70 to make the reservation

DON'T FORGET: Tarp, warm sleeping bag, waterproof matches, bug spray, clothes for all weather, fishing licence and proof of reservation. Collect firewood along the way to the campground in late summer. Campsites have bear lockers and tent pads. Leashed dogs allowed; toilets are open-air but private.

TOUR COMPANIES: None

INTERESTING FACT: Henry McLeod was the first European to see Maligne Lake while scouting routes for the Canadian Pacific Railway in 1875. The trail at Coronet Creek Campground is named after him.

Backpacking
The Skyline Trail
in Jasper National Park

□ ■ □ □

Backpacking the Skyline Trail in Jasper National Park rewards you with incomparable mountain views for almost two-thirds of its 44 km (27 mi) length. It's a world-class trail that ranks up there with the best of them in Canada. That said, the season for hiking it is short. Don't even think of booking campsites until mid- to late July, after the snow has disappeared from the Notch. By the end of September, the season is over.

A successful hike on this trail also requires a little bit of luck with regards to the weather. Because so much of the trail lies above the tree line, you are at the mercy of the wind and storms. The high ridges and passes are no place to be caught in an electrical storm. Snowstorms can happen at any time of the year too.

Elevation gain over the length of the trail is 1,205 m (3,953 ft), a tolerable amount of climbing over two to three days and easier than many of the other backpacking trips in this book. There is the option to start at the Signal Mountain Trailhead and make the hike harder by adding 530 m (1,738 ft) of elevation gain, but who wants to do that?

Hikers must climb three mountain passes: Little Shovel Pass, Big Shovel Pass and the Notch. The climb to Little Shovel Pass begins after Evelyn Creek. A series of switchbacks delivers you to the tree line in no time. On the other side of the pass is Snowbowl Campground, a good place to aim for on your first night out. Big Shovel Pass begins shortly after leaving the campsite. Views of Curator Basin from this pass are superb. It is from here that you can see the Notch — the wall at the far end of the basin. The Notch is the highest point of the trail and the crux, as it holds onto snow even into August.

Kilometres of ridge-walking come after the Notch. They are by far the most exposed section of the trail, but also the most glorious for views. Cross your fingers that the weather gods are on your side.

Tekarra Campground is a good place for your second night out. Except for one gradual climb out of the campsite, it's largely downhill from the ridge top. The trail ends on a low note with an 8.5 km (5.3 mi) mostly viewless descent on a fire road back to the trailhead. Fortunately, you can dispatch it in just a few hours.

The Skyline Trail provides a superlative mountain experience on a trail that delivers expansive scenery for the majority of its length.

HIGHLIGHTS: Hiking above the tree line for 30 km (19 mi), mountain vistas, meadows, wildflowers, caribou, grizzly and black bears

DISTANCE: 44 km (27 mi), elevation gain of 1,205 m (3,953 ft) and a loss of 1,735 m (5,692 ft)

TIME NEEDED: 2–4 days

GRADE: Moderate

WHERE: Signal Mountain Trailhead is 9.4 km (5.8 mi) from downtown Jasper on an unmarked road off the Maligne Lake Road. If parking lot is full, drive another 0.8 km (0.5 mi) to Maligne Canyon parking lot. The shuttle picks up there too. Maligne Lake is an hour's drive from Jasper.

HOW: Reserve by calling 1-780-852-6177 three months ahead of start date.

WHEN: Mid-July to late September

COST: $9.80 pp/night for a backcountry campsite, $9.80 pp/day national parks entrance fee, $11.70 reservation fee

DON'T FORGET: Book a seat on the Maligne Lake shuttle from Signal Mountain parking lot if you want to leave your vehicle at the end of the hike. Bus leaves at 9:00 a.m. for the Maligne Lake Trailhead and costs $25 pp. No dogs because of the caribou. No open fires, stoves only. Bring bear spray and bug dope.

OPTIONS: Stay at Shovel Pass Lodge half-way along the trail if you'd prefer not to carry a heavy backpack. The 13 km (8 mi) Watchtower Trail provides an escape from the Skyline Trail if weather turns.

TOUR COMPANIES: Snowy Mountain Alpine Tours, Canadian Skyline Adventures

INTERESTING FACT: The mountains along the Skyline Trail were completely covered in ice during the last ice age, hence their more rounded appearance.

Walking the trails of
Dinosaur Provincial Park
in eastern Alberta

■□□□

Dinosaur Provincial Park, a UNESCO World Heritage Site, contains more complete dinosaur skeletons than any other place in the world. About thirty-five species of dinosaurs have been found, in addition to fossils of turtles, fish, lizards and flying reptiles. Once you know what you're looking for, it isn't hard to find dinosaur bones, some of which date back seventy-five million years.

And that's all great, if you love dinosaurs.

Let me be clear, though: I am not a dinosaur fan. I don't know my Leptoceratops from my Stegosaurus, but that didn't stop me from enjoying several hikes in the park, particularly the guided Centrosaurus Quarry Hike. The reasons: the impressive badlands scenery and the fact that the guides are able to bring the dinosaurs to life. I joined a group, which I am normally loathe to do, because it's the only way to get access to the off-limits section of the park. The actual hike itself is easy, though I can't imagine it would be too much fun on a hot day. Our guide told me they cancel the hikes when the temperature gets above 34°C. And if it rains a lot, the bentonite clay underfoot becomes as slick as dinosaur snot — the guide's words, not mine.

To begin, you are shuttled out to the start of the trail, which is included in the price of your ticket. It's an out-and-back hike through a fabulous country of wildly eroded buttes and hills in a variety of colours from soft yellow to buff, cream, red, grey and black. There is little elevation gain or loss.

On the hike towards the quarry, you stop frequently as the guide offers clues as to why there have been hundreds of dinosaur skeletons discovered in such a relatively small area. It's not until you come to the end of the hike that you get the full picture . . . and the pièce de résistance, a well-preserved dinosaur skeleton. Then you are left with some time to wander and explore on your own at the end of the trail, which will be appreciated by any photographers in the group.

Although this is one of the easier adventures in the book, it's altogether different from anything else. The landscape is unique, exceptionally beautiful and harsh all at once. Even if you're like me and care little about dinosaurs, it's hard not to fall in love with this land.

HIGHLIGHTS: Dinosaur bones, badlands, UNESCO site

DISTANCE: The quarry hike is 2–3 km (1.2–1.9 mi) return. Add another 5 km (3.1 mi) if you do the interpretive hikes.

TIME NEEDED: Minimum of a half day, a full day to explore the park in depth. Allow an hour for the Visitor Centre.

GRADE: Easy and family-friendly

WHERE: The park is 48 km (30 mi) northeast of Brooks and 225 km (140 mi) east of Calgary.

HOW: Reserve by phoning 1-403-378-4344 or book online at **albertaparks.ca**.

WHEN: Mid-May to mid-October if you want to do the guided Centrosaurus Quarry Hike.

COST: $15/adult and $8/youth

DON'T FORGET: Dress for summer heat, bring lots of water and watch for prairie rattlesnakes. Keep your hands away from holes and crevices, which may house black widow spiders and scorpions. Dogs are allowed on interpretive trails but not on the Quarry hike.

OPTIONS: Book the Great Badlands hike through **albertaparks.ca**. Tours run from end of June to end of August. They showcase beautiful and desolate sections of the park which are otherwise inaccessible.

TOUR COMPANIES: All hikes on interpretive trails are with Alberta Parks people, even if organized by another company.

INTERESTING FACT: Located in the warmest and driest sub-region of Alberta, the park boasts the largest badlands in Canada.

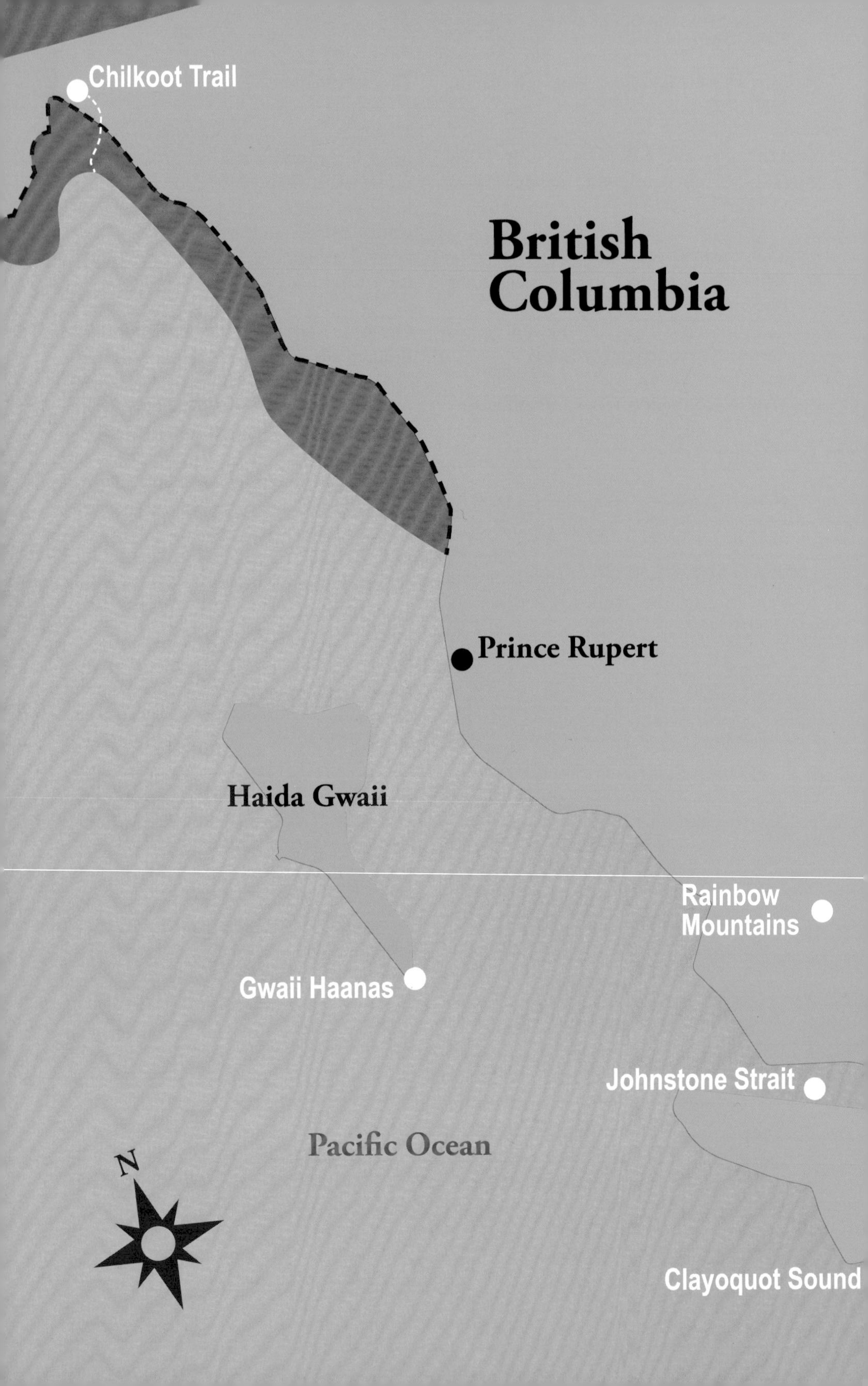

Chilkoot Trail

British Columbia

Prince Rupert

Haida Gwaii

Rainbow
Mountains

Gwaii Haanas

Johnstone Strait

Pacific Ocean

N

Clayoquot Sound

British Columbia Adventures

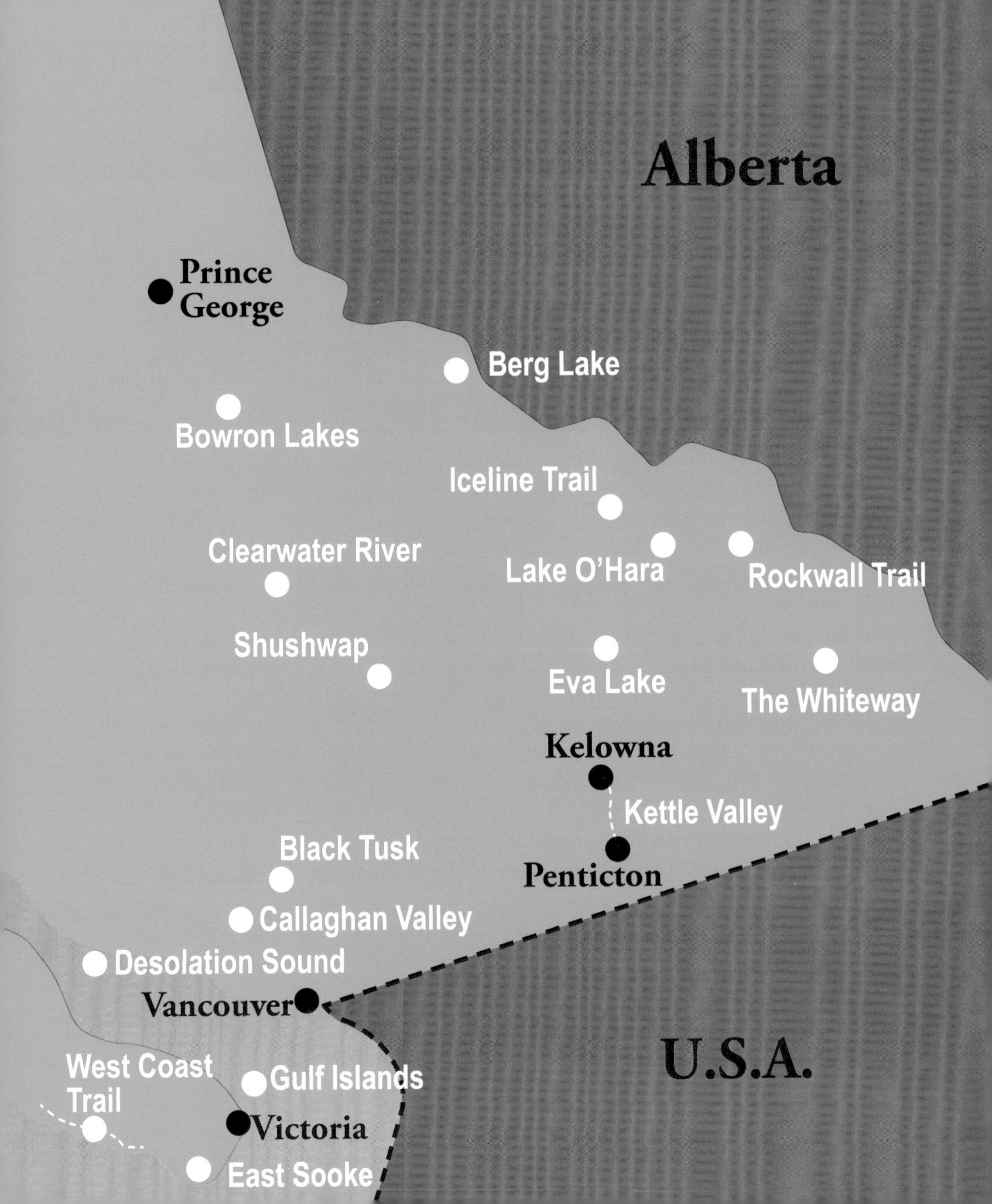

Alberta

● Prince George

○ Berg Lake

○ Bowron Lakes

○ Iceline Trail

○ Clearwater River

○ Lake O'Hara

○ Rockwall Trail

○ Shushwap

○ Eva Lake

○ The Whiteway

● Kelowna

Kettle Valley

○ Black Tusk

● Penticton

○ Callaghan Valley

○ Desolation Sound

● Vancouver

U.S.A.

West Coast Trail

○ Gulf Islands

● Victoria

○ East Sooke

Hiking
The Coast Trail
in East Sooke Regional Park

□□■□

The best outdoor scenery is usually reserved for backpackers, mountains climbers and people who have earned the chance to see it by schlepping big packs for many days. But not everyone has that kind of stamina or time. Enter the Coast Trail in East Sooke Regional Park, only forty-five minutes from downtown Victoria.

The hike along the Coast Trail is a standout from start to finish. Spectacular coastal scenery alternates with a temperate rainforest of massive, moss-hung cedars and firs. Throw in pocket beaches, tide pools, views of the Olympic Mountains, windswept pines and red-barked arbutus trees and you'll quickly understand the appeal of this hike.

It's not easy though; the 10 km (6 mi) hike takes a solid five hours. The trail moves back and forth between shaded valleys and narrow cliff-side paths. Other than the walk in and out of the parking lot at the northern trailhead, it's nothing but continuous ups and downs. And in wet weather, it can be slick.

Transportation to and from the trail will need some planning. A car shuttle or a drop-off is ideal because that way you'll only need to hike one way. Otherwise, count on a brutal 10+ hour day.

You can start at either Pike Road at the northern end of the trail or Aylard Farm at the southern end. Also consider doing a loop beginning and ending at Aylard Farm by taking the interior trail out to Cabin Point and returning to the parking lot via the Coastal Trail. Don't worry about finding your way. Signage is excellent with an easy-to-understand map at every intersection. The loop hike, at less than 10 km (6 mi), will take you three to four hours.

You can do this hike at any time of the year, but it's particularly lovely in spring when the wildflowers emerge. Avoid the trail during wind storms when groaning trees will unnerve you, or worse, topple over. It's a dog-friendly trail, but you can't camp overnight. Petroglyph seekers should check out the rocks at Aldridge Point along the coast.

If you only have a day to hike on the west coast of Vancouver Island, then this is the trail to do.

HIGHLIGHTS: Rugged coastal scenery, pocket beaches, tide pools, mossy rainforest, wild flowers, sea life

DISTANCE: 10 km (6 mi) one way

TIME NEEDED: Five to six hours to do the full trail with stops for beachcombing

GRADE: Difficult

WHERE: East Sooke Regional Park, 45 minutes from Victoria via Highway 14 and Gillespie Road

GETTING THERE: Drive two cars and park one car at either trailhead for a loop walk; or take BC Transit Bus #64 (Monday to Friday only) from 17 Mile House to East Sooke Road. There is a bus stop close to the Anderson Cove entrance which links to trails to the coast.

HOW: No special requirements, but visit **eastsookepark.com** to download a map

WHEN: Year round, though it tends to be rainy from November to March. Avoid hiking on very windy days. Park open from sunrise to sunset.

COST: Free

DON'T FORGET: It's always windy so dress appropriately. Cellphones work, but be mindful — you're close to the border so you may end up paying US roaming charges

OPTIONS: Do a circular route so you don't need to leave a car at either end. Aylard Farm to Cabin Point and back via the coastal trail would make a good hike.

TOUR COMPANIES: None

INTERESTING FACT: Every fall from mid-September until late October, various species of hawks gather in the park before flying across the Juan de Fuca Strait to Washington's Olympic National Park.

Backpacking
The West Coast Trail
in Pacific Rim National Park Reserve

The West Coast Trail is a physically demanding 75 km (47 mi) hike stretching along the west coast of Vancouver Island. Up to eight thousand people hike the trail annually. Don't go expecting solitude unless it's the shoulder season. Instead, enjoy the camaraderie you're likely to encounter. You can compare blisters.

Many factors will influence your enjoyment of this trail. Your physical condition and the weight of your pack are factors you can control; the weather you cannot. Do plan for rain, though; this is a temperate rainforest, after all. Sunshine is a bonus.

Before the hike you'll need to figure out which end to start at, how to get back to your start point and whether you're fit enough. Once these questions have been answered, you're off and running.

The trail offers a lot of variety: hike along root-covered trails, climb up and down endless ladders, hop into a cable car and pull yourself over roaring rivers, meander along sandy sections of beaches, curse the giant boulders and be cautious walking the slick, green, poorly maintained boardwalk sections. If it's a rainy year, be forewarned that mud can be knee-deep in places.

Highlights include the beautiful Carmanah Point and Pachena Point lighthouses, the section in and around Hole in the Wall and Tsusiat Falls, and the expansive views from Valencia Bluffs.

At the end of each and every day, deposit yourself on a gorgeous beach and absorb the endless ocean views. Take off your boots and marvel at the magic of the trail.

For my complete guide to the West Coast Trail visit http://bit.ly/1shci5g.

HIGHLIGHTS: Beautiful campsites, waterfalls, unspoiled beaches, fresh crab

DISTANCE: 75 km (47 mi) one way

TIME NEEDED: 6–8 days depending on fitness level

GRADE: Difficult

WHERE: Start at Port Renfrew, 110 km (68 mi) northwest of Victoria, or at Bamfield on the west coast of Vancouver Island.

GETTING THERE: Drive a car to the trailhead and leave it there, returning by bus or the Juan de Fuca Express boat. Reserve seat on **trailbus.com** for getting to the trailhead or back to your vehicle.

HOW: Reserve by phone from April 17 — for June 15 to September 15. From Canada or US, call 1-866-727-5722; international 1-250-726-4453. Online reservations at **reservation.pc.gc.ca**

WHEN: May 1 to September 30; trail closed October 1 to April 30

COST: $127.50 pp to hike; $24.50 pp for reservation, but 10 walk-ons per day allowed (5 at either end of the trail); $30 pp cash for boat ferry

DON'T FORGET: Mandatory safety talk before embarking. The last Gordon River boat crossing is at 4:00 p.m. Bring gaiters, hiking poles, tide charts, waterproof matches, bear spray, cash for fresh crab at Nitinat Narrows, insect repellent.

OPTIONS: It's easier hiking the first day out from Bamfield than from Port Renfrew.

TOUR COMPANIES: Sea to Sky Expeditions, BikeHike Adventures

INTERESTING FACT: The West Coast Trail started as the Dominion Lifesaving Trail. It was built in 1907 to facilitate rescue of shipwreck survivors since the coastline running parallel to the trail is part of the treacherous Graveyard of the Pacific.

Kayaking
Clayoquot Sound
on the west coast of Vancouver Island

◻ ◼ ◼ ◻

Clayoquot Sound, on the remote west coast of Vancouver Island, is a remarkable spot for a kayaking trip. It's ruggedly beautiful with classic west coast mountain and ocean scenery, plus a number of stunning white sand beaches. It's also the site of one of the world's largest temperate rainforests, as well as the traditional home of the Ahousaht, Hesquiaht and Tla-o-qui-aht First Nations people.

There are a number of ways you can explore Clayoquot Sound, depending on how much time you have and what kind of kayaking skills you possess. If you only have a day, plan to paddle to Meares Island to marvel at some of the oldest and biggest trees in British Columbia. Do it on your own, or with a guided group if you are new to paddling. Boat and seaplane traffic, as well as currents, can be challenging in Tofino's harbour. Once you've kayaked to the trailhead, it's a 3 km (2 mi) round-trip hike through the forest on a boardwalk to the famous Hanging Garden Tree, a western red cedar with a massive 18.3 m (60 ft) circumference.

If you have three days, a circumnavigation of Meares Island is possible. Or you can head to Milties Beach on Vargas Island and set up camp for a few days. From there, walk across the island and enjoy the spectacular beach and the wildness of the area, without any of the risks of a surf landing.

The best trip, though, providing you have at least five days, is to head to Hot Springs Cove. There are two ways to do this trip: either paddle on the mostly calm backside of Vargas and Flores Islands so as to avoid heavy swell and surf landings, or paddle the very beautiful outer coast. The outer coast does require excellent kayaking skills, however, and it's not for the faint of heart. Don't attempt it if the seas are above 2 m (6.5 ft) or the wind is blowing more than fifteen knots; definitely don't do it if it's getting dark or it's foggy. There are not many safe landing spots.

As a staging area for Hot Springs Cove, aim for beautiful Halfmoon Beach on the northwest side of Flores Island. It's a great place to set up camp for a few days. From there, it takes about an hour to paddle to the hot springs. Bring money for coffee and baked goods at the government wharf, and a towel and bathing suit for the hot springs. From the wharf, it's a 2 km (1.2 mi) walk along a most interesting boardwalk inscribed with the names of visitors, both boats and people. Enjoy a long soak before retracing your steps.

Clayoquot Sound is the sort of place that will call you back repeatedly over your lifetime.

HIGHLIGHTS: Deserted sandy beaches, possible gray whale and sea lion sightings, abundant bird life, Maquinna Marine Provincial Park hot springs, mountains, coastal temperate rainforest

DISTANCE: Varies. Study marine charts to plan your route.

TIME NEEDED: Day trips are good, but 5–7 days even better.

GRADE: Moderate to difficult, depending on whether you paddle the inside passage or the exposed coast. Paddling against the current or in big swells increases the level of difficulty.

WHERE: Begin in Tofino on Vancouver Island. Tofino is 315 km (196 mi) north-west of Victoria, and 200 km (124 mi) west of Nanaimo via Highway 4.

HOW: A self-guided trip is easy to do if you have the paddling and navigation skills; otherwise, join a tour.

WHEN: May to early October

COST: Sea kayak rental in Tofino, free camping, $3 for hot springs

DON'T FORGET: Exercise caution around heavy boat and seaplane traffic in Tofino harbour. Bears are common on the mainland. Do not land on Indian Reserve land (marked IR on charts) without permission from the band office.

OPTIONS: Set up a base camp on Flores Island and do day trips out from there.

TOUR COMPANIES: Tofino Sea Kayaking, Paddle West Kayaking, Majestic Ocean Kayaking, Black Bear Kayaking

INTERESTING FACT: In 1993, Clayoquot Sound was the site of the largest-ever act of civil disobedience in Canada. Ten thousand protesters journeyed to the Peace Camp from both Europe and North America to save the giant trees of Clayoquot Sound.

Kayaking in
Gwaii Haanas National Park
in Haida Gwaii

□■■□

Be prepared to be wowed by a visit to Gwaii Haanas National Park. Located at the southern tip of Haida Gwaii in British Columbia, the park offers intermediate to advanced paddlers the chance to explore the world the Haida people have lived in for over twelve thousand years. Experience the gorgeous sand beaches and dense rainforests of the west coast, incomparable marine life and First Nations culture.

One of the most popular kayaking routes in the park takes you from Rose Harbour to Burnaby Narrows, or vice versa, with a stop at the former nineteenth-century Haida village of SGang Gwaay. At this UNESCO World Heritage Site, you will see the beams and posts of long-ago Haida longhouses and the weathered remains of totem poles, both standing and fallen. A tour with one of the Haida Watchmen is a must.

Getting to Rose Harbour via a shuttle with Moresby Explorers takes three to four hours, so don't count on much paddling the first day. Rose Harbour is an abandoned whaling station, named for the way the blood of butchered whales once reddened the waters of the bay. Now, it's a beautiful spot with only remnants of rusted whaling equipment lying in the long grass. Consider camping nearby, because this part of the rainforest offers soft, thick moss that makes for very comfortable sleeping. I also recommend making reservations for a dinner prepared by Susan Cohen in her home next door to the Rose Harbour Guest House. And if you're a risk-taker, be sure to try out her giant swing in the back.

From Rose Harbour, most people head west to SGang Gwaay. It requires an open-water crossing, so assess the weather before you commit. Allow at least three hours on the island as there's plenty to see and lots of history to absorb. From there, paddle over to Gordon Island for an example of the exposed west coast. Always be alert for whales and sea lions; I had the memorable experience of suddenly finding a humpback whale swimming under my kayak. Continuing north, you must paddle a short section of Hecate Strait, which boasts some of the most dangerous waters on the planet. Proceed with caution and be prepared to pull in and wait for better paddling conditions. Head west once you reach Skincuttle Inlet. The waters are noticeably calmer once you get here. The Burnaby Narrows are next. Ideally, you will want to time your float through this section with a very low tide. The constant flushing of nutrients has created the richest intertidal life in the world — something you can only appreciate from your kayak, as walking would crush unique and rare organisms found nowhere else on the planet.

Haida Gwaii is recommended by National Geographic as a place to visit in 2015. I couldn't agree more.

HIGHLIGHTS: Whales, sea lions, seabirds, world's richest intertidal life, SGang Gwaay, Haida Watchmen tour

DISTANCE: Varies, depending on the winds and weather

TIME NEEDED: At least a week

GRADE: Moderate to difficult, depending on wind and waves

WHERE: Start in Sandspit on Haida Gwaii. Fly from Vancouver or ferry from Port Hardy to Skidegate.

HOW: The park has a quota system, so reserve dates by calling the Gwaii Hanaas office. Mandatory orientation at 9:00 a.m., Monday to Friday (and Saturdays in summer). If self-guided, arrange boat shuttle and kayak rentals from Sandspit with Moresby Explorers.

WHEN: Early April to late September. July and August have the best weather.

COST: Tours start at $1,800/week. For self-guided trip, budget for park entrance of $19.60 pp/day. Shuttle is $205 pp to Burnaby Narrows, $250 pp Rose Harbour; $270/week for single kayak rental, $380/wk/double

DON'T FORGET: Water-resistant tent, quick-dry clothing, kayaking gloves, sun hat, lip protection, extra food, water filter

OPTIONS: Paddle around Burnaby and Lyell Islands, or other First Nations sites of Tanu, Skedans, Windy Bay and Hot-springs Island.

TOUR COMPANIES: Green Coast Kayaking, Ocean Sound Kayaking, Tofino Expeditions, Kingfisher Wilderness Adventures

INTERESTING FACT: Haida Gwaii is on the Queen Charlotte Fault and has had over 15 earthquakes registering more than 5.0 on the Richter Scale.

Backpacking
The Chilkoot Trail
on the Alaska–British Columbia border

□ □ ■ □

The historic Chilkoot Trail offers a unique backpacking opportunity on the gold rush trail of the late 1800s. It begins on tidewater in Dyea, Alaska and climbs up over the Chilkoot Pass at the United States–Canada border and then down into a barren but very beautiful landscape. Hiking over the next few days takes you through forests, over a pass and along a series of lakes to reach the end of the trail in Bennett, British Columbia. From here you can take the White Pass and Yukon Route Railroad. An alternative allows you to bypass Bennett and hike out at the end on a cutoff trail to Log Cabin on the Klondike Highway, where you can catch a pre-arranged bus back to Whitehorse or Skagway.

The Chilkoot Trail is short but don't let the distance mislead you. There are challenging sections, initially with mud and tree roots to trip you, giving way to boulder scrambling especially on the day over the Chilkoot Pass. Snow is always a possibility especially early in the season, and you can count on a snowfield on the Canadian side of the pass even in the height of the summer. The area is also renowned for its cold rain so there's a very real possibility of hypothermia. Look out for bears, too — both black and grizzly. It's imperative to put your food in bear-safe caches or hang it from the poles.

Don't overestimate your hiking ability, particularly because you'll be carrying a heavy backpack for the better part of a week. This is important because you must pre-book each campsite along the way. There are nine in total, as follows with distances from the trailhead: Finnegan's Point (7.9 km/4.9 mi), Canyon City (12.5 km/7.8 mi), Pleasant Camp (16.9 km/10.5 mi), Sheep Camp (20.9 km/13 mi), Happy Camp (33.0 km/20.5 mi), Deep Lake (37 km/23 mi), Lindeman City (41.8 kms/26 mi), Bare Loon Lake (46.7 km/29 mi) and Bennett (53.1 km/33 mi). Keep in mind that Sheep Camp gets very busy and fills quickly because it's the last one before the pass.

To get to the Chilkoot Trail, fly into Whitehorse or Skagway. There is a bus from Whitehorse to Skagway and it's easy to get a taxi to the trailhead once you're in Skagway. (Buy a bus ticket online at **yukonalaskatouristtours.com**)

If you plan to exit the trail via the train from Bennett make sure your exit day corresponds to the train schedule. Visit **wpyr.com** for more information.

If you are prepared, then you're likely to have a great time. It's a memorable trail, not only for the scenery and history but for all the people you meet along the way.

HIGHLIGHTS: Klondike history, lakes, picturesque campsites, international border, wildlife, historic train ride

DISTANCE: 53 km (33 mi) one way. The high point is at Chilkoot Pass at 1067 m (3,057 ft)

TIME NEEDED: 3–6 days

GRADE: Difficult

WHERE: Dyea Trailhead just outside of Skagway, Alaska, located 176 km (109 mi) south of Whitehorse

HOW: Unless on a tour, book campsite from early January by phone 1-800-661-0486, Monday to Friday, 8 a.m. to 4 p.m. PST. Know what campsites you want before calling. Only 50 hikers/day are allowed to cross the pass. For more info, search Chilkoot Trail on **www.pc.gc.ca**.

WHEN: July and August are best. In June, trails could still be snow-covered.

COST: Chilkoot Trail permit $50.30 pp; campsite $9.70/tent/night plus $11.70 pp reservation fee; $9.80 pp/day parks fee in Canada

DON'T FORGET: One-hour time difference between Whitehorse and Skagway. Buy bear spray in Whitehorse or Skagway, and bring hiking poles, insect repellent, head net, toilet paper, waterproof map, permits, passport and visa, money, 8 m (25 ft) of rope and carabiner plus bag to hang food.

TOUR COMPANIES: Cabin Fever Adventures, Nature Tours of Yukon, Packer Expeditions

INTERESTING FACT: In 1897, a horse-powered tramway was built to haul loads up the final 183 m (600 ft) to the pass. The cost was 1¢ per pound to use it!

Hiking
The Rainbow Mountains
in Tweedsmuir Provincial Park

☐ ■ ☐ ☐

The relatively unexplored Tweedsmuir (South) Provincial Park offers isolated wilderness on a grand scale. It's famous for Hunlen Falls (one of Canada's highest waterfalls), the Turner Lake Chain favoured by canoeists, fabulous salmon fishing and the eye-catching mountains that make up the Rainbow Range. This hike features numerous small lakes and brimming tarns. On a summer's day, the combination of wildflower-filled meadows, deep blue mountain lakes and the multicoloured Rainbow Mountains is enough to take your breath away. Wildlife flourishes, including mountain goats, moose, deer, wolves, cougars and coyotes. The area also has one of the highest concentrations of grizzly and black bears in the world. This world-class hike is not for everyone. Although only moderately difficult, this is true wilderness. Plan to be self-sufficient and bear aware. Help is far away.

The trailhead for the Rainbow Range is easy to find. Signage just west of Heckman Pass directs you to a parking lot to the north of the highway. Three trails start from here: the Rainbow Range, Octopus and Crystal Lake Trails. Stick with the trail to the Rainbow Range. The other two take you to the intersection with the Alexander Mackenzie Heritage Trail, a 420 km (261 mi) overland route between Bella Coola and Quesnel. Also known as the Grease Trail because fish oil was once carried along it into the interior, much of this trail is in poor shape. But for the adventurous, it's a historical route through pine forests and meadows, all against a stunning backdrop.

For the Rainbow Mountains, signs will advise you to angle north and begin a gentle one-hour climb through a 2009 burn where great swaths of pink fireweed and yellow arnica now thrive against a dramatic blackened background. After that, you're only about fifteen minutes away from the high alpine and the start of some seriously amazing mountain scenery. As you climb, turn around periodically to check out the views of the Coast Mountains in the distance.

Cairns point the way when the trail starts to die out. After 8 km (5 mi), you'll find yourself looking down on an unnamed lake with the sweep of the Rainbow Mountains beyond. For some, this is a good turn-around spot, having had a taste of what the Rainbow Range is all about. But if you have time, continue following cairns and see where they take you; just keep your bearings straight.

The hike can be done comfortably in five hours, but it's worth going slowly to take in the peace and beauty of the area. Overnighting in the high alpine is even better. Bear-proof boxes can be found by a small lake on the trail to the big unnamed lake. It would make a perfect base camp for a few days of exploration. Be prepared to be gobsmacked by the Rainbow Range.

HIGHLIGHTS: Rainbow coloured mountains, beautiful alpine lakes and tarns, wildflowers, big vistas, solitude, wildlife

DISTANCE: 8 km (5 mi) each way (with a 300 m/984 ft elevation gain), but once you're in the high alpine, you could hike for days on unmarked trails.

TIME NEEDED: 5–6 hours at a minimum

GRADE: Moderate

WHERE: The Rainbow Range is located in central BC, approximately 354 km (220 mi) west of Williams Lake and 872 km (542 mi) north of Vancouver.

GETTING THERE: The well-signed trailhead is on the north side of Highway 20 shortly after you enter Tweedsmuir Provincial Park. It's 35 km (22 mi) from Anahim Lake.

HOW: No permits are needed but do let someone know of your plans.

WHEN: July to mid-September; if you're planning a longer multi-day hike, late summer is best when water levels are lower.

COST: Free

DON'T FORGET: Bear spray, bear bangers, first aid kit, insect repellent

TOUR COMPANIES: Rainbow Mountain Outfitting (hiking and horseback riding), Kynoch West Coast Adventures

INTERESTING FACT: All the extraordinary colours that you see in the Rainbow Range are caused by minerals involved in the volcanic formation of the mountains.

Canoeing
The Bowron Lakes Circuit
in Bowron Lake Provincial Park

□ ■ ■ □

Outside Magazine calls British Columbia's beautiful Bowron Lakes Circuit in the Cariboo Mountains one of the world's Top Ten Canoe Trips. The 110 km (72 mi) Bowron Lakes Circuit involves six major lakes and two rivers linked by numerous portages, and is typically paddled over six to ten days. A canoe cart is highly recommended to make the portages tolerable.

The circuit opens on May 15 and remains open until September 30. Visit in May, June or September for solitude, but even in the height of the summer, chances are you'll have most of the campsites to yourself. Every day a total of twenty-one canoes or kayaks are permitted to start. In total, roughly 3,500 adventurers paddle the circuit every year. Reservations can be made up to two days beforehand and four spaces are held every day for walk-ons on a first-come first-served basis.

The weather is notoriously unpredictable: rain, wind and thunderstorms are common, and it can snow at any time of the year. Hypothermia is a real risk. Bowron Lake Provincial Park publishes a downloadable pre-trip booklet with a list of essential items. Don't leave home without them. Also, bring clothing for four seasons and a few days' extra food in case of emergency. Wind can keep you shorebound for a day or two.

The route itself is easy to follow, but before you paddle your first stroke you must deal with the longest of the seven portages: a 2.4 km (1.5 mi) tramp through the woods to the shores of the diminutive Kibbee Lake. This is great moose country, so paddle quietly across to the next portage, an uphill hike that takes you to Indian Point Lake, the destination of many for the first night. Be prepared to share one of the six campsites that are spread along its shoreline. The next portage takes you to Isaac Lake, the longest of the lakes. Stay close to shore, as winds can blow up quickly here. Exit Isaac Lake via the chute. Experienced paddlers can run it and save themselves 1.6 km (1 mi) of portaging, but the lower half of the Isaac River must be portaged. McLeary Lake and the fast-flowing Upper Cariboo River are next. Look out for sweepers and deadheads. You end up in Lanezi Lake, a murky greenish lake with few campsites. Camp on Sandy Lake instead. From there, two short portages deposit you on the shores of Spectacle Lake, and then it's a lovely meandering paddle through Bowron Slough and down the length of Bowron Lake to the finish.

Stunning mountain vistas, clear lakes, wildlife and solitude make this a first-class experience. This is one canoe trip that paddlers return to year after year.

HIGHLIGHTS: Wildlife including moose, bear and deer; swimming, mountain vistas, solitude

DISTANCE: The total distance is 116.4 km (72.3 mi) including 14 km (8.7 mi) of river paddling and 10.4 km (6.5 mi) of portages.

TIME NEEDED: 6–10 days for the full circuit, 1–3 days to paddle the lakes on the park's west side. The maximum time allowed on the circuit is 14 days.

GRADE: Moderate if you use a cart; difficult otherwise

WHERE: The circuit is in Bowron Lake Provincial Park in central British Columbia, about 120 km (75 mi) east of the city of Quesnel. Driving time from Vancouver is approximately 9 hours.

HOW: Reservations can be made on the Discover Camping website beginning January 2. Book a required orientation when you make your reservation. You can book with a live person but that will cost you $5 more. Phone: 1-800-689-9025 or 1-519-826-6850.

WHEN: Registration is required between May 15 and September 30.

COST: $60 pp to paddle the circuit, $30 pp to paddle the west side; $18/vessel reservation fee

DON'T FORGET: Bear spray, binoculars, a fishing licence; do not bring commercially packaged beverage or glass containers.

OPTIONS: Paddle the west side of the park for a few hours or a few days.

TOUR COMPANIES/CANOE RENTALS: Bear River Mercantile, Bowron Lake Lodge, Pathways Tours, Whitegold Adventures

INTERESTING FACT: The record for completing the circuit is 11 hours.

Rafting
The Clearwater River
in Wells Gray Provincial Park

□ ■ □ □

Rafting the Clearwater River isn't an experience you're likely to forget. Even before you reach the first rapid, there's an extraordinary side trip awaiting you. Just across the river from the launch site is the trail to Moul Falls, which are 31 m (102 ft) high. But this pretty waterfall isn't simply for admiring; a walk behind it will leave you gasping. And if that isn't enough, you can wade through the pool at the bottom of the falls, which is like having continuous buckets of cold water dumped on your head — nothing short of exhilarating. But you don't have to take my word for it.

Then it's back to the river and onto the rafts. The Clearwater, the largest tributary of the North Thompson River, dishes out one gnarly set of rapids after another. With names like Shark's Tooth, Shane's Demise, Buckaroo and Sabretooth, you know you're going to be hit with not only giant waves but one adrenaline rush after another. When you do get a chance to finally catch your breath and your adrenaline levels have returned to baseline, look around. You're in Wells Gray Provincial Park for the entire ride — a pristine section of British Columbia's interior — and on one of the few rivers of this size still in its undammed natural state.

The biggest rapid of the day — Sabretooth, also the only Class IV rapid to run — is the first one you hit. It's a white-knuckle, heart-pounding kind of rapid, and you don't want to flip or you'll be swimming the next set of Class III rapids. Fortunately, it's a rare boat that flips.

By the time you reach the pull-out for lunch, you'll be ready for a breather. The afternoon begins with an agreeable — read: no chance of flipping — section of floating. That doesn't mean that there aren't kilometres of wild water! There are, but there's plenty of time to sit back and just admire the scenery. You do have to sidestep the raft around a Class VI rapid that even from shore looks menacing. A few people have tried it over the years, but none would attempt it again.

On the last few kilometres of the river, signs of civilization appear — first roads, then cottages. When you finally raft into town you'll be a short distance away from where you started your day. The Clearwater River rafting and hiking combination provides a remarkable experience. It's one of only a handful of rivers that really offer a true wilderness experience in just one day.

HIGHLIGHTS: Class III and Class IV whitewater, legendary rapids including Sabretooth (one of the biggest in British Columbia), pristine beauty of Wells Gray Provincial Park, Moul Falls, walking through and under waterfalls

DISTANCE: 8 km (5 mi) for the 3-hour trip, 25 km (15.5 mi) for the 1-day trip, and 37 km (23 mi) for the 2-day trip

TIME NEEDED: 1 day

GRADE: Moderate

WHERE: Meet in the town of Clearwater, 127 km (79 mi) north of Kamloops. All the rafting companies are located along a stretch of Old North Thompson Highway Road West, approximately 2 km (1.2 mi) west of the Highway 5 intersection.

HOW: Reserve ahead of time, especially for summer weekends. Minimum age is 12.

WHEN: Mid-May until the end of September or early October, depending on water levels and weather

COST: Approximately $169 pp plus tax and tip

DON'T FORGET: Bathing suit, and a towel for the bus

OPTIONS: Choose from half day, family-friendly options, or a 2-day trip

TOUR COMPANIES: Interior Whitewater Expeditions, Liquid Lifestyles, Riverside Adventures

INTERESTING FACT: The Clearwater River flows through Wells Gray Provincial Park for all but the last 5 km (3 mi).

Backpacking to
Berg Lake
in Mount Robson Provincial Park

□ □ ■ □

Are you looking for big, bold Rocky Mountain scenery, the kind that takes your breath away? The trail to Berg Lake offers just that. The backdrop — should you be lucky enough to see it, as it's often shrouded in mist or cloud — is Mount Robson, the highest mountain in the Canadian Rockies rising 3000 m (9,843 ft) above the valley floor. It's so big that it makes its own micro-climate, a good thing if you're keen to hike by mid-June as it's warmer than nearby Jasper.

Not only is Berg Lake a first-class destination, but the trail up to the lake offers an astounding variety of scenery. It starts gradually, climbing alongside the Robson River through a micro rainforest of hemlock and cedar. The year I did it was a wet one and large sections of the trail for the first few kilometres were underwater.

Kinney Lake is the first major landmark you reach and the location of the first of seven campsites. It's also the end of the trail should you be riding a bike. Next up is the fantastic Valley of a Thousand Falls, accessed via a very steep climb. Named waterfalls you pass include White Falls, Falls of the Pool and Emperor Falls. From Emperor Falls it's another 3 km (1.9 mi) to reach the shores of Berg Lake. Look for the Berg Glacier as you continue along the trail. Sometimes you might even see a recently calved iceberg. Look up too. The face of Mount Robson rises over 2,300 m (7,546 ft) above the lake.

Many people call it quits at the Berg Lake Campground since it's got a cabin for cooking indoors, a plus when you consider that the climate here is notoriously wetter than in either Banff or Jasper National Park. But if you want a taste of solitude continue to the Rearguard or Robson Pass Campgrounds, 1 and 2 km (0.6 and 1.2 mi) away respectively. Almost no one goes there.

Try to allot a few extra days in the Berg Lake area and use them to explore Snowbird Pass and/or do the Hargreaves Glacier/Mumm Basin Route. Both offer outstanding vistas and wonderful wildflowers in summer.

The Berg Lake Trail wins the popularity award for the Canadian Rockies. It sees more backpackers — almost 4,000 per year — and day hikers than any other trail in the Rockies. But don't be put off by this fact. There is a good reason so many people hike to Berg Lake: extraordinary scenery and an extraordinary experience.

HIGHLIGHTS: Mount Robson, Valley of a Thousand Falls, glaciers, wildflowers, marmots, black and grizzly bears, mountain caribou, whitetail and mule deer, grey wolves

DISTANCE: Gain of 800 m (2,625 ft) over 23 km (14.3 mi) to Robson Pass Campground, 21 km (13 mi) to Berg Lake

TIME NEEDED: Minimum 2 days; 5 if exploring Hargreaves Glacier or Snowbird Pass

GRADE: Difficult

WHERE: The trailhead is at Visitor Centre, 80 km (50 mi) west of Jasper, 320 km (199 mi) northeast of Kamloops

HOW: Get backcountry permit at Visitor Centre on Highway 16; reserve for summer on Discover Camping website from January 2, or call 1-800-689-9025.

WHEN: Mid-June to September

COST: Backcountry pass is $10 pp/night, $5 pp/night for under 16; reservation is $6 pp/night to a maximum of $18. Add $5 if reserving by phone. Reservations optional.

DON'T FORGET: Rain gear, pack cover, three-season sleeping bag

OPTIONS: From Berg Lake Campground, do the 21.2 km (13.2 mi) round trip to Snowbird Pass; or hike 1 km (0.6 mi) to Toboggan Falls; or do the 12 km (7.5 mi) Hargreaves/Mumm Basin Loop.

TOUR COMPANIES: Yamnuska Mountain Adventures, Discover West Canada

INTERESTING FACT: Mount Robson Provincial Park, a UNESCO World Heritage Site, offers 200 km (124 mi) of trails and hosts 182 species of birds, 43 species of mammals and 4 species of amphibians.

Hiking
The Iceline Trail
in Yoho National Park

□■□□

If you're looking for a moderate day hike in the Canadian Rockies that delivers high impact scenery within sixty minutes of hitting the trail, then the Iceline would be an excellent choice. The only downside is that it's a popular trail.

Superb views of not just Takakkaw Falls but the mountains and glaciers of the Yoho Valley will take your breath away. And if you're willing to climb 690 m (2,264 ft) to the high point on the trail — the amphitheatre at the base of Emerald Glacier — then your reward is expansive vistas of three peaks: the Vice President, Whaleback and Isolated Peaks.

The trail starts from the Takakkaw Falls parking lot and climbs steeply for about 400 m (1,300 ft) to reach the tree line. Although it continues to be steep at times, the sublime views should alleviate any pain you feel.

There are a lot of variations to this hike. You can do it as an out-and-back hike — and decide based on weather and energy just how far you want to go. To the highpoint and back is 12.8 km (8 mi).

Alternatively, try one of these scenarios:

- Do a full loop that takes you from the Iceline Trail down into the subalpine forest past the Stanley Mitchell Hut onto the Little Yoho Valley Trail but do it as a 20 km (12.4 mi) day hike. You'll enjoy the best views by doing this.

- Hike up the Yoho Valley Trail from the Takakkaw Trailhead to the Stanley Mitchell Hut and spend the night, or camp in Little Yoho Valley just a few hundred metres farther along. Allow a day to investigate the fabulous landscape around the President Range. The next day complete the loop via the Iceline Trail.

- Hike 5.7 km (3.5 mi) up the Iceline Trail to the junction with the 4.2 km (2.6 mi) Celeste Lake Trail. Stay on it until it intersects the Little Yoho Valley Trail to complete a shorter loop of 16 km (9.9 mi). On this loop you'll miss some of the wonderful scenery farther along the Iceline Trail. Consider the Celeste Lake Trail as an option in a storm because you drop back down into the trees.

No matter what option you choose, the Iceline will astound you with its picture-postcard scenery.

HIGHLIGHTS: Spectacular vistas of Yoho Valley, Emerald Glacier, Takkakaw Falls, glacier-fed streams

DISTANCE: 12.8–21.1 km (8–13 mi) with 690 m (2265 ft) elevation gain

TIME NEEDED: 5–8 hours as a day hike, or as part of a multi-day backpacking trip

GRADE: Moderate

WHERE: Yoho National Park Visitor Centre in Field is 58 km (36 mi) east of Golden. From Field the trailhead is 17 km (11 mi) north via the Yoho Valley Road accessed from the Trans-Canada Highway. From Alberta turn north 12.5 km (7.8 mi) past the BC–Alberta border.

WHEN: July to mid-September

HOW: Buy park day pass in Field, or on summer weekends on the access road going into Takakkaw Falls. Reserve Stanley Mitchell Hut 4 to 6 months ahead. Passes bought in Banff National Park work too.

COST: $9.80 pp/day for park pass, $9.80 pp/day for backcountry camping permit, $11.70 for camping reservation; Stanley Mitchell Hut $36/night or $25/night for Alpine Club of Canada members

DON'T FORGET: Dress in layers. For mountain and glacier views, hike this trail on a sunny day.

TOUR COMPANIES: REI Adventures and Yamnuska Mountain Adventures as part of multi-day trip

INTERESTING FACT: Takakkaw Falls is fed by the Daly Glacier so the water volume remains high all summer. The 384 m (1,260 ft) waterfall is the third-biggest in Canada.

Hiking the
Lake O'Hara Alpine Circuit
in Yoho National Park

□ □ ■ □

The Lake O'Hara Alpine Circuit is one extraordinary hike that over-delivers when it comes to mountain scenery. From start to finish, this soul-stirring hike will amaze and inspire you. There are few equal to it in Canada or anywhere else.

The alpine circuit connects seven trails to create a loop, which you can hike in any direction. It's good to know that numerous exit locations are there should bad weather arrive — high on a mountain is no place to be caught in a storm. Start the hike at Lake O'Hara. It begins with a stiff climb up to the Wiwaxy Gap, but that way you can dispatch with the worst of the day's elevation gain while your legs are fresh. The next hour will be a test of your ability to withstand trails which are, while wide enough to walk on and not technical (meaning they don't require climbing equipment), high and frightening. Mountaineers call these high, narrow sections of trail 'airy.' Slowly make your way down to Lake Oesa, but stop occasionally so that you can take in the sight of brilliant turquoise lakes, glaciers and rugged mountain peaks.

From Lake Oesa, it's an easier hike up to the Opabin Plateau via the Yukness Ledge Alpine Route. The narrow level paths crossing the face of the mountain are called ledges or shelves; they are far easier to negotiate than the descent from Wiwaxy Gap. But pay attention to the cairns (piled stones) that mark the way to the ledges, as it's a bit confusing through here. Once you reach the top, savour the spectacular views of Lake O'Hara.

At the beautiful hanging valley of Opabin Plateau, you have the option of returning to Lake O'Hara in less than an hour by either the East Opabin or West Opabin trails. Otherwise, continue until you reach Old Soul's, an arduous section of the trail often omitted on the circuit because it retains snow longer than the rest of the route. After a stiff climb, descend to Schaffer Lake and continue from there to Lake O'Hara over easy, well-marked trails.

The high alpine circuit is a truly outstanding hike, delivering gloriously unimpeded views of alpine scenery almost every step of the way.

HIGHLIGHTS: Alpine scenery, plateaus, turquoise lakes, ledges, wildflowers, yellow larches in fall

DISTANCE: A loop hike is 9.8–12.4 km (6.1–7.7 mi), with an elevation gain of 495 m (1,625 ft).

TIME NEEDED: 6–7 hours

GRADE: Difficult, with exposed ledges

WHERE: Turnoff for Lake O'Hara parking lot is 200 km (124 mi) west of Calgary and 21 km (13 mi) from Lake Louise off the Trans-Canada Highway, across the Alberta–BC border on the BC side. Catch the bus at the trailhead off the highway.

HOW: Reserve bus and camping 3 months ahead. Call 1-250-343-6433, have credit card ready and be flexible with your dates. Groups limited to 6 people and 2 campsites with 1 tent/campsite.

WHEN: July to late September for high alpine route. Access Lake O'Hara by bus from June 14 to September 30. Don't attempt circuit until snow melts in mid-July.

COST: $9.80/night camping fee, $14.70 pp for a return bus ride, $9.75 pp/one-way bus ride, $11.70 non-refundable reservation fee, $9.80/pp/day national park pass.

DON'T FORGET: Sturdy boots and clothes for all weather. Pick up map at Le Relais Day-Use Shelter where bus drops you off.

OPTIONS: Try the easy hike to Lake Oesa if an exposed high-alpine route isn't your thing.

TOUR COMPANIES: Great Divide Nature Interpretation

INTERESTING FACT: The high alpine route was beautifully designed by Italian stonemason, former coal miner, climbing guide and park warden at Lake O'Hara, Lawrence Grassi.

Backpacking
The Rockwall Trail
in Kootenay National Park

□ □ ■ □

The Rockwall Trail, located in Kootenay National Park, is one of the premier backpacking trips in the Canadian Rockies. This tough trip of steep ascents and knee-crunching descents is amply rewarded by the Rockwall, a limestone cliff 35 km (22 mi) long, and glorious Floe Lake, as well as wildflower-filled meadows, hanging glaciers, Helmet Falls and the ochre-coloured Paint Pots.

For this one-way hike, arrange a car shuttle beforehand or plan to hitchhike back to your car. Start from either the Floe Lake trailhead, which I recommend, or Marble Canyon, both of which are a 2.5 hour drive from Calgary. Begin the 10.7 km (6.7 mi) hike to Floe Lake by crossing the Vermillion River. The trail then heads up through a wildflower-filled burn created by a 2003 forest fire. A series of steep switchbacks follows, but the reward is a beautiful campsite at the base of the Rockwall, 697 m (2,286 ft) higher than the parking lot.

The next day, continue on the Numa Pass Trail to Numa Pass, the highest point on the Rockwall trail. From there it's a tough 830 m (2,722 ft) descent into Numa Creek Basin. Look for the Numa Creek Campground, 10.2 km (6.3 mi) from Floe Lake. (Note that access back to the highway is no longer possible from here or from the Tumbling Creek Trail at the next campsite.)

On the third day, hike 7.1 km (4.4 mi) to the Tumbling Creek Campground. Cross gorgeous Tumbling Pass at 4.8 km (3.0 mi), but make lots of noise through what writer Graeme Pole calls a "grizzly bear grocery store" because of its abundance of berries. Continue over rock and scree to a view of the Tumbling Glacier. Cross a lateral moraine and then descend steeply to Tumbling Creek and a campground.

Aim for the Helmet Falls Campground on the fourth day, 12.7 km (7.9 mi) away. After a steep climb you enter the beautiful subalpine meadows that make up the Wolverine Plateau. From there, hike over two passes and the Limestone Summit before descending to the campground. If you still feel energetic continue for another 8.4 km (5.2 mi) to the Tumbling/Ochre Junction Campground. Then, on the last day, it's only 5.2 km (3.2 mi) out past the Paint Pots to the trailhead by Marble Canyon.

Make lots of noise while hiking this trail. Bear activity is monitored by rangers, but you still need to use common sense and keep your tent free of food and fragrances. All the same, don't let the possibility of a bear sighting stop you from hiking the Rockwall Trail.

HIGHLIGHTS: Floe Lake, the sheer lime-stone cliffs of the Rockwall, Wolverine Plateau, Helmet Falls, Paint Pots, spectacular alpine views, wildlife

DISTANCE: 55 km (34 mi) one way with a total elevation gain of 2,260 m (7,415 ft) and a loss of 2,225 m (7,300 ft)

TIME NEEDED: 3–5 days

GRADE: Difficult

WHERE: The Floe Lake Trailhead is located 23 km (14 mi) south of the Kootenay–Banff National Park boundary just off Highway 93 on the southwest side. From Calgary it's around 200 km (124 mi) away.

HOW: Make a reservation up to 3 months beforehand by calling any Parks Canada Visitor Centre in the Rockies.

WHEN: July to late September

COST: $9.90 pp/night for a backcountry permit. You must also have a valid Park Pass displayed on your vehicle.

DON'T FORGET: Bear spray, bear bangers, water filter

OPTIONS: Hike a section of the trail from the Marble Canyon end.

TOUR COMPANIES: Canadian Rockies Hiking by Yamnuska, White Mountain Adventures

INTERESTING FACT: Helmet Falls is one of the highest waterfalls in the Canadian Rockies with an approximate fall of 352 m (1,155 ft).

Skating or cross-country skiing
The Whiteway
on Lake Windermere

■ ☐ ☐ ☐

Lake Windermere, which is in fact just a widening of the Columbia River, is located in the Columbia Valley between the Rocky Mountains to the east and the Purcell Mountains to the west. The lake is the winter home of the Whiteway, one of the newest additions to a cold-weather line-up of outdoor adventures in the Invermere area. The Whiteway is now a Guinness World Record holder, holding the title as the longest naturally frozen skating trail in the world with 29.8 km (18.5 mi) of cleared ice.

Every winter, once the lake freezes solidly enough to be safely walked upon, the Toby Creek Nordic Ski Club goes to work. A path of ice 6 m (20 ft) wide is cleared around the circumference of the lake. It started off several years ago as a 15 km (9 mi) loop, but has grown to include the whole lake and is now 31 km (19 mi) long. As the ice is cleared, snow is piled up on one side of the skating surface to form a base for skiing. Once there's enough snow, the club sets the track for cross-country skiing. There's also enough room for skate-skiers to use it.

For a family-friendly outing, you can't beat the Whiteway. On a sunny day, the view of the mountains from the lake is outstanding. Bring the dog (make sure you pick up after it), strap on some skis or lace up some skates and head out with the whole family for an hour or a day. You have the option to do shorter loops, or you can do an out-and-back and just go as far as you want. Hardcore skaters and skiers can knock off the loop in about two hours.

Mountain cycling is also permitted on the ice, but because of the wind chill, it's a good idea to bring extra face protection.

Of note is the fact that cars and trucks are permitted to drive on the lake, but they are forbidden from using the Whiteway.

HIGHLIGHTS: Beautiful Columbia Valley mountain scenery, family- and dog-friendly, great sense of community

DISTANCE: 29.8 km (18.5 mi)

TIME NEEDED: One hour up to a full day

GRADE: Easy

WHERE: There are three official entrances: at the Kinsmen Beach in Invermere; near the Invermere Bay Condos in Invermere; and at Windermere Beach. Invermere is located 275 km (171 mi) west of Calgary and 17 km (11 mi) south of Radium Hot Springs.

HOW: Bring your own mountain bike, skates, skate-skis or cross-country skis. You can rent skates or skis at the Inside Edge Sports Store in Invermere.

WHEN: The season varies from year to year. Typically, it runs from late December until early March. The Whiteway is not lit at night, but in theory it's open 24 hours a day.

COST: Non–Toby Creek Nordic Ski Club members are asked to pay a day-use fee of $5 pp. Donate online or put cash in secure donation boxes at information kiosks around the Whiteway.

DON'T FORGET: A potential risk is thin ice. Dress in layers as it can get windy on the lake. If you're planning to be out for a half day or more, take water and food, as there is nowhere to buy anything.

OPTIONS: There is excellent cross-country skiing at nearby Lake Lillian and at the Panorama Nordic Centre.

TOUR COMPANIES: None

INTERESTING FACT: Lake Windermere is shallow with an average depth of just 4.5 m (14.8 ft).

Hiking to
Eva Lake
in Mount Revelstoke National Park

□ ■ □ □

Access to the turquoise jewel of Eva Lake is via a trail located at the top end of the 26 km (16 mi) Meadows in the Sky Parkway. The road switchbacks sixteen times as it climbs Mount Revelstoke, gaining 1,600 m (5,249 ft) by the time it arrives at the parking lot by Balsam Lake. From there, you have the option of hopping on a shuttle, but it's nicer to walk the easy 1 km (0.6 mi) Upper Summit Trail through the beautiful subalpine tundra to the Eva Lake Trailhead.

The trail to Eva Lake changes character as you hike. Initially, it passes through a forest of subalpine fir, Englemann spruce and mountain hemlock, with intermittent views of the Columbia River thousands of feet below. The forest occasionally opens into wildflower-filled meadows; consider planning your hike for early to mid-August, when they're at their prettiest.

After you pass though the last of the meadows, you enter a world of rocks and boulders. You may be startled by the peeps of pikas and the whistles of the hoary marmots who make their home there. At the 5.4 km (3.4 mi) mark, the trail intersects with another one that heads off to Miller Lake. As it's only 0.4 km (0.2 mi) away, you can easily do it as a side trip. A few steps later, there's another intersection, this time to Jade Lake. Stay left, and in roughly fifteen minutes you'll arrive at the stunning Eva Lake. Every step of the trail around Eva Lake offers a different vista, and even though all are beautiful, you shouldn't miss the one across the Coursier Creek Valley. It's directly opposite the cabin on the far side of the lake. The 1928 cabin, just up from the lake, is now a federal heritage building. Inscribed with hundreds of names, it provides a refuge in a storm. You can camp overnight at the lake in one of the four backcountry campsites which are available on a first-come basis.

Eva Lake epitomizes the unique beauty of the subalpine landscape.

HIGHLIGHTS: Beautiful subalpine lake, wildflowers in season, mountain vistas

DISTANCE: 12 km (7.5 mi) return with a shuttle. Add another 2 km (1.2 mi) return if you don't take the shuttle. Elevation gain is 209 m (686 ft).

TIME NEEDED: 5–6 hours

GRADE: Moderate and family-friendly

WHERE: Start at the Meadows in the Sky Parkway, accessed from the Trans-Canada Highway just a few kilometres east of Revelstoke. Revelstoke is roughly halfway between Calgary and Vancouver.

HOW: Buy a park pass at the gate and get there early on a weekend or you'll have to park your car some distance away.

WHEN: Late June to late September

COST: $7.80/adult/day; a backcountry pass is $9.80/person/night.

DON'T FORGET: Bear spray. Bear-warning signs should be taken seriously, though on crowded weekends they are less of a concern. Dogs are not allowed on the shuttle and must be kept on a leash at all times.

OPTIONS: For a longer hike, head to Jade Lake via Jade Lake Pass.

TOUR COMPANIES: None

INTERESTING FACT: The Meadows in the Sky Parkway took 16 years to build and wasn't completed until 1927.

Cycling
The Kettle Valley Railway
from Myra Canyon to Penticton

□ ■ □ □

Winding across the Okanagan and Similkameen region in southern BC is the Kettle Valley Railway (KVR), an abandoned railroad track that offers over 800 km (497 mi) of cycling. The jewel of the KVR is the 12 km (7.5 mi) section through Myra Canyon. After a 2003 forest fire destroyed thirteen of its eighteen wooden trestles, this National Historic Site of Canada was rebuilt and reopened in June 2008. It now draws up to a hundred thousand hikers and cyclists annually.

At the entrance, there is a large parking lot and a bike rental company. Reserve a bike ahead of time for summer weekends or you may be out of luck. If you choose to ride all the way to Penticton, you'll want to arrange a shuttle or go with a tour company. Most cyclists bike the Myra Canyon section as a return trip and don't continue all the way to Penticton. Some turn around at the Chute Lake Resort, 35 km (22 mi) away.

The ride through Myra Canyon is glorious, with a gentle grade that lets you enjoy the view and feel the airiness of the trestles. When you reach #6, the highest trestle on the line, you're midway and 55 m (180 ft) above Pooley Creek. Look for the rock oven 0.7 km (0.4 mi) after passing Trestle #2. It once baked two-and-a-half-foot loaves for the railway crews; each crewman ate one a day.

After you get through Myra Canyon, it's another 25 km (16 mi) of pleasant cycling with occasional Okanagan Valley views to reach the Chute Lake Resort. Some cyclists on multi-day trips may opt to spend the night at the resort, but most people are happy to just dig into a piece of pie with ice cream and pour back a cold drink.

From Chute Lake Resort, continue to descend on trails with an average grade of 2 percent. In roughly 12 km (7.5 mi) you'll reach the Adra Tunnel bypass, which was put in after the Adra Tunnel was closed for safety reasons. From there through to Penticton the cycling is sublime. Pine forests and expansive views of Lake Okanagan and the Naramata Bench keep you pedalling. Be tuned into your surroundings, though; this is rattlesnake and black bear country.

Roll by the Hillside Winery at 70 km (43.5 mi) into the ride — or stop for a tasting. Then it's an easy cycle into Penticton past orchards and wineries. Finally, what better way is there to finish up an 80 km (50 mi) day than to jump in Lake Okanagan for a refreshing swim?

HIGHLIGHTS: Historical Kettle Valley Railway (KVR), 18 trestles, Okanagan Lake views, vineyards, orchards, wildlife possibilities

DISTANCE: 80 km (50 mi) from Myra Canyon to Penticton

TIME NEEDED: A full 8–9 hour day to do the whole ride; just 2–3 hours for a return trip though Myra Canyon

GRADE: Moderate, because of the distance

WHERE: Start at Myra Canyon in Myra-Bellevue Provincial Park, accessed via McCulloch Road and Myra Forest Service Road out of Kelowna.

HOW: Drive or get a shuttle to the trailhead at Myra Canyon. Leave another car in Penticton or get someone to pick you up.

WHEN: The 3rd weekend in May until mid-October

COST: Free if you do it on your own

DON'T FORGET: Spare inner tubes, bicycle pump, lunch, first aid kit, extra water. Cash if you want to purchase food or drinks at Chute Lake Resort

OPTIONS: Do an out-and-back ride so you don't have to arrange a shuttle.

TOUR COMPANIES: Monashee Adventure Tours, Myra Canyon Bike Rentals, Free-wheeling Adventures (for a week-long KVR tour)

INTERESTING FACT: The Kettle Valley Railway was opened in 1915, with the purpose of getting the rich mineral wealth from the Kootenay region to Vancouver's seaport. By 1961 parts of it were abandoned and by 1989 it was totally decommissioned.

Cycling the trails of
The Shuswap Region
in the Okanagan

□ ■ □ □

The North Okanagan–Shuswap region — encompassing the towns of Salmon Arm, Sicamous, Chase, Sorrento, Enderby, Armstrong and Falkland — has over 675 km (419 mi) of cycling trails. They range from the epic 40 km (25 mi) Larch Hills Traverse to mellow hour-long trails in some of the local parks. You can decide by trip length, choose between road or mountain bike, or base your choice on theme, such as visiting birding hotspots, wineries, beaches or local farms. Shuswap Tourism offers full online guides to help make those decisions easier.

I chose to explore the area by cycling out and back on the Sunnybrae–Canoe Point Road near Salmon Arm. Side trips include an easy walk to the very beautiful Margaret Falls (named for the first white woman to see it), a visit to the Sunnybrae Vineyard & Winery (one of the most northerly wineries in the world), and beaches that are perfect for summertime swimming and picnicking, as well as the chance to pedal past picturesque Canoe Point farms. The route takes you up and down along the north side of Shuswap Lake, a huge lake with over 1,000 km (621 mi) of shoreline that is fed by melting snow and glacier ice from the Monashee Mountains.

Initially, the road is quite flat with only a bit of residential traffic. In the summer, traffic is heavier, so aim for an early start. Drivers are courteous, but still take care as the road has no shoulder. The traffic thins the farther out you go.

Your conditioning program will be tested well before you reach Margaret Falls. Once there, lock your bike and take the short trail to the falls to find a green, mossy world full of monstrously large fir trees. If you have energy to burn and want a bird's-eye view of the falls, hike the steep Upper Canyon Trail, accessible via nearby Herald Provincial Park.

From Margaret Falls it's another 9 km (5.6 mi) to reach Robinson Creek Park, which is very small and a perfect picnic and swim stop. From there it's just a short ride on a gravel road past Canoe Point farms with wonderful Shuswap Lake views to the end of the road at Canoe Point. Return the way you came, enjoying a well-earned 2.5 km (1.6 mi) downhill with a 4.5 percent grade.

HIGHLIGHTS: Shuswap Lake views, Margaret Falls, beaches, Canoe Point farms, Sunnybrae Vineyard & Winery, Herald Provincial Park, Robinson Creek Park

DISTANCE: 36 km (22 mi) return

TIME NEEDED: Half day

GRADE: Moderate

WHERE: Start on the Sunnybrae–Canoe Point Road, 15 km (9.3 mi) north of Salmon Arm. Sunnybrae Park is approximately 450 km (280 mi) east of Vancouver and 125 km (78 mi) north of Kelowna.

HOW: Park your car at Sunnybrae Park, 3.7 km (2.3 mi) along the Sunnybrae-Canoe Point Road from the Trans-Canada Highway.

WHEN: Mid-April to October

COST: Free unless you rent a bike

DON'T FORGET: Picnic, a bathing suit in summer, water

OPTIONS: Check out the Shuswap Tourism website for a full map and other options.

TOUR COMPANIES: Rent a bike from Skookum Cycle and Ski in Salmon Arm.

INTERESTING FACT: There are over 30 cycling routes in the area, averaging 40–50 km (25–31 mi). Every year there are community bike rides out of Armstrong and Salmon Arm. The Okanagan Shuswap Century Ride occurs on the last Sunday in May from Armstrong. Salmon Arm's Bike for Your Life Century Ride takes place on the third Saturday in September.

Hiking to
The Black Tusk
in Garibaldi Provincial Park

□□■□

The unmistakable volcanic dome of the Black Tusk is visible from many vantage points along the Sea-to-Sky Highway connecting Vancouver to Whistler, and you can't miss it from the top of the highest chairlift in Whistler. Although it rises to a height of 2,319 m (7,606 ft), you don't have to go to the top to feel like you've hiked it.

Most people start out for the Black Tusk from the Rubble Creek parking lot. Initially it's a tedious 6 km (3.7 mi) of switchbacking to reach the junction to Garibaldi Lake, but the grade is moderate and you can hike this section quickly. It also doesn't take too long to hike the next 1.5 km (0.9 mi) to Taylor Meadows, where the views begin. From the Taylor Meadows Campground, the trail steadily winds its way up through more meadows and over countless streams. In the summer the area is alive with wildflowers, and in autumn it's ablaze with fall colours. It can be very wet through here, too — even in July, if there was a lot of snow. Occasional views of the Black Tusk make it look farther away than it really is.

Once through the last of the trees, it takes roughly 90 minutes to hike 7 km (4.3 mi) up the moderately steep black talus slopes to the shoulder at the base of the Black Tusk. This section is often snow-covered until well into the summer. When you need to catch your breath, turn around and enjoy the views; they become more amazing with each step you take.

At the shoulder, you can decide whether to call it a day or continue to the top of the Black Tusk. The route up from here is well worn and obvious. It's the final bit to the top — along a narrow, enclosed path known as a chute — that might make your stomach flip, as it's vertiginously airy and the rock is crumbly. There's a serious gap you'll need to cross with one giant step, but once over you're only metres away from the summit. Now take the time to absorb the views of Garibaldi Lake to the south, Helm Lake and Cinder Flats to the east and the Tantalus Range to the southwest.

The Black Tusk is one of the must-do hikes in southern British Columbia. It never fails to amaze.

HIGHLIGHTS: High alpine meadows, wildflowers, spectacular mountain views, Garibaldi Lake

DISTANCE: 29 km (18 mi) return from the Rubble Creek parking lot, with a vertical gain of 1,735 m (5,691 ft); 14 km (8.7 mi) return from Garibaldi Lake

TIME NEEDED: 8–10 hours as a day hike; 5 hours as a day hike from Garibaldi Lake, Taylor Meadows or Helm Creek Campgrounds

GRADE: Difficult

WHERE: Garibaldi Provincial Park, about 100 km (62 mi) north of Vancouver and 19 km (11.8 mi) south of Whistler

GETTING THERE: To get to the Rubble Creek parking lot from Vancouver, take Highway 99 north 100 km (62 mi) and turn right (east) onto a road signed for the Black Tusk. From Whistler, drive south 19 km (11.8 mi) and turn east.

HOW: Start from either the Rubble Creek parking lot or the Cheakamus Lake Trailhead.

WHEN: July to early October

COST: May 1–November 15 camping fees are $10/adult/night and $5/child/night (6–15 years old). Pay online or bring cash. Parking is free.

DON'T FORGET: Dogs are not allowed. Bring bug spray in the summer months.

OPTIONS: Camp on a first-come basis at Taylor Meadows (40 tent sites), Garibaldi Lake (50 tent sites) or Helm Creek (9 tent sites) and do the Black Tusk or nearby Panorama Ridge as day hikes.

TOUR COMPANIES: None

INTERESTING FACT: The Barrier is an unstable lava dam retaining Garibaldi Lake. Don't linger below it.

Cross-country skiing at
Callaghan Country
near Whistler

■■☐☐

The Ski Callaghan region, covering Whistler Olympic Park and the Callaghan Country Wilderness Adventures area, is about a two-hour drive from Vancouver, and just forty minutes from Whistler. Once you turn off the Sea-to-Sky Highway, it's a 10 km (6 mi) drive up the mountain on an excellent road to reach the main parking lot. It's a whole other world up at the top, nothing at all like the town of Whistler.

The first thing you notice is the vast amount of snow. The area reportedly receives up to 4 m (13 ft) of snow per year, one of highest amounts in Canada. The size of the snowbanks on the drive up will attest to that fact. Then you'll see the day lodge. What you won't see are hotels, restaurants or condominiums. It's wilderness up here, a place where you can't help but enjoy the solitude of the woods and the unfettered mountain views. And it's quiet, save for the odd snowmobile.

Whistler Olympic Park was the site of the Nordic events for the 2010 Winter Olympic and Paralympic Games. You can see the ski jumps and follow the trails the Olympians skied. Trails are in amazing shape: track set, groomed and very wide to accommodate skate-skiers. Trails are well signed, too, but because there are 130 km (81 mi) of trails between the Olympic and the Callaghan areas, covering all ski levels, it's worth taking a few minutes at the start of the day to get your bearings and to formulate a plan. Don't forget to pick up a map.

Most visitors stick to the trails that make up Whistler Olympic Park, but there is a wilder, even more scenic option: the network of trails accessible from around the Journeyman Lodge called the Callaghan Country Wilderness Adventures area. Generally, they're only used by the guests of the lodge — who can either ski up or be shuttled up via snowmobile — but if you're a particularly strong skier you can get up and down within a day, and enjoy a home-cooked lunch while you're at it. Some of the trails up here head into avalanche country, so go prepared if you venture onto them.

Ski Callaghan enjoys wide appeal. Every type of skier — from beginner to expert, out of shape to endurance athlete — will find plenty of trails to choose from and lots to smile about at the end of the day.

HIGHLIGHTS: Well-designed cross-country trails, mountain views, Olympic venue, warming huts with leather chairs and gas fireplaces

DISTANCE: Depends how far you want to ski

TIME NEEDED: Half to full day

GRADE: Easy to moderate

WHERE: 120 km (75 mi) north of Vancouver and 16 km (10 mi) southwest of Whistler via a 10 km (6.2 mi) mountain road after turning off Sea-to-Sky Highway

HOW: Call Whistler Tourism at 1-800-944-7852 to reserve on Whistler ski shuttle. Departs 9:00 a.m. from several locations in Whistler; returns 3:30 p.m. There's no public transportation.

WHEN: November to early April, 9:00 a.m.–4:30 p.m. (5:00 p.m. weekends). The Callaghan Country Wilderness area is closed Wednesday and Thursday, but all other trails are open.

COST: Day pass $23.50/adult, $12.15/youth, $3/pet. A $75 ticket includes ski shuttle, ski pass and ski rentals. Rent classic and skate skiing equipment, snowshoes, child carriers on skis, toboggans and helmets at lodge.

DON'T FORGET: Driving there when it's snowing can be harrowing. Winter tires are essential. Bring chains and a shovel.

OPTIONS: Ski 13.5 km (8.4 mi) from the parking lot to stay at the Callaghan Country Journeyman Lodge. Snowshoeing is an option.

TOUR COMPANIES: None

INTERESTING FACT: Whistler Olympic Park was built at a cost of $119.7 million and completed in time for the 2010 Winter Olympics.

Kayaking
Johnstone Strait
on the north end of Vancouver Island

□ ■ ■ □

Johnstone Strait, a narrow body of water along the northeast coast of Vancouver Island, is home to the largest number of resident orca whales in the world. It's possible to kayak in their presence, especially in the summer as they congregate to feed on salmon. Large numbers of orca whales, also called killer whales, come to rub their bellies on the pebble beaches of Robson Bight, partway down the strait, but unless you're a researcher this area is strictly off limits.

The possibility of paddling among the orcas — an exhilarating though scary experience — is not the only reason to visit Johnstone Strait. The area is home to a huge amount of sea and animal life. It's quite likely you'll see bears, seals, sea lions and dolphins or porpoises. On one kayaking trip I witnessed a pod of dolphins that was at least a half mile long.

The Johnstone Strait area — though busy with fishing boats, whale-watching boats and cruise ships — still retains a wild feeling to it compared to its counterpart, the Discovery Islands, located to the south. Maybe it's the climate. The water is colder, it's foggier and the weather is far less predictable. Or maybe it's because most of the Native sites have been gobbled up by the rainforest and apart from Telegraph Cove the coastal villages have almost disappeared too. You might feel like you've fallen off the map, especially if you paddle into the Broughton Archipelago where you might not see anyone for days at a time.

Another bonus to kayaking the Johnstone Strait area is the sheer beauty of it all. Chances are you'll have a fabulous campsite, perhaps on a small rocky beach, where you can enjoy a fire and views of the rainforest and mountains shrouded in mist — or in sunshine if you're lucky.

A note of caution is in order. The currents are usually a manageable one to two knots but there are areas where they top ten knots at full flow and can be dangerous. Combined with wind and boat wake, Johnstone Strait can become treacherous quickly. Never try to out-paddle a cruise ship either. If you see one, even off in the distance, let it pass before you continue your crossing.

HIGHLIGHTS: Orca whales, sea lions, seals, Pacific white-sided dolphins, porpoises, snowcapped peaks of Vancouver Island

DISTANCE: Varies. Paddling to Kaikash Creek near Robson Bight takes a full day.

TIME NEEDED: 2–4 days, and up to 10 to explore the Broughton Archipelago

GRADE: Moderate to difficult depending on winds, currents and boat traffic

WHERE: Start in Telegraph Cove, 350 km (218 mi) north of Nanaimo.

HOW: Rent kayaks from North Island Kayak at wharf in Telegraph Cove and leave right from the dock.

WHEN: Late April till October but best in the summer

COST: Parking at Telegraph Cove is $6/night or $25/week. Launch fee $7/kayak. Free camping on first-come basis. Kayak rentals with safety gear start at $100/single/two days. Four-day tours are about $995 pp.

DON'T FORGET: Binoculars, camera, wet weather gear, warm clothing, fishing licence. Consider bringing a wet suit.

OPTIONS: Johnstone Strait is the gateway to the Broughton Archipelago where you can quite literally go for weeks.

TOUR COMPANIES: North Island Kayak, Ecomarine Paddlesport Centres, Spirit of the West Adventures, Out for Adventure

INTERESTING FACT: The Johnstone Strait is home to the largest number of resident orca whales in the world, with a population in summer approaching 200 whales.

Kayaking
Desolation Sound
off the Sunshine Coast

■■□□

Desolation Sound, located off the northern end of British Columbia's Sunshine Coast and 144 km (90 mi) north of Vancouver, is world-famous for its summer boat cruising. It also draws lots of sea kayakers, from novice to expert, not only for the spectacular beauty of the Coast Mountains but for the fact that the waters are some of the warmest ocean waters north of Baja California in Mexico, warm enough for swimming in the summer.

You can easily spend a week to 10 days in this area poking around the islands, islets, sheltered bays and pocket coves. Some of the kayaking you'll likely do is in Desolation Sound Marine Provincial Park, but there are a number of campsites just outside the park that are quieter and equally pretty. At low tide look for giant sunflower stars, purple stars and sea cucumbers. Seals are common, Pacific white-sided dolphins and orca whales less so. But there's enough bird life that you'll want to keep a pair of binoculars handy.

Most paddlers launch from Lund or Okeover Inlet. I prefer Lund so I can stock up at Nancy's Bakery, a stone's throw from the launch site, before heading out. Also, the very beautiful Copeland Islands are just a short paddle away and they make a great first or last night's camping spot.

Leaving Lund, you might wonder what you've got yourself into. Sailboats and yachts chug up and down the coast off the Malaspina Peninsula, most seemingly oblivious to the fact that you're in a kayak. Fortunately they like to hang out in groups so if you avoid their anchorage spots, particularly Prideaux Haven, you can find the quiet and beauty you have come for.

Apart from the boat traffic, the biggest downside to Desolation Sound is finding a prime camping spot in high season. Most of the shoreline is jagged rock covered with razor-sharp oysters, both of which can wreak havoc on kayaks. If you can score a campsite on the Curme Islands then you're very lucky, but be prepared to share. The Martin Islands offer lots of accessible camping spots whereas Kinghorn Island, though beautiful, is very difficult to access. Other camping spots to consider, if you're prepared to add a few miles to your trip, include Forbes Bay in the Homfray Channel, Roscoe Bay Marine Provincial Park and Cassel Lake located at the end of Teakerne Arm.

Kayaking in the warm waters of Desolation Sound is truly an exceptional experience and not anywhere as bleak as Captain Vancouver, who named the place, would lead you to believe.

HIGHLIGHTS: Mountains, warm water for swimming, pretty islands, fresh oysters, marine life

DISTANCE: Varies, depending on how far up Desolation Sound you want to kayak

TIME NEEDED: 3–10 days

GRADE: Easy to moderate

WHERE: Launch from the wharf in Lund on the Sunshine Coast.

HOW: Lund is accessible from West Vancouver via two ferries: the Horseshoe Bay Langdale ferry and the Earls Cove Saltery Bay ferry. There is an 84 km (52 mi) drive between ferries and a further drive of 57 km (35 mi) from Saltery Bay to Lund. You can also launch from Cortes Island.

WHEN: May to early October. It can be busy in late July and August.

COST: Allow for ferries and kayak rentals, and $7/day or $43/week at Dave's Parking in Lund.

DON'T FORGET: Boat traffic and boat wakes can be a problem.

OPTIONS: Continue north of Desolation Sound and explore the farthest reaches of Toba Inlet; or head to the north side of Cortes Island and explore the Discovery Islands.

TOUR COMPANIES: Powell River Sea Kayak, Spirit of the West Adventures, Wild Coast Adventures

INTERESTING FACT: Desolation Sound is at the confluence of two tidal streams entering Vancouver Island's inside passage. As a result, the tides have a limited ability to flush the water and the water temperature markedly increases, making it the warmest ocean water north of Baja California in Mexico.

Cycling
The Southern Gulf Islands
south of Vancouver Island

■■□□

It's hard to beat island-hopping with your bike. Mild temperatures, sunshine, low rainfall, and a mix of pastoral and coastal scenery on quiet, hilly roads make Victoria and the Gulf Islands superb cycling destinations. Your toughest decisions will be choosing which island to visit next.

From Swartz Bay Ferry Terminal, get a taste of Vancouver Island by cycling along the easy Lochside Trail, a dedicated bike path that goes to the provincial capital of Victoria. After that, return to Swartz Bay for the voyage to Salt Spring, the largest Gulf island in both area and population, where there are two moderately strenuous cycling loops 35 km (21.7 mi) and 50 km (31 mi) long. Strong cyclists could cover the whole island in a day, but two days lets you enjoy more of the island, including ocean and lake swimming, dozens of hiking trails, kayaking, and an extensive self-guided studio tour of the many local artists. Food stops include artisanal cheese shops, wine tastings at two local vineyards and a spectacular Saturday farmer's market in the town of Ganges.

Great cycling can also be had on the smaller Galiano, Mayne, Pender and Saturna Islands. Coming from the mainland, the first one you'll see is Galiano. This second-largest of the Gulf Islands has hilly cycling along with some great hiking, excellent kayaking and lots of beaches. Cycle to the far end of the island for the best coastal views.

Mayne, with only nine hundred inhabitants, has roughly 30 km (18.6 mi) of mostly easy cycling with a great short side trip to Georgina Point Lighthouse. Pender Island is actually two islands joined by a one-lane bridge: peaceful, rural South Pender, and North Pender where most of the two thousand residents live. Quiet back roads take you through orchards and farmland, a vineyard, and artists' studios if you want a break from the bike. Follow the trail to the summit of Mount Norman, the highest point on the island at 244 m (800 ft).

Rural Saturna, home to only three hundred full-time inhabitants, is the most southerly of the Gulf Islands. The best cycling on the island follows the coast along East Point Road (which becomes Tumbo Channel Road). Enjoy a picnic at the end of the road and admire the view of the San Juan Islands in Washington State.

HIGHLIGHTS: Rugged coastal scenery, ferry rides, beaches, farmer's markets, opportunities for hiking and kayaking, whale watching, galleries, craft stores, local cuisine, wineries

DISTANCE: Highly variable depending on what island or islands you cycle

TIME NEEDED: 1–7 days depending on how many islands you want to visit

GRADE: Easy to moderate

WHERE: The southern Gulf Islands are located south and immediately east of Vancouver Island. All the islands are readily accessible via ferries from Tsawwassen and Swartz Bay. There are smaller inter-island ferries too.

HOW: Ferry reservations are not needed for passengers travelling with bikes but make sure you arrive at the ferry terminal at least 20 minutes prior to loading. Check out **BCFerries.com** for current schedules. Many of the Gulf Islands offer bike rentals but the downside is that you will have to return to that island. Rent a bike from Coastal Cycles, Sports Rent or Selkirk Station Bicycle and Kayak in the Victoria area.

WHEN: April to mid-October

COST: Budget for ferries, accommodation, food, bike rentals and other activities. Bikes are allowed on all ferries at a cost of $2/bike.

DON'T FORGET: A bike lock

OPTIONS: There are an infinite number of routes and combinations. Half the fun is planning your route.

TOUR COMPANIES: Bicycle Adventures, Great Explorations, CycleTreks

INTERESTING FACT: There are 13 major islands and approximately 450 smaller islands that make up BC's Gulf Islands.

The North Adventures

N

Beaufort Sea

U.S.A.

Northwest Territories

Yukon

Tombstone

Dawson City

Cameron River

Yellowknife

Auriol Trail

Whitehorse

Yukon River

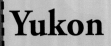Tatshenshini River

British Columbia

Baffin Bay

Auyuittuq

Pangnirtung

Iqaluit

Nunavut

Thelon River

Hudson Bay

Manitoba

Hiking
The Auriol Trail
in Kluane National Park

■ □ □ □

Kluane National Park — together with its neighbour, Wrangell-St. Elias National Park and Preserve in Alaska — was declared a UNESCO site in 1979. Host to the world's largest non-polar icefields, the two parks offer a rich variety of ecosystems in a pristine environment. The easy 15 km (9.3 mi) Auriol Trail, while close to civilization and only a ten-minute drive from Haines Junction, manages in just 8 km (5 mi) to take you through the boreal, subalpine and alpine climate zones.

Beginning in open grass fields, which are ablaze with colour by the end of August, the trail follows an old wagon road/cross-country ski trail for the first 2 km (1.2 mi). It climbs gradually through a forest of white spruce, aspen and poplar to reach a junction and the start of the loop section of trail. It's here that the dramatic views begin. Stay left on the loop for an easier ascent. You'll cross a number of streams and pass through meadows where moose may be spotted. Continue past swaths of arctic flora until you reach a wilderness campsite on the banks of a river at the 7.3 km (4.5 mi) mark, where you'll find tent pads, a pit toilet and a bear-proof pole for hanging your food. Hikers with the time and interest can explore the high alpine off-trail via a spur trail from the 8.2 km (5.1 mi) marker. Many peaks, both named and unnamed, can be climbed from here as well. From this vantage point, the views of the Auriol Range are superb.

Continuing past the campsite, it's 0.5 km (0.3 mi) to the high point of the trail before it begins its descent. To complete the loop, descend for 5.7 km (3.5 mi) to reach the junction. The path is steeper than it was for the ascent, but only for short stretches. Don't miss the short side trail offering superb views of not just the Auriol Mountain Range but of Haines Junction and the scenic valley.

Kluane National Park is largely inaccessible unless you're prepared to backpack for many days, but the Auriol Trail is a scenic introduction to the area and one of the best hikes to do if you're just passing through the park. It will whet your appetite for more.

HIGHLIGHTS: Beautiful Auriol Mountain Range views, Arctic flowers, range of eco-systems, wildlife

DISTANCE: 15 km (9.3 mi) roundtrip with a 397 m (1,302 ft) elevation gain

TIME NEEDED: 3–5 hours

GRADE: Easy

WHERE: The entrance to the park is at Haines Junction, 160 km (99 mi) west of Whitehorse or 238 km (148 mi) north of Haines, Alaska. The Auriol Trailhead is located 7.2 km (4.5 mi) south of Haines Junction.

HOW: Day hikes require no reservations.

WHEN: Mid-May until the end of October, though the park is best between June 15 and September 15. Bugs can be bad in June and early July. Fall colours are excellent in late August and September, which is also when there's a chance of seeing the Northern Lights.

COST: Backcountry camping permits are $9.80 pp/night. A day pass to the park is free.

DON'T FORGET: If you're planning to camp you must register at the park office. A bear-resistant food container is mandatory. Carry bear spray on all hikes and insect repellent in the summer months. Be prepared for any type of weather.

OPTIONS: Backpack the 85 km (53 mi) Cottonwood Trail over a 4–5 day period beginning at Kathleen Lake. Alternatively, ask the park personnel at the Visitor Centre in Haines Junction for suggestions.

TOUR COMPANIES: Kluane Ecotours, Up North Adventures, Alayuk Adventures

INTERESTING FACT: Kluane National Park is the most seismically active mainland area in North America, getting up to 3 tremors a day. That's what happens when tectonic plates collide.

Rafting
The Tatshenshini River
from the Yukon to Alaska

■ □ □ □

The best way to see the world's most scenic rivers has to be by raft. Considered one of the top ten river trips in the world, the Tatshenshini River is a wilderness experience on a grand scale where the reward is nature in its most pristine state. It's also your chance to see the world's largest non-polar icecap. Along with the Alsek River, the Tat — as it's commonly known — is part of the world's largest protected area, and now a UNESCO World Heritage Site. The number of permits given to access the rivers is tightly controlled to preserve the quality of the experience. You pay for the privilege, but it's one worth saving for.

The rafting trip can be done in one of two ways: self-guided or with a tour company. A self-guided trip might be cheaper, but even if you have the rafting skills the logistics will be daunting for most people. You have to go on a waiting list to get a permit, then be able to go as soon as your name comes up. Visit the Glacier Bay National Park website, **nps.gov/glba/**, and click on fees/reservations to get the process rolling.

The Tat flows from the interior of northwest British Columbia north into the Yukon, and then back to BC, where it joins the Alsek River. From there it flows across the Alaska Panhandle through the ice floe–laden Alsek Lake to empty into the Pacific Ocean in Glacier Bay National Park, Alaska. Most people join the river in the Yukon and raft it through to Dry Bay in Alaska. Rapids encountered are never more difficult than Class III (Class IV at peak flow times), and a real bonus is the total absence of any signs of human civilization such as garbage, towns or power lines. What you do find are wildflowers, glaciers and towering mountains, including 4,671 m (15,325 ft) Mount Fairweather. And if you're really lucky, you'll also see mountain goats, bighorn sheep, and black and grizzly bears.

For those on a tour, you'll find that once you're on the river, the days melt into each other in an easy rhythm of sleeping, eating and rafting. There's usually lots of time for bird watching, nature walks, photography and occasional all-day hikes. For the brave, there is always swimming in near-freezing water. Bugs, if you get them at all, will be earlier on in the trip. The temperatures, though never balmy, are comfortable, and often by noon it's short-sleeve weather. However, the closer you get to the coast, the cooler it gets.

Rafting the Tatshenshini River is truly a world-class adventure and great fun for all ages.

HIGHLIGHTS: Wildlife, bird life, icebergs in Alsek Lake, St. Elias mountains, 10,000-year-old ice in your drinks, the Walker Glacier, solitude, long hours of daylight

DISTANCE: The rafting trip begins at Dalton Post and ends approximately 225 km (140 mi) later at Dry Bay in Alaska. Tour companies fly people back to Whitehorse from there.

TIME NEEDED: 8–11 days

GRADE: Easy and family-friendly

WHERE: Start at Dalton Post beside Kluane National Park, 237 km (147 mi) southwest of Whitehorse.

HOW: Trips are popular, despite the cost, so sign up early.

WHEN: Mid-June to early September

COST: Tour prices start from $3,850 pp. Self-guided trips require a permit issued through the US Glacier Bay National Park and Preserve, and a BC Parks River fee of $125 pp/trip for Dry Bay take-outs in July and August.

DON'T FORGET: Rain gear, rubber boots with thermal insoles, binoculars, camera. Human waste needs to be carried out in a portable toilet affectionately known as an ammo can.

OPTIONS: Raft a short section of the Alsek River.

TOUR COMPANIES: Tatshenshini Expediting, Canadian River Expeditions, Sea to Sky Expeditions, Wilderness Adventures

INTERESTING FACT: The Tatshenshini and Alsek Rivers are the only major river drainage in North America to be completely protected from headwaters to source.

Backpacking through
The Tombstone Mountains
in Tombstone Territorial Park

☐☐■☐

World-class mountain scenery reminiscent of the mountains of Patagonia awaits those prepared to backpack into Grizzly, Divide and Talus Lakes in the Yukon's remote Tombstone mountain range. The trailhead — accessed from the Dempster Highway (also known as Yukon Highway 5), a 750 km (466 mi) dirt road connecting the Klondike Highway to Inuvik on the Mackenzie River delta in the Northwest Territories — is a seven-hour drive from Whitehorse.

To reach the jagged Tombstone Mountains — so-named because one of said mountains resembles a gravestone — you must hike through a challenging environment that takes you up and down lichen-covered talus slopes which can become extremely slick when wet. The landscape, though, is divine, and especially memorable in late August when the boreal forest and alpine meadows deliver a rainbow of fall colours. This backpacking trip is one of the most scenic ones you'll do in Canada, but go prepared. Many people backpack into Grizzly Lake, spend a night and hike out. But even for a short trip like that, you should dress for any kind of weather, and always carry bear spray because this is grizzly country.

To continue to Divide Lake you must cross Glissade Pass, which lives up to its slippery name when the temperatures drop towards freezing. It's a slog to the top, and then a steep, fast, kick-stepping descent to reach the bottom. From there, the hiking is easy all the way through to Talus Lake. At all times, the scenery is a knockout.

I'd list this backpacking trip as one of the top five in Canada. Make the effort to visit this remote and unforgettable destination, and if possible, allow a few extra days to explore more of the desolate Dempster Highway.

HIGHLIGHTS: Wildlife, fall colours in late summer, Arctic tundra, gorgeous mountain scenery

DISTANCE: 11.5 km (7.1 mi) to Grizzly Lake with 797 m (2,615 ft) of elevation gain; 6 km (3.7 mi) with gain of 411 m (1,350 ft) to Divide Lake; Talus Lake is a further 6 km (3.7 mi) with 191 m (625 ft) gain

TIME NEEDED: 2–4 days for backpacking trip. Allow 5–8 hours to Grizzly Lake, another 3–5 hours to Divide Lake, then 1.5–3 hours to Talus Lake.

GRADE: Difficult

WHERE: Trailhead located at KM 58.5 on Dempster Highway. The Tombstone Interpretive Centre is at KM 71.5.

HOW: Book backcountry sites on Yukon Parks website (**yukon.goingtocamp.com**) or show up at Interpretive Centre at 9:00 a.m at start of trip. Mandatory orientation given 4 times daily.

WHEN: Late June to mid-September

COST: $12/backcountry campsite/night, $60 cash deposit for mandatory bear-proof food canister. Campsites at Tombstone Mountain Campground near Interpretive Centre are on first-come basis.

DON'T FORGET: Bear spray, warm clothes including mitts and hat, rain gear, gaiters, tarp for keeping cooking tent warm. Buy food and cook stove fuel before you get to Dempster Highway.

OPTIONS: Goldensides and the Lookout Trail are easier day hikes that still give you a sense of the area.

TOUR COMPANIES: Sea to Sky Adventure Company, Cabin Fever Adventures, Ruby Range Adventure

INTERESTING FACT: At the northern edge of the Tombstone Mountains, you'll find Berengia, an area that escaped glaciation in the last ice age, which allowed people and animals to cross the Bering Sea.

Canoeing
The Yukon River
from Marsh Lake to Schwatka Lake

■ ■ ■ □

The 3,185 km (1,979 mi) Yukon River is the third-longest river in North America, stretching from the Coast Range Mountains in northern British Columbia through the Yukon and Alaska to empty into the Bering Sea. The river has played key transportation roles for the past 125 years, especially during the Klondike Gold Rush at the end of the nineteenth century and in the late 1950s as a shipping route until the Klondike Highway was finished.

Today, the Yukon River is a recreational paradise for paddlers. Every summer, canoeists with time and experience accomplish the epic trip between Whitehorse and Dawson City. But you can still get a taste of the Yukon River with this day trip. Launch at Marsh Lake, about a thirty-minute drive south of Whitehorse, and paddle all the way downriver to Schwatka Lake via Miles Canyon.

The Yukon River cuts through a scenic river valley lined with white cliffs composed of layers of sediment and volcanic ash. Look for swallows nesting in the cliffs, and if you're lucky you might see a moose or two coming down to the river to drink. You shouldn't have any trouble spotting bald eagles, either. The Yukon River is also an important river for salmon. At the end of Schwatka Lake, by the dam, look for the 366 m (1,201 ft) Whitehorse Fishway, which was built to help Chinook salmon return to spawn. It is reportedly the longest wooden fish ladder in the world.

The Yukon is a fast-flowing river, especially through Miles Canyon, but there are no rapids or portages to deal with on this section. A few hours into the paddle, campsites that double as picnic spots can be found on the east bank of the river. It's also worth stopping at the Canyon City Heritage Site, which for over two thousand years was an important campsite because it was the last safe place to stop before the dangerous White Horse Rapids. But in 1958 a dam was built, which formed Lake Schwatka and flooded the rapids.

Miles Canyon is definitely the highlight of the day. Rocks tower above you on all sides as the river narrows and picks up speed. But in just a few minutes, you're through it and into Schwatka Lake. The pullout is in a day-use park on the eastern side of the lake about a kilometre after exiting the canyon.

HIGHLIGHTS: Miles Canyon, wildlife sightings, bald eagles, Canyon City Heritage Site, scenic river valley

DISTANCE: About 30 km (18.6 mi)

TIME NEEDED: One day to paddle the Whitehorse section; or if you're ambitious, 15–20 days to paddle to Dawson City

GRADE: Easy as a day trip, moderate to difficult as a full trip to Dawson City

WHERE: Start at Marsh Lake, a 30-minute drive from Whitehorse, and finish at the day-use park on Schwatka Lake.

HOW: Rent a canoe or sign up with a local tour company.

WHEN: July to early September

COST: Prices start at $185 pp, depending on the number of participants and the tour company.

DON'T FORGET: Rain gear and warm clothes

OPTIONS: Other day trips to consider include Whitehorse to the confluence of the Takhini River or to Lake Laberge. For a multi-day trip, consider Whitehorse to Carmacks or Carmacks to Dawson City.

TOUR COMPANIES: Cabin Fever Adventures, Up North Adventures, Nature Tours of Yukon, Yukon Wide Adventures

INTERESTING FACT: The world's longest canoe and kayak race takes place every summer on the Yukon River. Called the Yukon River Quest, the 715 km (444 mi) race travels between Whitehorse and Dawson City. Winners have completed the race in under 41 hours.

Canoeing
The Cameron River
from the Ramparts to Yellowknife

■■■□

If you want a taste of canoeing in the Northwest Territories without the cost of a float plane trip, look no further than some excellent canoe routes within an hour of downtown Yellowknife. All are accessed via Highway 4, also known as the Ingraham Trail.

Your portaging skills should be good and you must be comfortable paddling on big lakes if you want to do the full trip from the Cameron River Ramparts to Yellowknife. If you'd rather not risk the possibility of big winds and waves, you can finish the trip at Powder Point on Prelude Lake — located on the Ingraham Trail, 40 km (25 mi) east of Yellowknife. It's also well worth adding several days to include a trip to Hidden Lake Territorial Park. Even as an overnight side trip, the park offers exceptionally beautiful paddling on a crystal-clear lake through a landscape of rocky islands with gorgeous campsites. It's accessed via two well-developed portage trails off the Cameron River. In calm weather or with favourable winds, the trip from the Cameron River Bridge at KM 55 on the Ingraham Trail to Yellowknife could be done in three days, but you would need to pull over quickly if a storm blew up or the waves got too big.

Almost immediately after launching, you must portage around the Ramparts, a set of waterfalls that would be impossible to paddle but are very pretty to admire. From there, it's 8 km (5 mi) to Cameron Falls with only one short set of easy rapids to run — or portage, depending on water levels. On this part of the river you might spot a moose or see your dinner in the shape of a large trout swimming beneath you. Because of the geography, you won't hear Cameron Falls as you approach, but it will be obvious when you're getting close. Pull out on the right before the pedestrian bridge and take some time to enjoy the scenic area around the falls. This portage is one of the prettier ones you're likely to do.

If you bypass Hidden Lake, Prelude Lake is next; it's accessed via a short, easy portage from Cameron River. To continue by the most direct route, hug the southern edge for 19 km (12 mi) until the lake empties into a slow-flowing, peaceful river that takes you into River Lake. Head for the southwest end to find some beautiful campsites on rocky points.

Two waterfalls will each require portages, after which a paddle around an unnamed lake will leave you at the sometimes treacherous Prosperous Lake. Exercise extreme caution on this lake. At the end of a 9–10 km (5.6–6.2 mi) paddle, either run or portage the Tartan Rapids. From there it's an easy paddle along the Yellowknife River to the Yellowknife River Bridge. Under optimal conditions, it's possible to paddle all the way back to Yellowknife via Great Slave Lake.

HIGHLIGHTS: Cameron Falls, Ramparts, Hidden Lake Territorial Park, beautiful campsites, bird life, fishing, swimming

DISTANCE: Varies depending on start and end points, but up to 65 km (40 mi) if you paddle back to Yellowknife.

TIME NEEDED: 3–5 days

GRADE: Easy through Hidden Lake Territorial Park; otherwise moderate to difficult, depending on wind and waves

WHERE: Start above the Ramparts at KM 55 on the Ingraham Trail (Highway 4), an hour from downtown Yellowknife on mostly dirt road. Start at KM 45 for access to Hidden Lake Territorial Park.

WHEN: July to early September

HOW: Canoe rental, food barrels, shuttle service from Overlander Sports in Yellowknife. Buy fuel in town and bring camping gear.

COST: $45/day for canoe, $15 for barrel, $1/km for shuttle service. Camping is free.

DON'T FORGET: Warm clothes and bear spray; cellphones work much of the time.

OPTIONS: Paddlers with more time can opt to start on Reid or Tibbitt Lake and paddle through to the Yellowknife River Bridge or Yellowknife.

TOUR COMPANIES: None, but check with Overlander Sports to see if there are any local guides.

INTERESTING FACT: Yellowknife is the diamond capital of North America.

Canoeing
The Clark and Thelon Rivers
in the Thelon River Sanctuary

□ □ ■ □

The Thelon River begins in the remote Barren Lands of the Northwest Territories and flows for over 900 km (559 mi) through Nunavut to ultimately drain into Hudson Bay at Chesterfield Inlet. The river and sanctuary are famous for a fantastic concentration of wildlife in a pristine wilderness environment. Also of interest is a stop at the cabin where John Hornby and his two companions starved to death in the winter of 1926.

Access to the Thelon is via an expensive float plane ride from either Yellowknife or Fort Smith, depending on which section you canoe. Our trip started on the Clark River, a tributary of the Thelon, but within four days we were paddling on the Thelon itself. From the confluence of the two rivers, it's mostly an easy paddle with only a few Class III rapids early on. Normally there are no portages, although we did have to make one due to pack ice early in the trip.

The topography changed dramatically over the course of ten days. In the beginning there was a lot of variation, but as we travelled it became more level until the land was pancake-flat, supporting only stunted trees and wildflowers. But such wildflowers! In the springtime heat and nearly round-the-clock sunshine it felt like we were watching a time-lapse movie seeing the flowers go from snow-covered to full bloom in just over eleven days.

Muskoxen, caribou herds, wolves, grizzly bears and thousands of birds can be seen on this trip. Molting Canada geese will keep you entertained as they run along the banks, flattening themselves with their heads down in the hope you won't notice them. Listen for loons and the meow of the rough-legged hawk, and keep your eyes peeled for peregrine falcons and gyrfalcons, as this is their breeding ground.

The bugs aren't bad if the wind is blowing, which it usually is. If you can't stand bugs, choose a trip late in the season when they're almost all gone. An added bonus of a later trip is the greater likelihood of seeing the Northern Lights.

For anyone who wants a taste of the north and the chance to visit a remote wilderness environment, this is definitely a trip worth considering.

HIGHLIGHTS: Pristine wilderness, Thelon Wildlife Sanctuary, caribou, wolves, muskoxen, grizzly bears, falcons, many types of geese, ducks, swans and loons, historic canoe route

DISTANCE: Depending on which tour operator you choose and where you finish, up to 275 km (171 mi)

TIME NEEDED: 10–12 days

GRADE: Difficult because of Class III rapids

WHERE: Start in Fort Smith, Northwest Territories and fly via chartered float plane to the put-in on the Clark River.

WHEN: Late June to late August

COST: $7,495 pp and up, including charter airfare

DON'T FORGET: Bug jackets, bug spray, a camera and multiple batteries, binoculars

BEFORE YOU GO: Read *Tundra* by Farley Mowat, *Thelon: A River Sanctuary* by David F. Pelly and *Discovering Eden: A Lifetime of Paddling Arctic Rivers* by Alex Hall.

OPTIONS: Theoretically, you could organize your own canoe trip, but the logistics are daunting.

TOUR COMPANIES: Canoe Arctic, Black Feather Wilderness Adventure Company, Nahanni River Adventures

INTERESTING FACT: According to the respected guide and naturalist Alex Hall, numbers in a caribou herd fluctuate dramatically and naturally. The Beverly herd, which frequented the Thelon River drainage basin, numbered 274,000 in 1994, but has now disappeared. The Bathurst herd, another of the four major northern caribou herds, has seen its numbers plummet from 350,000 to 20,000 over the same period.

Backpacking in
Auyuittuq National Park
on Baffin Island

□ □ ■ □

If you're looking for a remote wilderness backpacking experience that carries you across the Arctic Circle, then Auyuittuq National Park on the Cumberland Peninsula of Baffin Island in Nunavut Territory is a great choice. The trek takes you through a powerful landscape of rugged mountains, glaciers, and roaring rivers where only the hardiest of plants and animals survive and the weather can change in a heartbeat. The Arctic is an unpredictable place that demands self-reliance.

Most hikers choose to start at the trailhead at Overlord, accessed via a ninety-minute boat ride from Pangnirtung, though it is possible to hike, or rather, slog the 31 km (19.3 mi) distance from Pangnirtung to the park in two to three days. The trail, unmarked save for the occasional inukshuk pointing to the safest route, follows the Weasel River across the Arctic Circle. It passes Mount Thor whose massive cliff face — the largest in the world — rises a kilometre above the valley floor. The end of the trek is Akshayuk Pass at Summit Lake, a desolate spot famous for its extreme winds. From there it's possible to do a long day-hike to see the two cylindrical towers and flat summit of Mount Asgard, made famous by the James Bond movie *The Spy Who Loved Me*.

The hike is normally done over eight to twelve days. Although the daily hiking distances aren't high, you have to factor in that a very heavy pack means you'll be moving far more slowly. Eight days is very doable if the river levels are cooperative, and you do probably want to add in a day for Mount Asgard. But if the rivers are running high, you might have to delay a day and cross in the early hours of the morning when water levels typically drop. River crossings pose the greatest danger; drowning is the leading cause of death in the park. Follow the tips provided by parks personnel to stay safe.

With average monthly temperatures in July of 7.6°C (46°F), Auyuittuq lives up to the translation of its name: the land that never melts. The landscape reflects the Inuit belief that time is infinite and never-ending. Respect the landscape and you'll come away with a new appreciation for the Inuit ability to survive and thrive in the north.

If you're doing the hike on your own, you will need to get a detailed topographic map from the park's office and bring a SAT phone with extra batteries. Consider shipping food up ahead of time, along with bear spray and bear bangers. If possible, bring new fuel bottles and a new stove; if they look used, they might be confiscated by airline security. Buy white gas in the community. Plan to start the trip via the shuttle on a high tide. Take hiking poles, neoprene water shoes for stream crossings, and an all-season tent.

HIGHLIGHTS: Spectacular mountain vistas, Mount Thor, Mount Asgard, crossing the Arctic Circle, river crossings, wildflowers, sense of space

DISTANCE: The hike starts at Overlord at sea level and ends about 35 km (22 mi) later at Summit Lake; the elevation gain is 420 m (1,378 ft).

TIME NEEDED: 4–12 days, depending on whether you want to hike all the way to Summit Lake

GRADE: Difficult

WHERE: Start in Pangnirtung, accessed via a flight from Iqaluit. Book a boat shuttle to Overlord via **jalivaktuk@qiniq.com** or **peterkilabuk2005@qiniq.com**.

WHEN: July and August, though the water levels are typically highest in the last week of July and the first week of August.

HOW: Contact Parks Canada in Pangnirtung (1-867-473-2500) or Qikiqtarjuaq (1-867-927-8834) before booking any travel. Arrange for a mandatory 3-hour registration and orientation session.

COST: A Northern Park backcountry excursion pass is $147.20 pp. Add $24.50 pp/night in the park. The boat ride to the park is approximately $120 pp each way.

OPTIONS: Fly into Qikiqtarjuaq and do a one-way trip to Overlord so you don't have to retrace your steps. I wish I'd done this!

TOUR COMPANIES: Black Feather Wilderness Adventure Company, Equinox Wilderness Expeditions, Inukpak Outfitting

INTERESTING FACT: The Penny Ice Cap, which is the dominant feature in Auyuittuq National Park and larger than the province of PEI, is a remnant of the continental ice sheet from the last ice age.

Packing Lists

There's a good chance you already know what to pack for your next adventure. But sometimes a checklist is helpful — and it might give you some new ideas.

Here are links to three detailed packing lists — covering kayaking, backpacking and cycling. The kayaking checklist could easily be modified for a canoe trip. Take along a cooler if you don't have to portage, and food barrels with backpacking straps if you do.

- The Kayaker's Checklist — 100 Items You Can't Leave Home Without
  http://www.hikebiketravel.com/21466/the-kayakers-checklist-100-items-you-cant-leave-home-without/

- What to Pack on a Multi-Day Cycling Trip
  http://www.hikebiketravel.com/32456/what-to-pack-on-a-multi-day-cycling-trip/

- Packing List for a Remote Two Week Backpacking Trip (This can be easily modified for shorter trips.)
  http://www.hikebiketravel.com/26246/packing-list-remote-week-backpacking-trip/

PHOTO CREDITS

• The Cabot Trail by Parks Canada – J. Pleau • The Length of PEI by Parks Canada – John Sylvester • The Green Route by Freewheeling Adventures Inc. • The Magdalen Islands by Gustave Pellerin • Niagara Parkway by Niagara Parks Commission • Killarney Provincial Park by Ontario Parks • Sentinel Pass by Rebecca Curran • Clayoquot Sound by Barry Giles • The Chilkoot Trail by Cabin Fever Adventures • The Clearwater River by Interior Whitewater Expeditions Limited • The Rockwall Trail by Donna McKean • Johnstone Strait by Barry Giles • Desolation Sound by Barbara Arnold • Gulf Islands by Gustave Pellerin • The Tatsheshini River by Bruce Kirkby (Nahanni Adventures) • The Thelon River by Alex Hall

All pictures not noted above are by Leigh McAdam.

Acknowledgements

There are many people and companies that have helped make this book a reality. I am incredibly grateful to all of you.

THE FOLLOWING COMPANIES AND TOURIST ORGANIZATIONS OFFERED FREE TOURS, EQUIPMENT, PASSES AND/OR ACCOMMODATION

• Adventure Central Newfoundland • Algonquin Park • Cabin Fever Adventures — Yukon Territory • Churchill River Canoe Outfitters • Equinox Bike Rentals — Alma, Quebec • Eureka Canada, Canadian distributor of quality camping and outdoor gear (who provided me with a one-man tent) • Freewheeling Adventures — Hubbards, Nova Scotia • Go Western Newfoundland • Interior Whitewater Expeditions — Clearwater, British Columbia • Legendary Coasts — Eastern Newfoundland • Monte-Saint-Anne — Quebec • Monashee Adventure Tours • National Parks of Canada • New Brunswick Tourism • Ontario Parks • Saskatchewan Tourism • Seascape Kayak Tours — Campobello Island, New Brunswick • Shuswap Tourism • Ski de fond Mont-Tremblant • Tourism Laurentian • Tourism Outaouais • Travel Alberta • Travel Manitoba • Whynot Adventures — Kejimkujik National Park, Nova Scotia • Yukon Parks

THE FOLLOWING COMPANIES AND TOURISM OPERATORS KINDLY PROVIDED A DISCOUNT

• Baymount Adventures • Black Feather Wilderness Adventure • Fjord en Kayak • Green Coast Kayaking • Maligne Adventures • Nova Shores Adventures • Overlander Sports • Thousand Island Kayaking • Tourism Saguenay-Lac-Saint-Jean • Wolf Den Expeditions

The Skyline Trail, AB

Hopewell Rocks, NB

Index

Leigh McAdam plans to continue exploring Canada and travelling the world. Some of her more interesting adventures outside of Canada include cycling from Tanzania to Victoria Falls in Zambia, hiking in the remote Sierra Nevada del Cocuy region of Colombia, climbing Kilimanjaro, summiting thirty-five of Colorado's fifty-four 14,000-ft-plus peaks, and trekking around Manaslu in Nepal. Her next big trip involves a bike and a set of maps that will take her and her husband from Norway to Turkey via Eastern Europe.

Leigh is a contributor to the recently released *Fly Like an Eagle: Real Life Stories of Hope and Inspiration* by A Hopeful Sign and Gary Doi. Her life has included careers as a geologist, registered professional dietitian, flower shop owner and vice-president of Waterra, a company that sells equipment for groundwater monitoring. She will continue blogging at **HikeBikeTravel.com**, but hopes to also reach out via talks and presentations to inspire people to see more of Canada.

Since growing up in Ottawa, Leigh has lived in Hall's Harbour (Nova Scotia), Toronto, Niagara-on-the-Lake, Boulder (Colorado) and Vancouver. She now lives in Calgary with her husband John and dog Torrie, a rescue from the island of St. Maartens.